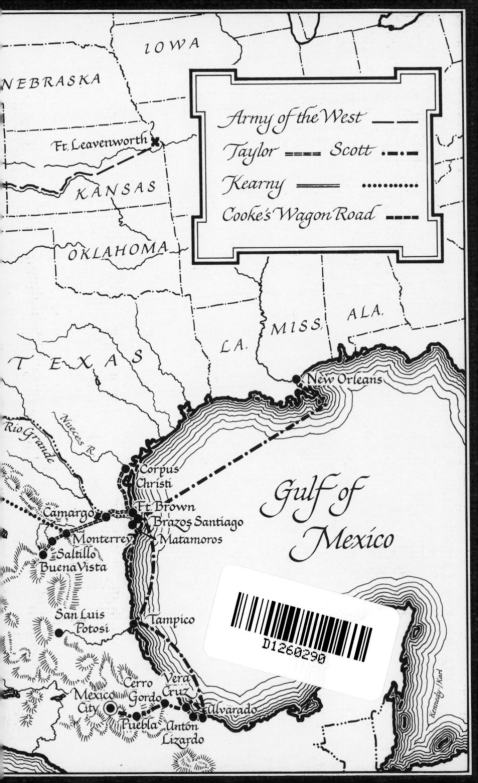

IOWA

NEBRASKA

Ft. Leavenworth

KANSAS

OKLAHOMA

ALA.

MISS.

LA.

T E X A S

New Orleans

Rio Grande

Nueces R.

Corpus
Christi

Camargo

Ft. Brown

Brazos Santiago

Monterrey

Matamoros

Gulf of
Mexico

Saltillo

Buena Vista

San Luis
Potosi

Tampico

Cerro
Gordo

Vera
Cruz

Mexico
City

Alvarado

Puebla

Antón
Lizardo

Army of the West _____

Taylor ==== **Scott** ·—·—

Kearny ═══════ ···········

Cooke's Wagon Road ━ ━ ━

Kennedy/Karl

D1260290

NORTH AMERICA DIVIDED

SEYMOUR V. CONNOR
AND ODIE B. FAULK

NORTH
AMERICA
DIVIDED

THE MEXICAN WAR
1846-1848

NEW YORK · OXFORD UNIVERSITY PRESS · 1971

COPYRIGHT © 1971 BY OXFORD UNIVERSITY PRESS, INC.
LIBRARY OF CONGRESS CATALOGUE CARD NUMBER: 77-161885

PRINTED IN THE UNITED STATES OF AMERICA

PREFACE

AMERICANS are a people peculiarly addicted to celebrating anniversaries, especially centennials. License tags denote the 100th or 150th anniversary of statehood, while cities celebrate the date of their founding with great gusto (as for example San Antonio with HemisFair in 1968 at its 250th anniversary). Even the centennial of the bloody Civil War brought four years and more of Civil War Round Tables, a plethora of books, and many local observances. And already the nation is beginning preparations for the granddaddy of celebrations at the bicentennial of the American Revolution. Probably this American desire to celebrate anniversaries comes from the youth of the nation and the striving for some unifying national heritage. However, one outstanding exception to such observances was the failure in 1946–1948 to note the centennial of the war with Mexico. No other such notable event in American history has been allowed to pass so unnoticed, so disregarded, so uncele-

brated. Even the national fatigue with war in 1946 does
not fully account for this strange omission.

The reason for this failure doubtless stemmed from a
national belief that the Mexican conflict somehow was wrong,
that the United States had been the instigator of the conflict with its southern neighbor, that, in fact, the war had
been peculiarly un-American. For a century and more historians have denigrated the American role in the conflict,
confusing it with the problems of the Civil War and reading into it motives that never existed in fact. Without
doubt much of what has been written about the war with
Mexico was penned to reinforce preconceived biases, perhaps more than with any other event in American history.
The New England interpretation of the war (if there can
be such) has dominated the textbooks of American history
to such an extent that even Southwestern college students
believe that President James K. Polk deliberately provoked
the conflict in order to expand the territorial limits of the
republic. Mexican historians, likewise trying to foster a spirit
of nationalism, too often in the past have cited American
authors to prove their country blameless. And, finally, no
event in American history—while simultaneously castigating the motives of the United States—has been written
so exclusively from American sources, excluding almost entirely those of the nation that was fought as well as the
sources of nations only peripherally involved.

We, the authors of this work, sought first to compile a
complete bibliography, one that did include both American
and Mexican (as well as peripheral) sources; this task proved
far more lengthy than first anticipated—as the bibliography
in this book attests. Next, our research convinced us that
the guilt for the outbreak of the conflict lay not with either
nation but with men and political factions within both;
for every bit of American guilt there is matching Mexican
guilt. Nor was there lack of bravery within the armies of
either republic. Finally, there was no great hatred at the

individual level, either by soldiers or civilians; the "gringo" and "greaser" explanation quickly fades in the face of compassion, even friendship, between Americans and Mexicans, both on and off the battlefield.

We deliberately chose not to footnote the narrative of this book, for the facts which we have incorporated are readily available to anyone pursuing the items in this bibliography. To our astonishment, we found that the mass of controversies which have generated much more heat than light within the ranks of historians quickly faded when put under glare of historical research—proving again that too many scholars who have written about this war did so from a position of preconceived bias, placing emphasis on such vaguely related issues as the slavery conflict, American "imperialism," the so-called Nueces boundary dispute, and the alleged intrigues of the much-maligned James K. Polk—(to the extent that they forgot other important considerations). For example, historians have worried so endlessly about when Polk framed his war message (before or after receiving notice from Taylor about the Mexican attack on Thornton's dragoons) that they have failed to note that Mexico already had declared war on the United States; they have argued the abstract concept of Manifest Destiny to the extent that they have forgotten the British desire for California; nor have they considered the British involvements in Mexico stemming from the English argument with the United States over the Oregon Territory.

It therefore is the purpose of this book not only to attempt to tell the story of the war without twentieth-century bias and to set it in proper nineteenth-century perspective, but also to synthesize the immense amount of recent scholarship in both Mexican and American history during this period. Finally, we believe that whatever the slant of those historians who use this work they will find the bibliography of great value.

In preparing this book for publication, the authors have

incurred numerous debts, as do writers of any book. Research funds from Texas Tech University and Oklahoma State University greatly facilitated the research, as did a grant from the Henry E. Huntington Library and Art Gallery in San Marino, California. Special thanks are due Sylvan Dunn and the staff of the Southwest Collection at Texas Tech University, the staff of the Oklahoma State University Library, and both libraries for their generous aid in acquiring materials. Appreciation also is extended to Gale Webber for her helpful assistance and to Bill Jones for his encouragement, criticism, and understanding. Finally, we wish to acknowledge the strong support and deft hand of the editorial staff of Oxford University Press, particularly Mr. Sheldon Meyer.

S. V. C.
O. B. F.

Lubbock, Texas
December 28, 1970

CONTENTS

NORTH AMERICA DIVIDED

CHAPTER ONE

ORIGINS OF THE WAR

THE ORIGINS of the war between the United States and Mexico, 1846–48, remain controversial even today. To most Mexicans the issue is simple—the United States fought Mexico in order to acquire the territory now called the American Southwest, including both Texas and California. Simple imperialism. To many Americans it is the same—the late Robert Kennedy once referred to the war as one of the most disgraceful episodes in the American past.

This war, fought in 1846 and 1847, actually began on September 16, 1810. On that day, in a little village church in Dolores about a hundred miles north of Mexico City, a parish priest named Miguel Hidalgo y Costilla initiated a movement that was ultimately to separate Mexico from Spain . . . and to divide the Mexican nation for over a hundred years. Father Hidalgo believed not only in the independence of Mexico but also in the principles of democracy and in the social and economic betterment of the lower classes. Others in Mexico, wealthy criollos (native-born of pure Spanish descent), had begun to desire separation from Spain but could not tolerate the ideas of social and economic equality. At first they failed to support the Mexican independence movement; later they and their successors established empires, monarchies, and dictatorships in the hapless Mexican nation. Always they opposed any democratic form of government because it could jeopardize their control of the land and wealth of Mexico.

Father Hidalgo strove mightily but unsuccessfully. In 1811, fleeing north, he was captured and beheaded. Two of his disciples carried the revolution into Texas, far from Mexico City and the potent royalist armies. One of these was Juan Bautista de las Casas, a native of that ancient Spanish province. Las Casas surprised and captured the governor and the military garrison at San Antonio in 1811, and detachments of insurrectionists possessed themselves of the villages of Goliad and Nacogdoches, the only other settlements in Texas. But a counter-revolution quickly mobilized under Juan Zambrano, wealthy rancher and supporter of the crown, and just as quickly restored Texas to the empire.

The second Hidalguista, Bernardo Gutiérrez de Lara, left his home in Tamaulipas in northern Mexico, tried to join Father Hidalgo, then fled to Texas, and with the failure of the Las Casas uprising, fled to Louisiana. Gutiérrez was a remarkable man with a tremendous survival instinct and an intense desire to liberate the Mexican people. He went at once to Washington where he had informal interviews with high officials and secured letters of introduction to important persons in New Orleans and Natchitoches. Thus, American interest in Mexican affairs was first piqued.

With the aid of a number of Americans, Gutiérrez put together an expedition to invade Mexico, consisting in part of American volunteers and in part of Mexican refugees of the Hidalgo movement. Gutiérrez had the idea, by no means illogical, that Texas was the place to begin the Mexican independence movement. It was a long distance from the capital in Mexico City, natives of Texas had demonstrated a propensity for liberal sentiments that seemed to ensure the success of the venture, and its nearness to the United States suggested the possibility of volunteer support. With Augustus W. Magee, who had resigned his commission in the United States Army, Gutiérrez occupied Nacogdoches in 1812, declared independence, gathered additional volunteers, and marched to Goliad, which was easily taken. Soon the insurgents moved on San Antonio to capture the capital city with little difficulty. There Gutiérrez established a revolutionary junta and began plans to extend the revolution into northern Mexico. He was doomed to failure. Joaquín de Arredondo, the royalist military commander for the region, marched against the revolutionaries (who may be called Mexican patriots), defeating them near San Antonio on August 18, 1813. Gutiérrez escaped with his life, having fled shortly before the battle.

Later, in 1815, in company with other Mexican patriots, he helped to organize a paper republic of Mexico in New Orleans, again enlisting the volunteer support of Americans. Spain protested but to no avail; the official United States policy was total neutrality, but what individual Americans did was their own business. Under Louis d'Aury a naval base was established on Galveston Island from which privateers raided Spanish commerce in the Gulf of Mexico. Gutiérrez, as a merchant, fenced the goods out of Natchitoches. The entire operation was not greatly unlike that involving Jean Paul Jones and Pierre Augustin de Beaumarchais when, under the name of Rodríguez, they sold British goods in Paris during the American Revolution. Before long the revolutionaries were ready to attack again, this time the northern coast of Mexico. Again their attack was a failure, and the survivors regrouped in New Orleans.

By then a treaty with Spain provided added provocation for American volunteer aid. In 1803 Jefferson had purchased the Louisiana Territory with undefined western boundaries.

For over a decade and a half diplomats had tried to settle the territorial margins. Finally in 1819 John Quincy Adams, then secretary of state, negotiated a treaty with Spain, ceding the American claim to Texas (based on La Salle's settlement there in 1685) for Florida and settling the monetary claims of American citizens against Spain for approximately $5,000,000, which was paid by the United States to the claimants.

This abandonment of its vague claim to Texas by the United States incited a small wave of protest, especially in the South. Gutiérrez hastened to take advantage of it and linked the Mexican independence movement to a filibustering (or freebooting) expedition organized by Dr. James Long, whose absurd goal was to "recover" Texas. Together with about two hundred Mexicans and Americans they entered Nacogdoches in 1819, and once again Gutiérrez proclaimed independence. Spanish royalists made quick work of the movement, but Long returned to Texas again in 1821 in consort with other Mexican liberals, only to be captured after he took Goliad, and later killed. Gutiérrez fled the first invasions, lived in Louisiana, and ultimately returned to his native Tamaulipas.

Although Texas had been the scene of action for Mexican independence, the Hidalgo movement was not dead in central Mexico. Guerrilla bands had harassed royalist troops and, more important, the wealthy criollos had become disaffected with the Spanish monarchy because of its acceptance of constitutional limitations. The criollos decided to join the Hidalguistas to effect complete separation from Spain. In 1821 Agustín de Iturbide marched out of Mexico City at the head of a royalist army, made a rendezvous with Vicente Guerrero, who headed a remnant of the Hidalguistas, and established the agreement called the Plan de Iguala, which provided that the two forces combine to overthrow Spanish rule and to create a constitutional monarchy in Mexico. It was a bedding of strange politics. The Hidalguistas did not believe in monarchy; the Iturbidista criollos did not believe in constitutional limitations. Yet the alliance worked, temporarily.

The combination forced the abdication of the Spanish viceroy and established the independence of Mexico. But soon these incompatible forces were to be at each other's throats. Pursuant to the Plan de Iguala, Iturbide called a congress to assemble in Mexico City. It produced nothing but dissension. Some wanted Iturbide to become the monarch of a new kingdom of Mexico, others wanted to invite a Bourbon prince to the proposed Mexican throne, and the liberals—the old Hidalguistas—desired the establishment of a republican democracy on the pattern of the United States. President James Monroe, guided by Secretary of State Adams, quickly recognized the revolutionary government, perhaps not understanding the complexities of the unstable coalition. Within a few months, Iturbide staged a demonstration, proclaimed himself emperor of Mexico, and dissolved the revolutionary congress. Monroe and Adams might have been less eager to recognize such a monarchy. The American mind was already stirring with the concept of Manifest Destiny in its original sense of spreading democratic government to the people of the western hemisphere.

In Mexico City at this time a number of foreigners were intensely interested in the course of the Mexican Revolution. There was Arthur Wavell, an Englishman of distinguished ancestry who had fought with Simón Bolívar in South America; Joseph Vehlein, a German merchant who seemed to be out for all he could get; and James Wilkinson, an American of shadowy background. Wilkinson had been a troop commander in the revolution against Britain, had become the United States military commander in Louisiana, was a known agent for the Spanish government at the time of the Aaron Burr conspiracy, had negotiated the Neutral Ground agreement with Simón de Herrera in 1806 establishing an "understood" boundary between Texas and Louisiana, and was the uncle of the wife of the filibusterer James Long. They, and others like them, were in the Mexican capital like jackals ready to gnaw on the decaying carcass of the Spanish North American empire.

Unlike them was a reluctant Stephen F. Austin. Austin had come to Mexico because of the first misunderstanding between government officials and Americans in Mexico. To Austin it was something of a defalcation of contract; to Antonio Martínez it was but fate—the spin of the wheel—and he had had no difficulty in turning his coat wrong-side-out and converting from the royalist governor of Texas to the revolutionary governor. God and Liberty! as he now signed his name. But Austin had other business. His father had received a grant to colonize Anglo-Americans in Spanish Texas but died before he could initiate his program. Stephen Austin inherited the grant and, with the approval of Martínez, began the settlement of colonists at the same time that Iturbide was driving Spain out of Mexico. Martínez soon notified Austin that the revolutionary government would not approve the grant and that the settlers must leave Texas or move to San Antonio. Austin persuaded him to stay the expulsion until he could make a personal appeal to the government in Mexico City. Thus was Austin in the capital, and because the plight of his colony fitted into the schemes of the would-be land speculators, they supported him. Iturbide soon approved the grant, but before Austin left, the emperor was overthrown, and the liberals took over the government, rescinding all the acts of the imperial junta.

Patiently Austin re-petitioned the new government, and while he waited for it to act, he translated the United States Constitution into Spanish for Miguel Ramos Arizpe, who headed the committee to draft a republican frame of government for Mexico. The Constitution of 1824, as it was called when adopted, was an excellent constitution and was, in some respects, more liberal in the area of natural rights than the American document, although it accepted Roman law as the basis of jurisprudence and Roman Catholicism as the state religion. Shortly after drafting the Constitution the liberal congress granted Austin's petition and soon thereafter opened the borders of Mexico to American immigration in an act called the Federal Colonization Law.

It is highly significant—and too often overlooked—that both the Constitution of 1824 and the Federal Colonization Law demonstrated the friendly attitude of the liberal faction in Mexico toward the United States. And the feeling must have been mutual, for with the passage of state land-grant laws a small tide of Americans began flowing into Mexico. A few settled in Santa Fe and Taos, more in California, where immigrants were magnanimously given eleven leagues of land (nearly 50,000 acres), and still more in Texas, which was nearer but where they received one league (about 4500 acres). These land grants quite definitely provided the impetus for American migration to Mexico; in the United States a settler had to pay $1.25 per acre for unoccupied land. The implication by some historians that Americans "infiltrated" Mexican provinces with conspiratorial designs to wrest them away from Mexico is nonsense. They came for the free land offered to them by a generous and apparently democratic government.

But the Mexican people, tragically, were unequipped by the past to maintain a republican form of government. The history is a tortuous one, and the details are unimportant here. Suffice it to say that in the first national elections in 1828, the results of the polls were overturned at musket point, and after considerable turmoil the aristocrats came into control of the government. The Centralist-Federalist dichotomy in Mexico had begun. The Centralists advocated any form of authoritarian government that might succeed— imperialism, monarchy, dictatorship. The Federalists supported the Constitution of 1824. A Federalist uprising against the Centralist government erupted in 1829, and a dynamic military chieftain named Antonio López de Santa

Anna rose to lead the Federalists. By 1832 he had harried the Centralists out of the capital and assumed the reins of government.

During the time the Centralists had been in power, one of their earliest acts had been to halt all American immigration to Mexico and to put settlements of Americans under military surveillance. This Law of April 6, 1830, has often been interpreted as a reflection of a general Mexican attitude toward Americans. It was anything but that; instead, it was clear-cut evidence that Centralists could not tolerate Americans or American ideals. From this time until the outbreak of war between the United States and Mexico the relations between the two nations ebbed and flowed with the rise and fall of Centralism.

The story is involved. The Federalist leader Santa Anna installed as president the man who had been declared the victor in the 1828 election. He had but a few months to serve. New elections held early in 1833 gave Santa Anna himself the presidency. Again a mockery of the democratic process followed. Santa Anna refused inauguration and his vice president, Valentín Gómez Farías, took office. Santa Anna's purpose was insidious; he would let Gómez Farías, an ardent liberal, initiate reforms while he stood on the sidelines and tested the reaction of the Mexican people. After each reform that proved unpopular, Santa Anna took over the presidency. Five times the men exchanged the office while Santa Anna craftily gauged the public sentiment. In 1834 he assumed the presidency permanently and, by that time, after secret intrigues with Centralist leaders, had become in reality the leader of the Centralist faction in Mexico. It was his natural role.

Before his erstwhile Federalist followers realized his duplicity, he had dismissed congress and replaced the Constitution of 1824 with a document known as the *Siete Leyes* (Seven Laws) which established a centralized dictatorship over tragic Mexico. States became departments; state legislatures were dissolved; elected governors were replaced by Santa Anna appointees; and in some cases the *ayuntamientos* (town councils) were removed. By the summer of 1835 his dictatorship was complete.

Federalists, taken by surprise, had been unable to organize resistance until it was too late. But revolution was in the making. The stalwart citizens of Zacatecas rejected a disarmament decree but were ruthlessly punished by the dictator. Separated by distance from retaliation, the government of California refused to acknowledge the Centralist tyranny. In Monclova the government of the combined state of Coahuila and Texas tried to flee northward to establish a Federalist capital in San Antonio but was entrapped by Martín Perfecto de Cós, Santa Anna's brother-in-law.

Once again Texas was to become the stage for Mexican patriotism as Federalists fled the wrath of the government. Most noteworthy of the refugees was Lorenzo de Zavala, one-time governor of Yucatán and later of the Federal District of Mexico City and one of the foremost liberals of the time. The situation was confusing to the American settlers in Texas. In 1832 they had endorsed Santa Anna's military campaign against the Centralists—but, then, he was in the guise of the Federalist leader. In 1834 Santa Anna, posing as a Federalist, had repealed the hated Law of April 6, 1830. The Texans, Anglo and Hispanic alike, were slow to realize the truth. It came to them, as it had come to the people of Zacatecas, in the enforcement of the disarmament decree.

Ordered to surrender a cannon which they had been given for protection against the Indians, the people of Gonzales resisted. On October 2, 1835, the affair known as the Texas Revolution began. It was not, as it has so often erroneously been depicted, a revolution against Mexico. It was a revolt against the Centralist dictatorship and a part of the general uprising in Mexico against the abrogation of the Constitution. There was fighting at Goliad and at San Antonio. A convention assembled and declared by more than a two-to-one vote that the purpose of resistance was to restore the Constitution. On December 10, 1835, Centralist forces in San Antonio were compelled to surrender and accept what must have seemed rather ignominious terms. The officers were to swear not to interfere with the restoration of the Constitution; soldiers who wished to support the Federalist cause could remain in Texas and join the resistance; the rest must withdraw below the Rio Grande and promise never to re-enter Texas. Because of the absence of detailed records it is not known how many of the troops accepted the offer to remain and defend the Constitution. It is known, however, that approximately one-fourth of the land grants that were later made for military service to Texas went to persons with Hispanic surnames.

The dictator could not afford to let this defeat go unpunished, for Texas could become the rallying point for Federalism. Quickly he amassed an army under his personal command and marched toward Texas. There, conditions were chaotic. A provisional government under the defunct Constitution of 1824 had been disintegrated by petty bickering; a volunteer army had been rendered impotent by dissension; and a populace had become divided by a desire to declare independence rather than to continue the support of the Federalist cause.

Even as Santa Anna's forces invested San Antonio and began the attack on the Alamo, a new convention assembled at Washington-on-the-Brazos, and on the urgence of Lorenzo de Zavala declared the independence of Texas from Mexico. Zavala reasoned correctly that a movement for Texas independence would elicit more volunteer support from the United States and at the same time would not greatly impair liberals in Mexico. A constitution for the Republic of Texas was written and another acting government was created, with Lorenzo de Zavala as vice president. But the defenders of the Alamo knew nothing of the March 2 declaration of independence and died to a man on March 6 in defense of the Mexican Constitution.

Santa Anna had entered Texas much sooner than anyone had anticipated with a much larger force than was expected. General José Urrea was sent with one army to extirpate James W. Fannin at Goliad, while Sanata Anna with about six thousand troops marched on San Antonio. Almonte, his aide-de-camp, noted as they entered the city that the flag of the state of Coahuila y Texas was flying over the Alamo. It was within the walls of that old mission that William B. Travis had gathered the Texas volunteers when the Centralist army was sighted, despite orders from his commander-in-chief, Sam Houston, to demolish the fortifications and withdraw. In a desperate appeal for aid, Travis had written that "our flag still waves proudly"—but it will never be known whether it was the state flag that Almonte had seen, or the flag of the New Orleans Grays which was later taken to Mexico City, or the Mexican national flag of 1824, which seems most likely. (The flag of the Republic of Texas was not designed until nearly three years later.)

The heroic defense of the Alamo has gone down in the annals of military history. Approximately 180 men, including 32 volunteers from Gonzales who slipped into the Alamo at the penultimate moment, stood off the seige and attack by Santa Anna's vastly superior forces for thirteen days. And then, on the morning of March 6, they repulsed two attempts by the Centralists to broach the walls, only to succumb to a third wave of soldiers prodded into the melee by the bayonets of their officers. When it was over, the bodies of the defenders were burned on a grisly pyre at the orders of Santa Anna, despite a few protests from some of his officers.

Just as Houston, at the head of the remnant of the Texan forces, determined to make a stand at the Colorado River, he learned of the defeat of Fannin by Urrea and the brutal massacre of the Texan prisoners there. With less than four hundred men to stop Santa Anna's bloody invasion, Houston knew he could not risk a pitched battle against thousands. He retreated three times, drawing the Mexican forces further into Texas, stringing out the Mexican army and lengthening its supply lines. Volunteers augmented his little army to nearly twelve hundred. Santa Anna went after Houston in hot pursuit, the taste of victory keen on his tongue. But the weather favored the Texans. Heavy spring rains had swollen all the creeks and rivers. Santa Anna was unable to move his forces over the flooded streams and muddy roads as rapidly as he desired. In a monstrous error in judgment he finally took about nine hundred mounted men and swam the Brazos in an effort to catch David G. Burnet, Zavala, and the *ad interim* government of Texas.

Houston then realized that his only chance had come; Santa Anna had separated himself from his main army. He closed on the generalissimo at the San Jacinto battlefield with slightly over eight hundred effective troops. Santa Anna suddenly saw what he had done and kept his troops on the alert throughout the night, hastily stacking baggage and throwing up earthworks for protection against a Texan attack. The night was quiet as Houston's forces prepared a hot meal and bedded down, but there was no question in the minds of the Mexican staff that Houston would attack at dawn. When the sun rose on April 21 there had been no charge from the Texan lines. Mid-morning saw General Cós arrive with some five hundred reinforcements. Santa Anna relaxed. At noon he ordered a hot meal prepared—his men had neither slept nor eaten for twenty-four hours—a skeleton guard was mounted, and he allowed his forces to relax.

No one will ever know the reasons behind Houston's decision, but at three thirty he assembled his forces. Quietly they slipped across the prairie toward the Mexican lines, and incredibly they were not spotted until they were within two hundred yards. Suddenly bedlam reigned. Shouting "Remember the Alamo! Remember Goliad!" the Texans charged the nearly sleeping Mexican camp. The attack was over in seventeen minutes. For three days the Texans rounded up prisoners from the scattered and demoralized Mexican forces.

Santa Anna himself was captured while trying to escape in the uniform of a private soldier. It was this second piece of good fortune that made the Texan victory secure, for Santa Anna had some eight thousand troops in Texas, whereas Sam Houston's army numbered about twelve hundred in all. Had Santa Anna been able to rejoin his main army, then under Vicente Filasola, the fighting would have continued, and Texas would inevitably have been beaten. Instead, under pressure from his captors, the Centralist dictator ordered Filasola to withdraw all Mexican troops south of the Rio Grande and a few weeks later signed a treaty accepting the independence of Texas with the Rio Grande as the Texas-Mexico boundary.

Constitutional government was organized in Texas shortly thereafter, and, after many months of frustration and nearly a year after the battle at San Jacinto, the United States recognized it. Later the Republic of Texas was recognized by France, Britain, Holland, Belgium, and other European principalities. Mexico never did. It was somewhat like the situation in the American Civil War; Lincoln, who maintained that secession was illegal *ab initio,* could not logically recognize the existence of the Confederacy despite the fact that he was fighting a major war against that government. There was a difference in the Texas-Mexico situation. The Centralists in Mexico made no effort to re-establish domination over Texas. (Two token invasions in 1842 were repelled below the Rio Grande.)

In Mexico the fight against Centralism had continued after the capture of Santa Anna. Yucatán absolutely refused the noxious mantle of autocracy. In the north, Federalists attempted to separate portions of Tamaulipas, Nuevo León, and Coahuila from the dictatorship in emulation of Texas by creating the Republic of the Rio Grande. It was a failure, in part because it did not receive sufficient aid from American volunteers (although several hundred Texans—Hispanic and Anglo—enlisted in its army) and in part because of the defection of some of its military leaders. The Republic of Texas supported the rebellion in Yucatán by leasing its navy to the Yucatán government, and Yucatán retained its virtual independence until after the Mexican War. California succumbed superficially to Centralism late in 1838, but by 1845 there were two governments in existence there.

Santa Anna had been returned to Mexico, via Washington, D.C., in 1837. When, in 1838, the French attacked Vera Cruz to collect the claims of French citizens against the Mexican government (the Pastry War), he had rushed to head the defense. France was repulsed, although the Mexican government paid the claims. Santa Anna was hit by a cannon ball and lost one of his legs, thereby becoming once again a hero of the people, and once again he put himself at the head of the opposition to the government. Federalists and disaffected Centralists flocked to his banner. By 1842 he was able to route the coalition which had usurped power when he had fallen prisoner to the Texans. In his curious Federalist-cum-Centralist-cum-hero role, Santa Anna ordered the election of a constituent assembly in June 1842. The Federalists won and seemed determined to restore the Constitution of 1824, whereupon Santa Anna dissolved the assembly. On June 12, 1843, he replaced the *Siete Leyes* with an even more stringent instrument of government. Poor Mexico. And poor disillusioned Federalists.

Revolution began anew in 1844. Opposition to Santa Anna rallied behind José de Herrera, who if not a Federalist was at least a moderate. In December of that year Santa Anna was forced into exile in Cuba, and Herrera was inaugurated as president. He prepared to put Mexico's international relations on a realistic footing, especially with the

United States. Diplomatic intercourse between these two nations had been inconclusive at best and agonizingly frustrating at worst. In 1836 Manuel de Gorostiza, Centralist minister in Washington, had called for his passport and, in a storm of fury, had left the country, maintaining that the United States had supported the Texas Revolution. There was truth in his accusation; many in Houston's army were recent volunteers from the American states, but the position of the United States government was strict neutrality. What individual citizens did was their own business, as in the machinations of Gutiérrez or as in the prelude to World War II when Americans by the hundreds joined Canadian forces to fight Hitler. Gorostiza's principal point was that General Edmund Pendleton Gaines took an American army across the Sabine, and occupied Nacogdoches. His indictment was that Gaines intended to aid the Texas forces against Santa Anna. However, Santa Anna was defeated and captured in April 1836, and Gaines did not cross the Sabine until August. Furthermore, Gaines entered Texas to put down a possible Indian uprising that threatened Louisiana. Gorostiza's polemic was aimed at Mexico and was convincing in some quarters there; the American answer by a state department official named William A. Weaver did not dilute the propaganda effects of the denunciation.

The problem was much more delicate than Gorostiza's indictment indicated. For eight years President Andrew Jackson had endeavored to make some collection on the claims owed by the various Mexican governments to citizens of the United States. Jackson was unsuccessful. His representative to Mexico, Anthony Butler, was led down first one blind alley and then another, being told that Mexico was remiss, that the individual American claimants must present themselves in Mexico City, that the documents were lost, that they should be presented to the courts, that they should be presented to the minister of foreign affairs, that no claims could be considered until all were presented, etc. Butler's successor, Powhatan Ellis, made repeated efforts to settle the claims issue in 1836; finally in exasperation he asked for his passport but was refused and he left Mexico without it. One may suspect that Gorostiza's diatribe against the United States was motivated in part by the impasse over the claims. The Centralists then dominated Mexico, and many of the claims were against the Federalist government.

Through the actions of both Gorostiza and Ellis, diplomatic relations between the United States and Mexico were broken off by the end of 1836. Through Richard Greenhow, a state department official who was knowledgeable of Mexican affairs, the two countries exchanged ministers and reopened negotiations. To the Centralists in Mexico the issue was American aid to the Texas Revolution; to the Van Buren government the issue was the claims owed to citizens of the United States. Although Van Buren received a minister from Mexico on October 20, 1837, he did not appoint a minister to that country until after the Centralists offered to sign an arbitration agreement on the claims. Powhatan Ellis reopened the American embassy in Mexico City in February 1839. In the interim France had attacked Vera Cruz in the "Pastry War" to collect the French claims, and British gunboats had forced the payment of claims to British subjects.

With Santa Anna and his ragged coalition then nipping at their heels, the Centralists desperately wanted to avoid further foreign problems. An arbitration convention with the United States was signed and ratified early in 1840; delegates from the United States and from Mexico were appointed, with the Baron Roenne of Prussia as the umpire. The Centralist delegation for nearly four months insisted upon a discussion of procedure, and it was not until December 1840 that the first case was discussed. The arbitration dragged on for over fifteen months; in disgust, the Prussian adjourned the session. Of the $11,000,000 in claims, $7,000,000 had been discussed—$2,000,000 was awarded to United States citizens and $5,000,000 had been tabled; the remaining

$4,000,000 had not even been taken up. Waddy Thompson re-placed Ellis as minister to Mexico, and it became his unenviable task to collect the $2,000,000 the arbitration court had awarded American citizens. But by then the Centralist government that had agreed to the arbitration had been overthrown and Santa Anna was back in power. Ever short on funds, Santa Anna simply refused to pay.

It was 1842, and a threat of war was in the air. Twice Santa Anna ordered token invasions of Texas. In a small Pacific harbor in Mexico, Commodore Thomas ap Catesby Jones commanded the American Pacific squadron. On the appearance of a printed broadside from the Mexican foreign office accusing the United States of violations of neutrality and seeming to imply a declaration of war, Jones decided that his country must have a port in the Pacific and sailed up to Monterey, California, which he occupied without opposition. When he found war had not been declared, he withdrew with chagrin and apology—and was relieved of command of his fleet.

In January 1843 Waddy Thompson was able to negotiate an installment payment on the $2,000,000, and, after much difficulty, a new arbitration convention in November 1843. Diplomatic affairs marched toward a climax. The United States insisted on Washington as the seat of the arbitration. Santa Anna insisted on Mexico City and refused to make the second payment on the $2,000,000. The new arbitration of the claims broke down; Thompson was replaced by Benjamin E. Green who was soon replaced by Wilson Shannon; Santa Anna sent his long-time minion, Juan N. Almonte, to Washington to represent his government. While Shannon tried to negotiate the second installment payment on the claims, Almonte established contacts with leading abolitionists in Washington and elsewhere, all the time asserting that Texas had been stolen from Mexico by a conspiracy of the slaveocracy.

Whigs and abolitionists had been able to defeat in the

Senate a treaty annexing the Republic of Texas to the United States. That issue then became one of the principal ones in the presidential campaign of 1844. Dark-horse James K. Polk, the Democratic candidate, adopted a frankly expansionist platform, calling for the annexation of Texas and the occupation of Oregon to the preposterous limit of 54°40'. The nation voted for "Polk and Dallas—Texas and Oregon," and the annexation of Texas became inevitable. Knowing that a treaty would fail to obtain the necessary two-thirds majority in the Senate, lame-duck president John Tyler engineered a joint resolution offering annexation to Texas, which passed by simple majority of both houses over the vigorous protests of the abolitionists and the valid objection that the procedure was unconstitutional. Tyler signed the offer on March 3, 1845. Almonte screamed that this was an act of aggression against Mexico, and abolitionist sentiment supported him. He demanded his passport and stormed out of Washington. His public position was that the joint resolution was tantamount to a declaration of war.

Almonte's private position, however, clarifies his action. He was the appointee of Santa Anna and an ardent Centralist. Santa Anna had been overthrown by Herrera, and Almonte could expect to be replaced momentarily. Furthermore, what could be more embarrassing to the new regime in Mexico City than to have the Mexican minister defy the United States? And too, there was still the pesky claims question. By this time Shannon had informed the state department that he would have nothing further to do with attempts to negotiate its settlement and, as early as mid-summer of 1844, had recommended that Congress take action on it. Then, in November 1844, he abruptly broke off diplomatic relations with Mexico. So Almonte really had nothing to lose by his petulant action—and much to gain.

His declarations were popular in Mexico and, as he had no doubt anticipated, provided a rallying cry for Herrera's opposition. By the summer of 1845 the American annexation of Texas had become the critical issue on the Mexican political scene, for Almonte was not the only Centralist working to overthrow Herrera. And Herrera, anxious to resolve his foreign problems, had added fuel to the fire. Through Lewis Pakenham, British minister to Mexico, and Charles Elliot, British chargé in Texas, he had offered to negotiate a treaty of recognition with the Republic of Texas. His foreign minister, Manuel de la Peña y Peña, explained that while Mexico might be justified in going to war with the United States over annexation, Texas was simply not worth it and Mexico would be wiser to accept the realistic position that Texas was already lost. Peña y Peña's moderate counsels were lost in the storm of patriotic fury that arose, for in July 1845 a Texas convention had accepted the offer of annexation and the Texas congress had rejected the Mexican peace offer, since it entailed a promise to refuse annexation to the United States.

Matters were made worse when it became known that Herrera had indicated a willingness to receive a minister plenipotentiary from the United States. This important arrangement was effected by William S. Parrott, Polk's special agent to Mexico, and was confirmed by both the American consul and the British minister. In October 1845, amid the shouts for war from the opposition, Herrera's congress met in secret session and approved Peña y Peña's declaration that the government would receive a representative from the United States with full power to settle the "present dispute." Pakenham, recently transferred to Washington, relayed the confirmation to the state department. Polk and his secretary of state, James Buchanan, understood the term "present dispute" to mean all issues between the two nations. Whether Peña y Peña so intended is a matter of contention, but it seems likely that he did, in view of the earlier attempt to negotiate with Texas. Polk promptly appointed John Slidell to negotiate with the Herrera government and gave him wide powers of discretion.

In the instructions to Slidell another thread affecting United States-Mexican relations became entwined—the matter of California. Many historians have flatly accused Polk of provoking war with Mexico in order to acquire California. But California was peripheral to the main issue—the arousing of Mexican nationalism (by Herrera's opponents) over the annexation of Texas. By the time of Slidell's appointment in November 1845 Herrera's overthrow was imminent and war was virtually inevitable. It really mattered little whether Polk was interested in California or not.

But he was. This is quite clear from several sources, although the extent and motivation of his interest are clouded. In California, Santa Anna's appointee (as governor), Manuel de Micheltorena, had been faced with revolution at the same time as his master and, like him, had been driven out. Pío Pico was established as provisional governor, with José Castro in command of the northern segment of the state. Soon conflict erupted between Pico and Castro, and for all practical purposes government in California disintegrated. The situation was complex. At this time there were almost seven hundred Americans in California, some of whom had taken advantage of the wildly generous land donation to immigrants and settled in the Sacramento valley. These people had generally joined in the opposition to Centralism but were somewhat irresolute in the split between Castro and Pico.

A number of contemporary observers declared that California was ready for separation from Mexico. Based on dispatches from British consuls, the head of the British foreign office stated that such separation was inevitable. The French minister to Mexico opined that it was a moot question whether Britain or the United States would take possession of the territory. The British consul at Monterey, California, wrote that Britain could easily acquire control of the area, and that fact became the subject of a major debate in the

United States Senate. There was also the problem in Oregon. Both British and American fur traders were in occupation, and Polk and the Democrats in 1844 had cried, "Fifty-four forty or fight!" The tension between Britain and the United States on the West Coast is often overlooked in discussions of California as a factor in causing the war. Nearly a century later, Franklin Delano Roosevelt believed that the implementation of the Monroe Doctrine required Polk to intervene in California. Writing when he was president of the United States and viewing the situation from the lofty perspective of chief executive, he said: "The War between the United States and Mexico came in an era when it was the fashion for strong European powers to build empires by hoisting their flags over weakly held territories in all quarters of the globe. Only a generation previously the Monroe Doctrine had been set forth with a view to preventing such encroachments within the Western Hemisphere. Yet rumor, suspicion and fear continued to play upon the American imagination while covetous statesmen in Europe did not cease to scheme for the control of more lands on the continents across the Atlantic." It is perhaps of little significance that Roosevelt discussed only British intervention in California as a cause of the war. But he unquestionably understood Polk's dilemma.

Polk, engaged in negotiations over Oregon, secretly instructed Thomas Larkin, the American consul in Monterey, California, to support any movement for separation from Mexico. He also sent secret dispatches by way of Marine Lieutenant A. H. Gillespie to Larkin and to John Charles Frémont. Frémont was in command of an ostensible exploring expedition in Oregon and northern California, having arrived there in December 1845. The events of 1846 and Frémont's involvement in the Bear Flag revolt are not germane to the origin of the war, but they do indicate American concern in California. However, that Polk would have gone to war with Mexico because of British intervention in an area that was already, de facto, separated from Mexico may seriously be doubted.

Polk did instruct Slidell to make an attempt to buy California from Mexico. Polk seems to have had an exceptional sense of responsibility and obligation. And his obligations in nineteenth-century terms were awesome in 1845. There was the situation in California with the possibility of British occupation; there was the problem in Oregon and the deterioration of relations with Great Britain; there was the claims question and Mexico's recalcitrant refusal to negotiate; and there was Texas whose independence and annexation had wounded the Mexican national pride. Did Polk provoke a war by giving Slidell enormous latitude in negotiation, or was he sincere in trying to find some solution to a situation, which even then, was unresolvable?

Slidell was empowered to accept the Nueces River as the southern boundary of Texas if Mexico would agree to a prompt settlement of the claims; to assume the claims (by the United States) if Mexico would accept the Rio Grande as far as El Paso del Norte; to add an additional $5,000,000 if Mexico would cede New Mexico to the United States; to offer another $5,000,000 for northern California; and to go as high as $25,000,000 for all of California (not including Baja California). While the focus of these instructions is frankly upon territorial acquisition, it should be recalled that they grew out of the diplomatic situation that Polk had inherited in March 1845. At that time Almonte had said that annexation meant war; Shannon had said that the claims could not be collected without a show of force; and John A. Forbes, the British consul, had said that Britain could easily take over California.

Texas was the most immediate of Polk's problems. On July 4, 1845, Texas had accepted the terms of the joint resolution of annexation. Polk ordered General Zachary Taylor, then in Louisiana, to occupy Texas and prepare to defend it from possible Mexican attack. Taylor took the Army of Occupation, as it was then called, to the mouth of the Nueces River and set up camp. His orders actually read "on or near the mouth of the Rio Grande," but the territory south of the Nueces, between that river and the Rio Grande, was totally unsettled and could provide no logistical support for a military encampment. So Taylor selected the south bank of the Nueces. Later the question was raised of whether the Nueces was the proper boundary of Texas, and there has been so much misunderstanding about it in relation to the cause of the war that it deserves special attention.

In the middle of the eighteenth century the territory along the Gulf of Mexico that is now Tamaulipas was unsettled and especially vulnerable to foreign attack. Spanish authorities commissioned General José de Escandón to establish settlements there and made him governor of the province which was named Nuevo Santander. One of the most massive colonization projects ever undertaken by Spain ensued. Between 1749 and 1755 Escandón established twenty-three villages and settled thousands of colonists. Two of the towns were located on the northern bank of the Rio Grande: Laredo and Dolores. Laredo endured, but Dolores soon succumed to weather and Indian attacks. Initially, the northern boundary of Nuevo Santander (and thus the boundary between it and the province of Texas) was set at the San Antonio River. In recognition of this Escandón required that the presidio and mission of La Bahía be moved to the San Antonio River to guard his northern frontier. Soon, however, the boundary line was shifted south to the Nueces River. When the Republic of Mexico was formed in 1824 the line between Tamaulipas (formerly Nuevo Santander) and the artificially cojoined state of Coahuila y Texas was defined as the Nueces River from its mouth to the road between San Juan Bautista (on the Rio Grande) and San Antonio de Bexar, and thence along that road to the Rio Grande.

At that time there was no settlement between the Rio Grande and the Nueces save Laredo, and only a few ranchers south of the river had cattle and land holdings to the north. As has been noted earlier, during the Texas Revolution the Rio Grande was simply accepted, without argument or contention, as the Texas boundary. It was across this river that Cós retreated in 1835, that Filasola withdrew in 1836, and that Texas forces twice chased Mexican armies in 1842. In December 1836 the First Congress of the Republic of Texas made the absurd claim that the southern and western boundaries of Texas were the Rio Grande from its mouth to its source and thence to the treaty line of 1819 on the 42nd parallel. This boundary statute was ridiculous, not because of the claim to the Rio Grande in its lower courses, but because the upper Rio Grande split the province of New Mexico, and on the side claimed by Texas lay Albuquerque, Santa Fe, and Taos.

In 1846 anyone in his right mind knew that the Texas claim to New Mexico was silly, but no one knew where the boundary between Texas and New Mexico was, for Spain had never troubled to define it. However, the claim to the upper Rio Grande did not become significant until after the war. What was important was that many people in the United States, apparently including President Polk, thought that the Texas claim to the lower Rio Grande was equally spurious—thus, Polk's instructions to Slidell to accept the Nueces if Mexico would pay the claims. Contrary to popular opinion, however, no official of any Mexican government had advocated publicly or officially that the Nueces be accepted as the boundary (and no evidence has yet been found that any did so privately). Every Mexican government claimed all of Texas to the Sabine, even the Herrera government while it was quietly trying to negotiate through British agents. In reality, then, there was no dispute over the Nueces, for Mexico never asserted it as the boundary until Taylor moved south to the Rio Grande.

Now back to the winter of 1845–46. The Texas electorate ratified a state constitution in October 1845, and on December 29, 1845, Polk signed the Texas Admission Act. Earlier that month Slidell arrived in Vera Cruz and was informed that Herrera would receive no minister from the United States until Texas was returned to Mexico—an impotent, foolish, romantic gesture designed to save face for Herrera, who was being desperately pressed by radical Centralists. In a final effort to save the Herrera government and to avert war, Manuel de la Peña y Peña wrote: "War with the United States in order to dislodge the occupation of Texas is an abyss without bottom which will devour an indefinite series of generations and treasure which the imagination is unable to calculate and in the end will submerge the republic with all its hopes for the future." But such admonitions were useless; radical thought prevailed.

With Santa Anna in exile, another opportunist, Mariano Paredes, chased fortune. Shouting denunciations of the Herrera government and its conciliatory attitude toward Texas and the United States, he mustered sufficient support to take over the capital without firing a shot. On the same day that Polk admitted Texas into the Union, Paredes entered Mexico City and assumed the powers of government. Perhaps it was all foreordained, for there can be no question but that the annexation of Texas precipitated a reaction among patriotic zealots in Mexico which produced war—California, Polk, Manifest Destiny, claims, Nueces boundary notwithstanding. In his revolutionary manifesto of December 14, among other villifications, Paredes charged that Herrera and Peña y Peña had repeatedly thwarted the army from attacking the Americans in Texas.

On receiving word of Slidell's rejection by Herrera as well as his description of conditions in Mexico, Polk sent orders to Taylor to take up a position on the northern bank of the Rio Grande and sent instructions to Slidell to try to negotiate with Paredes. The logistical problem still remained, and Taylor was slow to move south. Paredes was quick to rebuff Slidell in rude and abusive language—meant for the public, of course.

A revolutionary junta named Paredes acting president, rewarded Juan N. Almonte with the appointment as secretary of war, and reiterated the intention of going to war with the United States for the recovery of Texas. Indeed, as far as the Paredes government was concerned, a state of war already existed. Paredes at once began mobilizing his forces, reorganizing the army, and bombarding the Mexican public with violent anti-American propagada. A significant element in Paredes's preparations for war was his and his cabinet's belief that relations between the United States and Great Britain were so ruptured over the Oregon question that Mexico would receive substantial aid from Britain when the fighting commenced. The Paredes government also deluded itself with fantasies of aid from France.

Perhaps more important in the mounting tempo at the Mexican capital was the belief that Mexican arms were superior to those of the United States. Many foreign observers classed the Mexican military force as one of the strongest in the world—well armed, disciplined, and above all experienced. After all, Mexico had been in an almost constant state of war since 1821. The Spanish minister to the United States said bluntly that there were no better troops in the world than the Mexicans. Pakenham believed it impossible that American arms could defeat the Mexicans in their own territory. Charles Elliot commented that Mexican forces were quicker and could endure hardship longer than American troops. The London *Times* correspondent in Mexico was positive that Mexican soldiers were superior to American soldiers, and another British newspaper stated that American troops were contemptible and "fit for nothing but to fight Indians." Mexico's Regular Army was over four times the size of the American army and had more modern equipment. True, the United States population was greater, but to European and Mexican eyes this was but another drawback in that America had volunteers and citizen-soldiers to fight a war against professionals. Said Elliot of the American volunteers, "they are not amenable to discipline, they plunder the peasantry, they are without steadiness under reverses, they cannot march on foot." There is little question but that most Mexican leaders, especially those among the Centralists and in the army, believed in the superiority of Mexican arms. Some moderates, such as Peña y Peña, feared the outcome but most were cocky and confident. Almonte reported that the fear of war in the United States was great. And, indeed, his belligerent statements in March 1845 had produced a near panic on the American stock market.

Two other factors assured Centralist leaders in Mexico of victory: geography and political divisiveness in the United States. The war would obviously begin in Texas, far from the populated centers of America. Mexican armies would sweep through Taylor's meager defenses and possibly capture Natchitoches, New Orleans, and Mobile. It seemed inconceivable that logistic support could be provided an American army in Texas. The more volunteers, the greater the problem of supply. It was obvious to Centralist leaders that it would be a war of offense by Mexico and defense by the United States. But if American troops should break through and invade Mexico, what would they find? Desert, thinly populated northern Mexico, barren mountains, ever-lengthening supply lines, guerrilla warfare, and local resistance. Just as important as the geographical problem to Paredes's henchmen was the political division in the United States. Almonte assured them that the North, represented by abolitionists, would not support the war. Internal conflict would destroy morale, and there would be many in the United States who would be convinced that a war with Mexico was unjust. (There might even be a revolution.) Furthermore, the Indians would rise and join the Mexican army and slaves throughout the South would revolt against their masters.

Following a series of hostile pronouncements in the early

spring, Paredes ordered General Francisco Mejía, then in command of Mexican troops amassing at Matamoros, on April 4 to attack Taylor. Taylor had encamped at the mouth of the Rio Grande on March 23, 1846. An interchange of interesting correspondence ensued between Taylor and Mejía. Before advancing to the Rio Grande, Taylor sent word that the movement was pacific in intent. Mejía responded by charging that the Americans were not content to invade Texas, they were now invading Tamaulipas. It is worth noting that this is the first assertion that the Nueces was the boundary of Texas. From this point on, several Mexican leaders maintained that the crossing of the Nueces (it was not actually a crossing) was a further invasion of Mexico. Mejía did not comply with the April 4 order to attack. He was replaced by General Pedro de Ampudia, who ordered Taylor to withdraw to the Nueces and ordered American civilians to leave Matamoros because a state of war existed. Taylor responded by blockading the mouth of the Rio Grande with chains and requesting American gunboats nearby to deny the use of the river to Mexico.

On April 18 Paredes wrote to Ampudia: "At the present time I suppose you to be at the head of our valiant army, either fighting already or preparing for the operations of the campaign. . . . It is indispensable that hostilities be commenced, yourself taking the initiative against the enemy." On April 23 Paredes issued a proclamation declaring "defensive" war against the United States. It is a statement full of curious ambiguities: "At the time Mr. Slidell presented himself the troops of the United States occupied our territory [Texas]. . . . Hostilities then have been commenced by the United States of the north. . . . I solemnly announce that I do not declare war on the United States. . . . From this day commences a defensive war. . . ."

Ampudia was superseded in command on April 24 by Mariano Arista, who immediately ordered General Torrejón to cross the river with about 1600 cavalry. He notified Taylor that "hostilities have commenced." And they had. Torrejón isolated Captain William Thornton and about sixty American dragoons that afternoon and after intensive skirmish forced Thornton to surrender the following day. Taylor sent a hasty dispatch to Polk which arrived in Washington at about six o'clock on Saturday evening, May 9. On Sunday Polk drafted his famous war message, and on Monday, May 11, he presented it to Congress. Late the next day, following vituperative debate, a declaration of war was voted, and on Wednesday, May 13, Polk signed it. He did not know yet that Mexican forces had crossed the Rio Grande again and attacked Taylor in the battles of Palo Alto and Resaca de la Palma.

What, then, caused the Mexican War? It is not possible to answer this question without equivocation. The annexation of Texas touched off the Mexican War, but the annexation cannot be considered an act of hostility against Mexico; it was the outgrowth of a series of events over the previous two and a half decades, not the least of which was the abrogation of constitutional government in Mexico by the Centralists, which triggered the Texas Revolution. Centralists, however, used annexation to overthrow the Herrera government and to work large segments of the Mexican population into a war fever. Mexican foreign minister to state department, August 23, 1843: "The Mexican government will consider equivalent to a declaration of war . . . the passage of an act for the incorporation of Texas. . . ." Almonte to U.S. secretary of state, November 3, 1843: "The Mexican government [i.e. Santa Anna] is resolved to declare war as soon as it receives information [of annexation]." Mexican Secretary of War Circulars, July 12 and July 16, 1845: Army commanders must raise troops for the purpose of waging war against the United States. Mariano Arista, August 12, 1845: "The time to fight has come." Mariano Paredes, August 27, 1845: "Soldiers! A rapacious and grasping race have thrown themselves upon our territory and dare to flatter themselves that we will not defend [Texas]."

Thus, even before Taylor's Army of Occupation entered

Texas, Mexican Centralists were demanding war. Annexation was an excuse to attack the Herrera government, but it was also—and no mistake should be made about this—a blow to the national pride of Mexico. Of course, Texas was lost. Any realistic Mexican politician knew this, but none dared admit it, and many refused to believe it. As late as 1847, Texas was still listed in the official gazette as a department of Mexico. With the annexation of Texas and the overthrow of the Herrera government in December 1845, war was a foregone conclusion.

The claims question had twice ruptured diplomatic relations and in nineteenth-century thinking could be considered cause for war, but three different presidential administrations in the United States had made it clear that the country would not press war to collect the claims. California was a center of intrigue and of little-known British interest, but hardly a source for war—unless with England—because California, for all practical purposes, was already separated from Mexico and would sooner or later fall into either American or British hands. The Nueces boundary question and Taylor's move to the Rio Grande in March 1846 has been much touted as the provocation of the war. It was, in a sense, added provocation, but Mexican Centralists had never prior to that time quibbled over the Nueces; they believed the United States had invaded Mexico when it annexed Texas.

CHAPTER TWO

TAYLOR'S CAMPAIGN

ZACHARY TAYLOR did not need a declaration of war by Congress to know that Mexico already considered the war to have begun and to be aware that hostilities had commenced once Thornton's dragoons were attacked on April 24–25, 1846. Born at Montebello, Virginia, on November 24, 1784, Taylor was the son of Richard Taylor, a lieutenant colonel on George Washington's Revolutionary War staff. In the spring of 1785, the family had moved to Louisville, Kentucky, where Richard Taylor became a collector of customs and an influential man. Young Zachary was poorly educated, although privately tutored, for he was destined for an agricultural life on the family plantation. The death of an older brother changed the family's preferences, however. In 1808 Zachary Taylor was appointed a lieutenant by President Thomas Jefferson. First he was assigned to New Orleans, but a bout with yellow fever forced a temporary retirement. Then in 1810 he was promoted to captain and sent to the command of General William Henry Harrison, then governor of Indiana Territory.

During the War of 1812, Taylor won prominence when in command of Fort Harrison. There his small detachment of troops withstood an attack by four hundred Indians led by the famous Tecumseh. During that conflict he advanced to brevet major but after the war reverted to his permanent rank of captain. This so angered him that he resigned his commission and returned to Kentucky to raise "a crop of corn." Then in May 1816 President James Madison restored him to the rank of major and sent him to Wisconsin Territory to command the 3rd Infantry. Fifteen years of garrison duty followed in Louisiana and Minnesota. In 1832 he was promoted to colonel and, during the Black Hawk War, commanded the detachment that received the surrender of Black Hawk himself. After that excitement he returned to Fort Snelling as commanding officer. There a subordinate, Jefferson Davis, sought to wed Taylor's second daughter, Sarah, but Taylor disliked Davis and forbade his entry into his home. Davis later resigned his commission and in 1835 eloped with Sarah; three months later, at Davis's Mississippi plantation, she died of a fever.

In 1837 Taylor was assigned to fight the Seminoles in Florida, and on Christmas Day that year he inflicted a stinging defeat on them at Lake Okeechobee, for which he was breveted a brigadier general. Muscular and stocky, rarely in full uniform, he was dubbed Old Rough and Ready by his troops. In 1840 he assumed command of the Department of the Southwest, that year purchasing a house at Baton Rouge, Louisiana, which he thereafter considered his home. He also bought, in 1841, Cyprus Grove plantation near Rodney, Mississippi, thereby becoming a slaveowner. It was on May 28, 1845, that the course of his life shifted dramatically; that day he was ordered to correspond with the government of the Republic of Texas, then negotiating annexation to the United States, and to repel any invasion by Mexicans. Thus he moved to the mouth of the Nueces, and ultimately to the mouth of the Rio Grande. Arriving there on March 23,

1846, with some four thousand men, he occupied Point Isabel and constructed what would be known as Fort Brown, opposite the Mexican town of Matamoros. It was at Fort Brown that he received word of the attack on April 24–25 against Captain Thornton's dragoons.

The sixty-two-year-old general had as his second-in-command Brigadier General William J. Worth, ten years younger and a hard, efficient man. Despite Worth's fits of temper, an appetite for alcohol, and a penchant for bad decisions, he complemented Taylor's shortcomings. Other high-ranking American officers included Colonels William G. Belknap, David E. Twiggs, and William Whistler, and Lieutenant Colonel James S. McIntosh. All were more than fifty years old, and—as one journalist commented—were "prepared to fight in 1846 as . . . [the] army had fought in 1812." By the time of the attack, Taylor's command numbered 3880 troops, of whom about 500 were ill with amoebic dysentery, diarrhea, yellow fever, or a host of other diseases arising from the unsanitary conditions of the military encampments at Fort Brown, Point Isabel, and Fort Texas —a feeble precursor of the horrors to come.

Across the river, in Mexico, the commander was General Mariano Arista, born at San Luis Potosí in 1802. Arista had joined a provincial regiment at age fifteen, later serving in the Vera Cruz "*Lanceros.*" By 1821 and the arrival of Mexican independence he was a captain, but just six months later he had risen to lieutenant colonel. Then successfully riding the wave of revolutions and *pronunciamientos* in the next decade, he achieved the star of brigadier general. However, in 1833 he failed to side with Santa Anna's cause and was exiled, living in Cincinnati, Ohio. After Santa Anna's downfall in Texas, Arista returned from exile and in 1839 was commissioned to campaign against rebels near Tampico, with his headquarters at Monterrey. He arrived at Matamoros on April 24, 1846, to command the Army of the North, his red hair and sideburns in sharp contrast to the black hair and dark complexions of such subordinates as Generals Anastasio Torrejón, Luis Noriega, and José María García, and Colonel José López Uraga. His army numbered more than eight thousand and included such crack units as the Tampico veterans, the 2nd Light Infantry, the 4th and 10th infantries, and General Torrejón's lancers. These were experienced men who had demonstrated their competence in other engagements, veterans of discipline and courage. But most, as was usual in Mexican armies, were raw conscripts and convict soldiers, poorly trained and equipped, without experience, and prepared to desert at the first opportunity.

Taylor was at Point Isabel, his supply point, early in May strengthening his fortifications there, confident that both Fort Texas and Fort Brown could withstand siege. Then on Thursday, May 6, he issued an order that on the following afternoon at three o'clock the troops would march to Matamoros. He knew when he issued this order that Arista's troops were occupying the road between the mouth of the Rio Grande and Fort Brown. Conflict would result, he knew—and it did just eighteen miles and less than twenty-four hours after the march began. At the pond of Palo Alto his scouts reported the enemy a mile ahead and spread out more than a mile and a half in width. Taylor prepared to fight his country's first battle, his army mainly a peace-time one but officered at the junior level with men trained at West Point.

Between one thirty and two o'clock both sides prepared to fight in their characteristic national ways, Arista by riding along his line shouting *"Viva la República"* and making speeches that were almost drowned out by the noise of bands in the rear, and Taylor by slumping sidesaddle on his horse, chewing tobacco, spitting, and talking to anyone who wandered by. Then each side deployed. It was time for fighting —and dying—both sides sustained by the belief that they were battling for national territory.

Taylor allowed his troops a short rest, during which the

more farsighted filled their canteens, and then he aligned them for battle. Despite the advice of his officers, Old Rough and Ready chose to place his artillery in the center of his formation. He did this because he had 2 eighteen-pound siege guns, as well as a total of 16 batteries and 932 men from artillery units of the Regular Army, and he believed they would stand firm during battle. On his right and left flanks were infantrymen, with the dragoons guarding his wagon train. Arista, meanwhile, chose to station 150 horsmen under General Noriega to the right, then a four-pound cannon, then infantry, with the Tampico Veterans in the center, and on the left he had 5 of the four-pounders, more infantry, and, slightly in advance, the thousand mounted lancers. Interspersed was the remainder of his artillery, consisting of eight-pound guns, and some sappers. Between these two forces were boggy pools and fields of grass that was stiff and shoulder high.

Taylor advanced his troops to within half a mile of the Mexicans, who opened fire with their cannons. There Taylor halted and directed his artillery to return the fire. Brevet Major Samuel Ringgold, who commanded a battery for lightweight guns, moved forward rapidly, unlimbered his weapons, and at approximately three o'clock began firing. The Mexicans stood the cannonade with great bravery—and numerous casualties. In fact, Ringgold's fire was so devastating that soon huge holes appeared in the Mexican ranks. The Mexican cannons, by contrast, were old, and their copper shot reached the American lines only on the rebound; the troops simply dodged, jumped, or sidestepped to avoid the shot. An hour of such one-sided conflict forced Arista to order a charge by Torrejón's lancers toward the American right and rear with the intent of taking the American supply wagons, a tempting sight to Mexicans, to whom those wagons meant they would have the best meal they had received in weeks.

With lances extended, banners fluttering from their tips, the lancers charged in the best Spanish tradition. Taylor sent word to Colonel David Twiggs to keep a "bright look-out for them," which Twiggs did with his 5th Infantry drawn up in a square. The 5th advanced in this formation to meet the Mexican charge, which came in column, not in line; the Americans held their fire until the lancers were only fifty yards away, then shot with telling effect. Torre-jón's men recoiled to re-form and try a second time—with the same result. Then Randolph Ridgely and Sam French brought two pieces of Ringgold's light cannons, commonly and rightly called "Flying Artillery," and opened fire on the Mexicans, whereupon Torrejón and his lancers retired from the field to report their failure to the dismayed Arista.

At this juncture the prairie grass caught fire, probably from sparks from the cannons on one side or the other. Ocean breezes coming inland fanned the flames, which generated a smoke screen between the two armies. Behind this screen, both Mexicans and Americans maneuvered—Arista by pivoting his right side forward and his left side back, Taylor by moving his entire force forward on an oblique to his right at an angle of some thirty-five degrees. When the smoke cleared, both sides were still facing one another. Thereupon Lieutenant William Churchill opened fire with the eighteen-pounders, using grape and canister shot to open gaping holes in the Mexican line. Arista responded by sending troops forward to capture or destroy the eighteen-pounders, but the charging Mexicans were routed by the American artillerymen, who fought as infantry, and by the cannon fire they were seeking to halt. And when a Mexican force of cavalry and infantry sought to flank the Americans on the left, Captain James Duncan opened fire with yet more artillery and drove the attackers back twice. Similar success was had on the American left, so that by seven o'clock that evening the moment was ripe for an American charge. But darkness intervened, and both sides bivouacked on the battlefield. A count showed only 5 dead Americans, including the brave Major Ringgold, and 43 wounded; Ar-

ista later reported 250 dead or wounded, but a better esti-
mate would be approximately seven times the American casualties.

Little did Taylor realize tht evening, as he paced in the
full moonlight, the devastating blow to Mexican morale
wrought by his artillery. Nor could he know that subordinates were charging Arista with cowardice and treachery for
his failure to make a frontal assault at the beginning of the
encounter. Early the next morning Taylor gained an inkling
of his victory when the light of day revealed the Mexicans
retreating from Palo Alto. A council with his ranking officers produced a vote of seven to three in favor of entrench-
ing and waiting, but Taylor ordered preparations for an advance; he did choose to leave his wagons behind, and he sent
Captain George A. McCall with 220 men of the 4th Infantry
to follow the Mexicans and harass their rear units.

Arista retreated toward the Rio Grande, some seven
miles distant, until he entered a thick woods and arrived at
Resaca de Guerrero, an ancient channel of the Rio Grande.
There, in a three- to four-foot depression, the Mexican general implanted several of his artillery pieces and spread his
troops along both sides of the road, with his strength to his
right. His strategy was sound. The trees would negate the
effectiveness of the Americans' dreaded artillery, and his position effectively barred Taylor's road to Fort Brown. At this
spot, then, he and his demoralized troops waited.

Word from Captain McCall of the Mexican halt reached
Taylor shortly after noon. With some 1700 men, the American general advanced the five miles separating the two
forces, and then he sent Lieutenant Stephen Decatur Dobbins forward to draw the Mexican fire and thereby reveal
the location of their artillery. The strategy succeeded, for
Dobbins and two sergeants were wounded and a private killed
by a "shower of grapeshot." Lieutenant Randolph Ridgely,
who had replaced Ringgold, was then ordered by Taylor to advance and blast the Mexican artillery out of the road. Ridgely

advanced to within a hundred yards, firing as he moved, but he and his men were unable to silence the Mexican guns, whereupon Taylor ordered Captain Charles A. May and the dragoons to charge. This maneuver resulted in the capture of several enemy lancers, including General Rómolo Díaz de la Vega, yet did not quiet the Mexican artillery. Taylor thereupon ordered Colonel William G. Belknap, with the 8th Infantry and part of the 5th, forward with the command, "Take those guns, and by God keep them." Belknap and his men rushed forward in a headlong charge, reinforcing their courage with fiendish yells, and after hand-to-hand fighting captured the Mexican pieces.

The loss of these guns effectively turned the battle against Arista, although he was slow to realize it. While these early events had been transpiring, he had been in his tent writing in the belief that only a skirmish was in progress. When he realized his mistake, he rushed out to take personal command of Torrejón's lancers, dashed forward to lance a few Americans, and then retreated pell-mell to the Rio Grande and crossed downriver. The Mexican soldiers, seeing their commander flee, followed him as fast as possible; they rushed to board whatever boats were available, dropping weapons and clothing in their haste and in their fear that the Americans were pursuing them. Some tried to swim across the river—many of them drowned, as did those who fell from the overcrowded boats. Resaca de la Palma, as this battle became known, was another decided American victory. Arista's army had dwindled to some 4000 once it was regrouped south of the Rio Grande.

Taylor made no attempt to cross immediately to Matamoros and take advantage of his victory, but preferred instead to regroup and resupply his troops. He made a trip to the coast to secure supplies from the American naval vessels offshore, and only after this did he prepare to cross the river. Arista, meanwhile, had no source of supply. His funds were scarce, his troops were panicky, and his ammunition was almost gone. On May 17 the Mexican general sent a request to Taylor for an armistice, to which Old Rough and Ready responded with an emphatic no: "I must have Matamoros even if I am forced to batter down the entire town. I am fully prepared to do that very thing. These are my terms: The city must capitulate; all property must be surrendered; then and only then may the Mexican army march out and retire."

Arista, whose orders were to hold Matamoros as long as possible, counseled with his officers, who advised him that the city was indefensible. Instead of replying to Taylor's message—a reply was demanded by three o'clock on Sunday afternoon, May 17—Arista fled the city, leaving behind his wounded and part of his ammunition and supplies. Taylor learned of this flight the next day. Soon thereafter a delegation of civil authorities from Matamoros called on Taylor to ask for terms; he replied that he would respect persons and property, the Mexicans assented, and American troops crossed the river to Fort Paredes and raised the Stars and Stripes while they sang "Yankee Doodle."

Arista, fleeing southward, saw large numbers of his troops desert in fear of American pursuit with their deadly artillery. The route became lined with dead animals—and dead Mexicans who succumbed to exhaustion and some even to suicide. Arista arrived in Linares with 2638 troops. The reaction in Mexico to news of this disaster was shocked astonishment. All Centralist leaders had been predicting victory, even conservative General De la Vega, now a prisoner; and President-General Paredes was stunned, for he had believed the nation would rally behind him in victory and proclaim him king of Mexico. National confidence plummeted. In a move to restore confidence and rebuild shattered morale, the Centralists blamed the defeat on Arista, removed him from command of the Army of the North, and replaced him with General Francisco Mejía. This new commander, charged with rebuilding the Army of the North, was just twenty-four years old, a political appointee filled with bombast and self-importance, yet a liberal within the framework of Mexican politics. It became his task to prepare for another engagement with Taylor and the Americans.

In the United States, the reaction to Taylor's victories at Palo Alto and Resaca de la Palma was a soaring confidence in the army and the volunteers. Taylor was the hero of the hour, and he was breveted a major general and named commander of the Army of the Rio Grande. Congress voted him two gold medals, while the Whigs openly talked of running him for the presidency in 1848. One recruiting poster summed up the national attitude: "Here's to Old Zach! Glorious Times! Roast Beef, Ice Cream, and Three Months' Advance!" Volunteer regiments formed under such colorful names as the New Orleans Eagle Guards, the Jasper Greens, the Washington Cadets, the Cincinnati Cadets, and even the Fannin Avengers. A call for 2800 men in Tennessee saw 30,000 responding, some of the disappointed even trying to buy a billet; in Maine the Aroostook boys marched off to war, while in Connecticut there were twice as many volunteers as needed.

Yet at Fort Brown and Matamoros there was no real happiness among the troops. The young officers were cursing Taylor as inept, bumbling, old, and foolish. George Meade, later a Union general in the Civil War, wrote that Taylor had a "perfect inability to make any use of information" supplied him. Nor were the enlisted men happy with the flesh-pots of Matamoros. The sickly climate, coupled with boredom, generated disillusionment and discontent; thus they flocked to the numerous gambling halls, cantinas, and brothels of the Mexican city for entertainment, and soon fell to brawling among themselves and pillaging the city. Their relationship with the Mexican women shifted from love to rudeness, even occasionally to rape. Taylor had no recourse but to move his headquarters to another location if he was to keep his army fit to fight.

On June 15 he sent Captain Ben McCulloch and forty

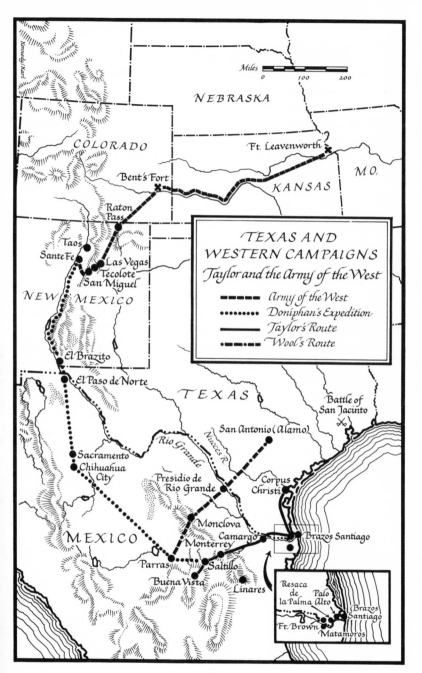

TEXAS AND
WESTERN CAMPAIGNS
Taylor and the Army of the West

▪ ▪ ▪ ▪ Army of the West
• • • • • Doniphan's Expedition
——— Taylor's Route
▪•▪•▪ Wool's Route

Texas Rangers southward to ascertain the best route to Monterrey, the nearest Mexican city of major size. And he worried about his troops. His army had grown to 8000 men, some of who were three-month volunteers and others who had signed for six months. Some of these men he sent home and more came. By August 1 he had nearly 20,000 men under his command along the Rio Grande. They had come to fight, not to drink brackish water, sweat out fevers, and watch their companions die of disease. Taylor ordered a move upriver to Camargo, the head of navigation on the Rio Grande, some to go by boat and some by land. On July 6–7 the 7th Infantry started this move, and by August 8 even Taylor and his staff had arrived at Camargo by steamer.

Camargo proved no more sanitary than had Matamoros. It was a place of death for 1500 Americans owing to heat and mud and the various diseases brought from Matamoros by the troops. So many died during the move itself that, it was said, the Texas mockingbirds learned to sing the death march from listening to the band. Camargo was walled in by limestone rock, and the air was motionless, hot, and humid. The men pitched their tents too near the camp supply of water, which was used for drinking, disposing of wastes, and bathing. Because of the blistering heat and the primitive sanitary conditions, sickness spread among the troops, already feverish, and many died. Young Lieutenant George B. McClellan commented, "I have seen more suffering since I came out here than I could have imagined to exist. It really is awful. I allude to the sufferings of the volunteers. They literally die like dogs." Lew Wallace, a volunteer from Indiana, wrote about another camp on the Rio Grande: "I cannot recall another instance of a command so wantonly neglected and so brutally mislocated." So many died that summer that military honors were no longer given at each burial; and when the supplies of lumber, gunboxes, and cracker-barrel staves were exhausted in making coffins, bodies were buried only in blankets.

Meanwhile, McCulloch and his Texas Rangers were scouting toward Monterrey. Taylor early had recognized the need for men such as the Rangers and had called for four regiments from Texas. Only three regiments were raised, forming a division under J. Pinckney Henderson, the governor of the state who took a leave of absence in order to participate in what to Texans was a popular war. Many residents of the Lone Star State remembered the Alamo and Goliad massacres and saw the war as an opportunity to even old scores; thus they happily joined the Rangers and rode south to kill. McCulloch's company was part of the regiment commanded by Colonel John C. Hays and was, according to one member of the company, "the best mounted, armed, equipped and appointed corps that was out in the ranging service." They had been recruited from along the Guadalupe River, a region where fights against Mexicans had long been common and where many old grudges with Mexico remained to be settled. These Rangers did not please the military sensibilities of Regular Army officers: they had no tents, and so constructed their shelters out of whatever came to hand, and they did not like to salute, to stand in formation, or to defer to men of rank. Yet armed with the new Colt six-shooter and the courage of the frontiersmen, they became demons feared throughout northern Mexico for their extreme anti-Mexican bias, thereby keeping Taylor's lines of supply and communication open.

With his forty picked men, McCulloch departed from Fort Brown on June 15 and rode toward Linares in the wake of Arista's retreating soldiers. They did not avoid ranches along the way; rather they depended on surprise and boldness to overrun those they encountered. They advanced to within sixty miles of Linares, only to learn that because of drought Arista's troops already had gone on to Monterrey. There ensued a time of waiting, during which the Texas Rangers made a general nuisance of themselves by their unmilitary conduct. They drank openly; they freely ate Mexican hogs and chickens; they disturbed Mexican fiestas and fandangos; and they did not hesitate to do violence to any Mexicans who resisted their demands.

By mid-August, Old Rough and Ready had his plans made and ordered the march on Monterrey to begin. Most of his troops he left on the Rio Grande. One division of volunteers would accompany two divisions of regulars, a total of 6640 men; the volunteers were under the command of Brevet Major General William O. Butler, a Kentucky lawyer of proven merit, while the two divisions of regulars were commanded by Brevet Major General Worth and Brevet Brigadier General Twiggs. The march south began on August 19 in two parallel—later converging—columns; those who marched considered themselves lucky to be escaping the heat, sickness, and death of Camargo, just as did the companies of Texas Rangers accompanying each column. Little opposition was encountered along the way, for the Rangers cleared out whatever hostile Mexicans were waiting, as at the villages of Ramos and Marín. In fact, as the Americans approached Monterrey, the troops were speculating that the Mexicans would not defend the city. Thus they marched to the outskirts of the city on September 19 and gazed across lush fields of corn and sugar cane at the town, the Rangers, as always, in advance under the command of J. Pinckney Henderson. All encamped for the night at Walnut Grove, a picnic ground for the fashionable citizens of Monterrey. That night it rained as men fitfully tried to sleep and thought of home.

Unknown to the Americans, the town was strongly defended. Command of the Army of the North had passed from the youthful Francisco Mejía to the more formidable General Pedro de Ampudia. Born at Havana, Cuba, in 1805, Ampudia had arrived in Mexico in 1821 to join at an opportune moment on the side of the rebels against Spain. Afterward he rose steadily in rank, fighting against the Spaniards in 1829 and against the Texans from 1840 to 1842. By September 1846 he was a general and was political chief and governor of Nuevo León. Ampudia bitterly despised Texans and was noted for his cruel and barbarous treatment of anyone he happened to capture; for example, in 1844 when the Mexican Navy captured exiled General Francisco Sentamanat, Ampudia ordered the general and fourteen of his aides shot and their heads boiled in oil so that their skulls could be displayed in iron cages.

Ampudia in September 1846 had orders to keep the 10,000 troops of the Army of the North at Saltillo to await the arrival of a new commander. He chose to disobey his orders and moved his men to Monterrey, for he believed the city of 15,000 to be a natural fortress which could not be captured; in fact, he proclaimed that it was impregnable. And so it seemed, for Monterrey was located on the north bank of the Rio Santa Catarina, hemmed in on the south and west by mountains; to the northeast by Fort Tenería, behind which was a stone tannery whose flat roof provided a parapet behind sandbags for a garrison of sharpshooters; and more to the northeast, on the Marín road, by an earthwork fort called El Diablo. Also to the north, just outside town, was the Citadel, housing 400 veterans and an eighteen-pound cannon. To the west, also outside town, was the Bishop's Palace atop Independence Hill, which with sandbags had become a fortress complete with cannon. In that vicinity was another fort, La Libertad, also with cannon, while more artillery pieces were at a post atop Federation Ridge called El Soldado. And in the center of the city at the cathedral, Ampudia had a large store of munitions. Thus he had good reason to believe he could hold the city.

Captain Richard A. Gillespie of the Texas Rangers and Major Joseph K. F. Mansfield provided scouting reports that made Taylor well aware of the stout defenses at Ampudia's command, and he carefully plotted his attack. Worth was to take 2000 men, skirt the Citadel, and sever Ampudia's supply line, the road to Saltillo; then they were to storm Independence Hill and move on to the town, this to be done while Taylor and the remaining troops made a diversionary attack on the eastern side of the city. When Worth made his major assault on Monterrey, then Taylor would commit all his forces, thereby making a two-front assault. Worth understood his orders, and at two o'clock on the afternoon of September 20 marched to take up his position, a move that took four hours. At the head of the column, as was becoming customary, rode the Texas Rangers. All encamped that night in a group of peasant huts, and they used the chickens and pigs they found there as food.

Early the next morning, September 21, the battle commenced. Worth first moved to take command of the Saltillo road, which brought a charge from 200 Mexican lancers. They came at McCulloch and the Rangers, both sides fighting with pistols and swords, while the American artillery poured a withering fire into the rear ranks of the Mexicans. The lines soon parted, the Mexicans leaving more than a hundred dead behind as the only obstacle between Worth and the Saltillo road. With that secure, Worth at noon ordered an attack on Federation Hill by four companies of artillerymen acting as infantry and six companies of dismounted Texas Rangers. The Texans calmly advanced while the Mexican artillery atop the hill fired grape and canister shot at them ineffectively; without a casualty the Texans reached the base of the hill and charged up it, whereupon the Mexicans abandoned their cannon to flee. The Texans then turned the gun on the retreating Mexicans.

Across the way the same process was taking place against Fort Soldado. Artillery, infantry, volunteers, and Rangers swarmed toward the top yelling loudy. Captain Richard A. Gillespie was first to cross the enemy breastworks, and the Mexicans there likewise fled. Worth then allowed his men to rest while he made plans for an assault on Independence Hill and the Bishop's Palace, to take place at three o'clock the following morning.

The attack began at the appointed hour— 450 men climbed the ridge of Independence Hill and, yelling wildly, stormed the Mexican defenders. Morale disintegrated and the Mexicans fled in panic. The American flag was unfurled from the position. Then at noon, Worth's men began cannonading the Bishop's Palace, which was so strongly defended that new tactics had to be devised. A feint by volunteers brought the Mexican infantry out in a charge, whereupon the volunteers began a retreat; the Mexicans, thinking the Americans were retreating, came storming after them. Suddenly a group of Rangers, who had been concealed, rose up and fired with deadly effect, demoralizing the Mexicans, some to retreat inside the Bishop's Palace, others to run for the safety of the city. A howitzer pounded open the gate of the Bishop's Palace, the Americans swarmed inside, and the remainder of the defenders, except for some thirty prisoners, fled to Monterrey. Worth had taken his major objectives with only thirty-two men lost in the two days of fighting.

Taylor's diversionary attack on the northeastern corner of the city had greatly aided Worth's movements. Old Rough and Ready had begun his effort with an artillery barrage from his heavy guns, then had ordered light batteries brought close to the city in an attempt to batter an opening in the walls. Next the 1st Division, commanded by Lieutenant Colonel John Garland (Twiggs had fallen ill) moved forward, along with Butler's volunteers and the Mississippi Rifles (who were commanded by Colonel Jefferson Davis). A murderous crossfire from the Citadel caused the volunteers to break and run. Yet the confusion was such that small clusters of men failed to hear the order to retreat; they managed to break into part of the city streets and to take El Tenería. Darkness fell at this time, and under its cover Taylor ordered a count of his casualties. He found that the one day of fighting had cost him 394 killed or wounded.

The next day, September 22, he allowed his troops to

rest. On September 23, as Worth and his troops entered the city from the far side, Taylor ordered his men to attack. The day was spent mainly in street-fighting, with men pushing from house to house and from block to block. As darkness fell, Taylor was ready to withdraw in order to join with Worth in a concerted attack the next day. But suddenly there was no need for further fighting. Ampudia had not been especially bothered by the house-to-house fighting, but the artillery changed his mind about continuing his defense. Worth's men had brought a cannon from Federation Hill to a point where it could shell the plaza of the city, while Captain Lucien B. Webster had placed a twenty-four-pounder at El Tenería; it also capable of bombarding the central plaza, and the cathedral, where the Mexican munitions were stored. General Ampudia and his best fighting men also were inside the cathedral. A shell landed so close that it scared the townspeople, the soldiers, and Ampudia. Immediately, the Mexican general sent Colonel Francisco Moreno with a flag of truce to ask that an armistice be arranged and that the Mexican soldiers be allowed to retire from the city, taking with them all military equipment and stores.

Taylor listened to Colonel Moreno and replied by demanding an unconditional surrender. Ampudia countered with a request for a personal interview with Taylor. The upshot of the negotiations was an agreement for commissioners to meet and work out details of an armistice. Worth, Jefferson Davis, and J. Pinckney Henderson represented the American side—and were bested by their Mexican counterparts. The terms of the armistice were that the Mexicans could retain their sidearms and accouterments, along with six pieces of artillery, and that the Americans would not pursue them for eight weeks. Thus on September 25, Ampudia and the Mexicans withdrew from the town, while Taylor and the Americans entered. Soon the Stars and Stripes was raised as twenty-eight guns boomed. Taylor had taken the "impregnable" city in just three days with the loss of 800 killed and wounded.

News of Taylor's conquest caused celebrations throughout the United States, yet in Washington there were many critics of his eight-week armistice. Some professional soldiers said Taylor's actions were unintelligent, but the most severe critics were Democratic politicians, including the president, who feared Taylor's growing popularity. To offset the increasing frequency with which Taylor's name was being mentioned as a Whig presidential candidate, Polk began openly criticizing the general: "In agreeing to this armistice Genl. Taylor violated his express orders & I regret that I cannot approve his course," he wrote. By late November the president was even more outspoken in his diary: "I am now satisfied that he is . . . without resources and wholly unqualified for the command he holds." Thus on January 26, 1847, he issued orders for Taylor to remain in the vicinity of Monterrey, while four-fifths of his troops were to be sent to accompany General Winfield Scott in an invasion of Mexico at Vera Cruz. The president thought that Taylor would have only enough men left to remain on the defensive—and, in fact, so ordered Taylor.

While the Americans quarreled for political advantage, Ampudia had retreated from Monterrey not just to Saltillo but all the way across the burning desert and then southward, reaching San Luis Potosí in mid October. One day before his arrival with the remnant of his army, the new commander of the Army of the North had finally reached the city; the command was restyled the Army of Liberation! Replacing Ampudia was Antonio López de Santa Anna, the wily villain of so many Mexican disasters and a veteran of long military background. Santa Anna had entered the Spanish Army in 1810 as a cadet at the age of sixteen. Just twelve years later he was a brigadier general. After independence was gained, he fought rebels in Potosí, Yucatán, and Zacatecas. He defeated the Spaniards in 1829 and emerged as dictator in 1835. His career culminated in his exile in 1844 when he fled to Cuba; he was living there when war broke out in 1846. Carefully he approached the Polk administration through diplomatic channels, promising a quick end to the war if he could but return to Mexico. Polk believed him and issued the ex-dictator a safe-conduct pass through the American naval blockade. Reaching the Mexican coast in mid-August 1846, Santa Anna arrived at the capital on September 14 to carefully staged "Hurrahs" from assembled crowds. Three days later President General José Mariano Salas named him commander-in-chief of the Army of Liberation.

His commission in hand, Santa Anna went north to arrive at San Luis Potosí just in time to confront the retreating Ampudia. With Ampudia's troops and with the recruits he conscripted, Santa Anna soon had an army numbering about 20,000. His next decision was where to fight. This question was answered when his scouts intercepted a letter from Scott to Taylor ordering Old Rough and Ready to send all but 6000 of his troops to the coast for embarkation. Santa Anna deduced that most of the men who would remain with Taylor would be volunteers, largely untrained and suffering from the battle at Monterrey. Here, he thought, would be an excellent place to win a startling victory, one that would return him to the Mexican presidency, and he marched northward with his army to do battle, utterly ignoring his promises to the American government to seek peace.

At Monterrey, meanwhile, Taylor had determined to defy Polk's orders to remain on the defensive, which he chose to interpret as an opinion rather than an order. His first target was Saltillo, some seventy miles southwest of Monterrey and a town of some 15,000 inhabitants. On November 8, 1846, he ordered General Worth to prepare to march on Saltillo. Five days later the order was put into effect. Saltillo was taken on November 16 without a shot being fired, and by mid-January Taylor had a line of defense—and offense—stretching from Monterrey to the Gulf of Mexico, about four hundred miles in length. This daring move had been made possible by the arrival of six companies of regulars of the 6th Infantry, three companies of volunteers from Illinois, a company of artillery, and some units of Texas Rangers who were acting as scouts; all were under the command of Brigadier General John Ellis Wool, a sixty-two-year-old veteran. Born in Newburgh, New York, Wool had had little formal education. He entered the War of 1812 as a captain, and when that war ended, his record was so creditable that he was breveted a lieutenant colonel. In 1816 he became inspector general of the army with the rank of colonel. Twenty-five years later he was promoted to brigadier, a rank he had held by brevet since 1826. At the outbreak of the war with Mexico, he had mustered 12,000 volunteers into service in six weeks, then went to San Antonio, where he took command of 1400 men whom he marched to Saltillo, arriving there on December 22.

By mid-January 1847 the signs that a powerful Mexican army under Santa Anna was moving north were sufficiently strong to bring Taylor back to Monterrey from Saltillo. And he recalled Wool from an expedition under way against Parral, Chihuahua. Consolidating his force, he moved to take up a position just south of the town of Saltillo on the road toward San Luis Potosí, his camp at the hacienda of Agua Nueva, an unprotected position in the shadow of the mountains. Counting Wool's troops, he had 4759 men, of whom only two squadrons of cavalry and three batteries of artillery were regulars, a pitiful 476 men.

Scouts dispatched by Taylor, including the indefatigable Ben McCulloch, reported on February 21 that Santa Anna and his army of 20,000 were approaching, that, in fact, General Vicente Miñón's cavalry was trying to block the road between the hacienda of Agua Nueva and Saltillo. With great rapidity Taylor withdrew his troops to the hacienda of

Buena Vista, from which point he departed the seven miles north to Saltillo, leaving Wool in command. Wool ordered the occupation of high ground at a point known as La Angostura, there implanting an eight-gun battery of artillery under the command of Brevet Major John Macrae Washington in a position to cover the road to San Luis Potosí. He also located six companies of troops nearby, while the other 4000 men waited below.

Santa Anna, marching northward, had good information about the number and the composition of Taylor's army, and was supremely confident of an easy victory. On Monday morning, February 22, Taylor returned from Saltillo to receive an imperious note from Santa Anna: "You are surrounded by twenty thousand men, and can not in any human probability avoid suffering a rout, and being cut to pieces with your troops; but as you deserve consideration and particular esteem, I wish to save you from a catastrophe, and for that purpose give you this notice, in order that you may surrender at discretion. . . ." He gave Taylor an hour to respond. Old Rough and Ready's note was brief: "In reply to your note of this date summoning me to surrender my forces at discretion, I beg leave to say that I decline acceding to your request."

Of the two armies, Santa Anna's was in the poorer condition at that time. He had pushed northward so rapidly that his men had been able to get little rest, and his supply of food for them was low. When he arrived at Agua Nueva to learn that Taylor and the *norteamericanos* had departed in great haste, he deduced that they were fleeing in panic and should be pursued. Thus he ordered General Pedro de Ampudia to hurry his troops forward without rest while he brought the remainder along himself. To the Mexican general's dismay, he arrived at La Angostura to find that the Americans had not fled but had taken up a position of strength and in good order. Yet his troops outnumbered them three to one, and he had General Miñón in the rear with reserves. Thus he decided to commit Ampudia's troops at once against the American left, thereby pinning down the artillery, while other Mexicans worked around, skirted the base of the hills, and attacked from the rear.

To start this attack, Santa Anna first made a feint at the right side of the American line, which did not fool Taylor sufficiently to order it reinforced. Then Ampudia and 1000 infantry struck on the left. When this began, Taylor sent two regiments of infantry, along with three guns, under Captain John Paul Jones O'Brien, to strengthen that side. As the attacking Mexicans came forward, they were warmly greeted by Colonel Humphrey Marshall's Kentucky volunteers and by withering fire from O'Brien's three cannons. The 2nd Indiana Regiment, for unknown reasons, suddenly retreated, exposing O'Brien and the artillery to continued and reinforced Mexican attack; finally O'Brien had to withdraw, losing the four-pound gun (a captured Mexican piece) in the process but saving his other two guns. The Mexicans did reach the upper slopes of the highest peak and there entrench themselves before dark. Thus ended the first day of fighting of the battle of Buena Vista.

During the night Santa Anna allowed his men to cook a hot meal, their first in twenty-four hours and one that consumed the last of their rations. And he harangued them with one of his stirring speeches, promising them a good meal on the morrow from captured American supplies. Afterward he allowed a band to serenade his troops before shifting their position slightly. He had 8 eight-pound artillery pieces brought forward to fire on O'Brien, and he moved the *Batallón de San Patricio* (a small unit composed of American deserters fighting on the Mexican side), up with their eighteen- and twenty-four-pounders for use in attempting to break the American lines. That night a cold, drizzling rain fell on both Mexicans and Americans, while rumors of attack caused sleep to be interrupted several times on both sides.

Dawn revealed that 1500 Mexican light infantrymen had scaled the heights sometime during the night to join Ampudia's men. The Americans gulped down a cold breakfast, but Santa Anna's troops had to fight on empty stomachs. The Mexicans made the first move, coming forward in good order, their pennants floating from lance tips and their bands playing stirring music. Wool had only 3300 men to oppose the 12,000 Mexicans moving forward, for Taylor had taken 500 men to Saltillo and 700 were to the right in the gullies. Then the fighting began, as General Santiago Blanco attacked the American right. No advantage could be gained there, for Washington's artillery cut Blanco's men to pieces as they advanced up the road and they were repulsed.

Then the main Mexican force, under Generals Francisco Pacheco and Manuel María Lombardini, began attacking Wool's position on the plateau. Here Captain O'Brien and his two artillery pieces, along with three of Washington's guns that were shifted raidly, wrecked havoc. General Joseph Lane, who had arrived the night before to be given command of that section by Wool, ordered a charge when the Mexican line began to break. But Colonel William A. Bowles, an old commander and a political hack, countermanded the order by telling his bugler to blow retreat; the Indiana volunteers obeyed. Other Americans, seeing them withdraw, followed, and the retreat became a rout. O'Brien and his gunners again found themselves unprotected and again retreated.

This action left Marshall and the Kentucky volunteers exposed and alone before Ampudia's advance. Dragoons under Captain Braxton Bragg and others rode forward, and together they were able to halt the Mexican advance, but not to turn it. At this crucial moment General Taylor returned from Saltillo. Immediately he sensed the need for action and rode forward on Old Whitey to order Jefferson Davis and the Mississippi volunteers up to fight Ampudia's men. Davis responded with a courageous charge, and the Mexicans fell back before the demoniacal assault. Bragg and

O'Brien also charged, seemingly with their guns everywhere as they took them across ground considered impassable. Shortly after noon the Mexicans began to fall back, with artillery shells crashing in their ranks. Santa Anna immediately sent an officer forward under flag of truce to ask what Taylor wanted; while the emissary talked with Wool, the Mexicans withdrew out of cannon range.

After regrouping his force, the Mexican general ordered his troops forward again under General Francisco Pérez. Taylor, instead of holding a defensive position, called for the Illinois infantry to charge—into a superior force outnumbering them six to one; the volunteers soon broke under Mexican fire, their leader, Colonel John J. Hardin, dead along with Lieutenant Colonel Henry Clay (son of the famous politician). Only the artillery rushing forward under Major Washington prevented the entire force from being annihilated; Captain Bragg and Captain O'Brien also arrived with guns, and grape and canister again turned the tide of battle. By five o'clock that evening the center of the Mexican line had collapsed, and Americans were advancing as darkness fell.

During the night of February 23, Taylor counseled with his generals. Casualty reports for the day showed that 673 Americans had been killed or wounded. Taylor knew that Mexican casualties were higher, but Santa Anna still had a larger, fresher army capable of doing battle. Wool and the other generals advised a retreat, but Old Rough and Ready wanted to hold his ground. About three o'clock on February 24, reinforcements arrived from Monterrey, 400 men and 2 eighteen-pound cannons. Taylor decided to continue the fight but his decision came after the battle was over, although he did not yet know it.

Santa Anna had been considering his own position during that same night. His casualties numbered perhaps 1800, but the damage to Mexican morale was infinitely greater. Twice they had charged with victory seemingly within their grasp, and twice they had been routed by American artillery and the enemy's ability to rally. They were without food and almost exhausted, their ammunition largely expended. Santa Anna realized all this and knew that his army could not fight again. During the night he ordered the retreat to begin, leaving the wounded behind. And what began as an orderly retreat turned into a race of terror as his conscripts fled the scene of death; they pushed the sick out of the road, men discarded their weapons, many fled into the hills, and wagons broke down and blocked the road. The retreat to San Luis Potosí accounted for 7000 losses, so that the Army of Liberation shrank to only 11,000. Santa Anna fled in the vanguard of this army. He decided to make his next stand against Winfield Scott on the road between Vera Cruz and Mexico City at a site known as Cerro Gordo.

On the morning of February 24, the Americans thus rose ready to do battle only to see the enemy in full flight. Regulars and volunteers alike moved across the plateau giving food and water to the Mexican wounded, brought them to hospitals, and treated them with kindness. Taylor and Wool hugged each other with relief, for they had grasped victory. Old Rough and Ready had been criticized for failing to capitalize on his victory at Monterrey, yet he held fast at Buena Vista in the knowledge that his tired army could not pursue the retreating Mexicans. Thus he allowed his men to rest, writing to his brother, "The great loss on both sides . . . has deprived me of everything like pleasure." He remained in northern Mexico with his army, knowing that Scott already had captured Vera Cruz and was marching on Mexico City. The war had ended for him, and he knew it. But the Battle of Buena Vista did bring him an official vote of thanks from Congress, along with another gold medal— and the criticism of Polk. Late in 1847 he would return to the United States expecting both the Democrats and the Whigs to nominate him for the presidency and to campaign for the presidency in his own peculiar fashion.

CHAPTER THREE

NEW MEXICO
AND CHIHUAHUA

New Mexico east of the Rio Grande was claimed by Texas at the outbreak of the war, a claim of no legitimacy. However, that province was a tempting prize for American occupation in 1846, and President Polk was much aware of it. Santa Fe traders had long demonstrated the commercial value of that Mexican state, while the Mexican hold on it had declined steadily. Its citizens were not protected by the national government from the ravages of Indian incursions; in fact, the troops that were present were more a menace to the people than they were a source of protection. Taxes were exorbitantly high, and New Mexicans felt no great patriotism and, in fact, little accord or sympathy, for the nation that ruled them. Thus Polk's move to acquire New Mexico was strategically sound, and he wasted little time, for on May 13, 1846, he directed the governor of Missouri to raise eight companies of dragoons and two of light artillery for the conquest of New Mexico.

To command the Army of New Mexico—or the Army of the West as it would come to be known—the president chose Colonel Stephen Watts Kearny, commanding officer of the 1st Dragoons. Born in 1794, the fifteenth child of his parents, at Newark, New Jersey, Kearny had attended Columbia College until the War of 1812, when he entered the army as a first lieutenant of infantry. During that conflict, he showed great courage at the Battle of Queenston Heights, where he was wounded and captured. He emerged from that war a captain, stayed in the army, and served with few interruptions on the Western frontier during the next thirty years in Iowa, Nebraska, Missouri, and Oklahoma. He was promoted to major in 1829, lieutenant colonel in 1833, and colonel of dragoons in 1836. In 1846 he was commander of the Third Military Department (Missouri), and thus naturally was given charge of the Army of the West, a position that saw him promoted to brigadier general as of June 30, 1846.

Recruiting for Kearny's army proved easy. Missouri lads were anxious to serve, especially since they had heard so much about Santa Fe from the traders who annually had gone down the trail to the capital of New Mexico. The recruits thronged to Fort Leavenworth by companies, where a tent city housed them. They were enlisted under an act of Congress, dated May 13, which authorized the president to accept the services of 50,000 volunteers for twelve months' service. The largest group under Kearny's immediate command was the 1st Regiment of Missouri Mounted Volunteers, numbering 856 men.

Custom dictated that such regiments be allowed to elect their own officers, which the volunteers shortly did. Chosen colonel of the Missouri Mounted Volunteers was Alexander William Doniphan, a thirty-eight-year-old native of Maysville, Kentucky, and a graduate of Augusta College in 1826. Doniphan, a smiling six-foot, four-inch giant, had become a lawyer of such oratorical ability in Missouri that few juries could resist him. He had served as a brigadier general in the state militia, in which capacity in 1839 he had aided in driving members of the Church of Jesus Christ of Latter Day Saints out of the state; however, he had refused a state order to execute the Mormon leader Joseph Smith and had threatened his commanding officer with legal action if the order was repeated.

In addition to the Missouri Mounted Volunteers, Kearny also had two companies of light artillery, some 250 men with 12 six-pounders and 4 twelve-pounders, under the command of Major Meriwether Lewis Clark; an infantry battalion of 145 men; Kearny's 1st Dragoons, numbering 300 men; and Captain Thomas B. Hudson's unit, the Laclede Rangers, from St. Louis, which numbered 107 men and was attached to the 1st Dragoons. This totaled 1658 troops and sixteen cannons. As these men straggled into Fort Leavenworth, they were drilled briefly by officers and non-commissioned officers of the Regular Army, some twenty days' drill in all; this training consisted mainly of cavalry tactics, such as marching by fours, saber exercise, the charge, and the rally. Then it was the first of June, and the grass along the trail began to turn green; once it could support horses, the march on Santa Fe could start. On June 5 a detachment of dragoons moved out, and by the twenty-ninth all were on the road. Accompanying the Army of the West were 414 vehicles belonging to Santa Fe traders anxious to do business. Ahead of them were freighters under contract to provide them with food—100 wagons loaded with provisions and 800 beeves; however, the supply contractors failed to find the trail, their wagons broke down, and they lost valuable time.

Fortunately Kearny's troops had several weeks before they could expect to fight, fortuitous since all training at Fort Leavenworth had been at the company level and the men had never fought together as a regiment or as an army; also the horses supplied them proved wild and ungovernable, while bugle calls, artillery and rifle fire, and the clanking and rattling of sabers and equipment further scared these animals. Thus they crossed the prairies and plains—while Doniphan read a book loaned to him by Kearny, a tome on French dragoon tactics written for use by American officers. By July 5 the first units were at Council Grove, 150 miles from Independence, and there they rested for the 500-mile-trip to Bent's Fort. Once they had availed themselves of the repair facilities at Council Grove, they could depart down the trail in earnest.

Rain, sickness, thirst, dust, and heat were these troopers' lot until they arrived at the Arkansas River, which was reached by the main body on July 12. Also, buffalo and antelope became available in large numbers for the first time, and thus they had fresh meat, along with plums and grapes gathered from thickets along the river banks. Such provisions were welcome, for the government had failed to provide the Army of the West with spring carriages for ambulances, and those who became ill were forced to ride in unsprung freight wagons—an oversight that cost the Army of the West a number of lives.

On July 18 an informant returned from a spying venture at Santa Fe to make a report creating much excitement in the traveling camp. He reported that 2300 men had already been called to defend Santa Fe by the governor and that another army was assembling at Taos. Thus the Army of the West could expect a hot fight when it arrived at its destination. The report confirmed that the New Mexicans were expecting the Americans, and that their own spies had been active—a fact borne out by subsequent events.

Indeed, the governor of New Mexico, Manuel Armijo, was preparing for battle. A man of low birth in New Mexico, Armijo had arrived at power in his native province through cunning, energy, intrigue, bluster, and brains. He appealed to the lower classes through his choice of uniforms: blue coat, striped pants, and red sash adorned with gold lace. Success had come through affability and shrewdness, and his wealth was the result of the high taxes he had levied on the

Santa Fe traders (taxes which they could pay or else languish in jail). Armijo displayed his success in figure as well as in dress, for he had become grossly corpulent since assuming the governorship in 1837. Yet for all his success and his intrigue, Armijo was not a man of courage; in fact, one of his favorite sayings was, "It is better to be thought brave than to be so." Greed and cowardice—these in combination in the governor of New Mexico caused Kearny to hope that conquest might be achieved without excessive bloodshed, and this he worked to achieve.

As the American army traveled up the Arkansas River in the July heat, the officers worked for a cohesive military semblance among the volunteers. Then they moved out of the buffalo country as they approached Bent's Fort, and fresh meat became scarce. The troops could amuse themselves with nightly swims in the muddy waters of the river, with watching the comical prairie dogs, and with looking at the profuse wild flowers, but the sick list had grown to some one hundred men; others, not ill, had seen their horses break down and had to walk. The 1st battalion was five miles in front of the other troops, and its commanding officer decided to drill them until the others caught up; the result was a near mutiny and a growing hatred of West Point officers.

The first units of Kearny's army reached Bent's Fort on July 22, and the others streamed in during the next few days. At the fort they found the caravan of traders waiting for them to serve as an escort into the New Mexican capital. And at the post Kearny relaxed discipline and allowed his weary troops to rest from the strict orders of the trail; the Army of the West had been in Mexican territory for more than a week, and Cheyenne and Comanche raiders had posed an additional threat. While the men relaxed, Kearny searched for a specific way to utilize Armijo's greed and fear, and on July 27 a wagon arrived carrying the man who could help the general, James Magoffin. While Magoffin's sister-in-law, Susan Shelby Magoffin, was in William Bent's room having a miscarriage, Magoffin and his brother (and business partner) Samuel conferred with Kearny. James Magoffin had long been in the Santa Fe trade, he spoke fluent Spanish, and he was a friend of Governor Armijo; in addition, he had close ties with Senator Thomas Hart Benton of Missouri, and through Benton was known by President Polk and Secretary of War William L. Marcy. Magoffin arrived at Bent's Fort with letters from Polk and Marcy to Colonel Kearny, letters stating that Magoffin should be allowed to negotiate with Armijo. These orders did not anger Kearny, for they fitted in with his own hopes of a bloodless conquest.

The American colonel, after this conference, made several moves. First, he sent three captured New Mexican spies to Santa Fe to announce that the Americans would protect all New Mexicans who did not resist the occupation. Next, on July 31, he issued a proclamation promising civil and religious freedom to all New Mexicans who laid down their arms, a proclamation he agreed to send via Magoffin; the trader, in turn, asked for twelve dragoons to accompany him under a flag of truce. To command the dragoons, Magoffin asked for a young officer of talent—and discretion. Kearny selected Captain Philip St. George Cooke for this task. Magoffin and Cooke departed Bent's Fort that same day, July 31, heading through Raton Pass with Kearny's proclamation. The Army of the West waited only one day before it also set out marching for Raton Pass, New Mexico, and destiny.

Meanwhile, in New Mexico, Governor Armijo was busily preparing for battle. His spies had informed him of Kearny's advance, the intent of which was obvious, and on July 1 Armijo appealed to Mexico City for help in combating the American invasion. From the governor of Chihuahua came a promise of 500 cavalry and a similar number of infantrymen; the governor of Durango made a similar promise. But Armijo needed more than promises, so he conscripted local citizens, gathered the regulars, and readied an army. He did get some 3000 men together, but they were not reliable and he knew it; they were, for the most part, raw conscripts, militia-men, old soldiers, and presidial troops that had never seen formal battle. His was not a formidable army. Such was the condition of preparedness in New Mexico when on August 12 Magoffin and Cooke arrived to ask for a conference.

While Armijo made his preparations, Kearny and the Army of the West were marching. On August 1–2 they departed Bent's Fort, to begin climbing toward Raton Pass. The advance caused great hardship and suffering. Captain Henry S. Turner, a Regular Army officer, wrote his wife on August 5, ". . . Regt. to a man is sick & tired of the business. . . . No grass for 4 days. Regulars have spirit & volunteers would not make it without them" (Turner Collection, Missouri Historical Society, St. Louis). Rations had to be cut by one-half—and then more—until meals consisted of flour stirred in water and fried with tiny bits of salt pork. The trail through the pass was narrow and often blocked. Baggage and wagons had to be pulled up rocky slopes by the men, then eased down steep cliffs on ropes. Finally they reached the south side to find a cool valley containing fresh water and plenty of grass; there they were allowed to rest, for it was Sunday. Kearny wished to have the day utilized in instruction of the Missouri Volunteers, so he approached Doniphan and said, "Colonel, would you rather have me present or not when you drill your regiment?" Doniphan replied, "I do not suppose you can learn anything new. But I may learn much from your kindly criticism" (Doniphan Papers, September 19, 1883, Missouri Historical Society, St. Louis). He proceeded to move his men through a light drill that satisfied Kearny. Then his troops were allowed to eat, for they now had been cut to one-third rations.

On August 11 the Army of the West arrived at Rayado Creek, where that day a detail returned from Taos with fourteen prisoners as well as a copy of a proclamation by the prefect at Taos; this called on New Mexicans to rally to drive out the *norteamericanos*. And that day Kearny happily encountered a trader from Taos who had a load of flour; this was purchased to feed the troops, now ravaged by disease. Each of the preceding days had seen graves being dug. The news of an impending fight served to raise spirits in the army. They had come to fight, and they welcomed battle. And during those past few days, Kearny had interviewed several captured Mexican spies; these he released after allowing them a good look at his army, for he wanted them to carry reports of high American morale and fighting potential to Santa Fe.

On August 14 a Mexican lieutenant and three lancers rode into the American camp with a letter from Governor Armijo. In this message the governor acknowledged Kearny's letter claiming all land east of the Rio Grande, but said he could not recognize the validity of this claim. He also stated that the New Mexicans were armed and that they would fight. Kearny held the Mexican lieutenant through the remainder of that day. That evening, as the army approached the village of Las Vegas, he told the lieutenant that the road to Santa Fe was open and that he hoped soon to meet Governor Armijo; then he allowed him and his escort to ride away.

Early on the morning of August 15 the Americans entered Las Vegas just after a courier had arrived with Kearny's commission as a brigadier general, dated June 30. Unopposed, the army rode to the central plaza of the little village to be greeted in friendly fashion by the *alcalde* and the people. General Kearny climbed to a flat rooftop overlooking the plaza, in company with the alcalde, to address the local citizens. Doniphan later wrote of this incident, ". . . The Genl had the Mexican element assembled, men, women, children and donkeys. At his request I had written the substance of the oath proper to be administered & without his request of my own notion the points of a brief address touching their change of allegiance &c" (Doniphan Papers, September 19, 1883, Missouri Historical Society, St. Louis).

Kearny told the assembled New Mexicans, "We come among you for your benefit—not your injury," and announced that the territory had become American, that they would have freedom of religion and security of property, and that those who resisted would be hanged. Finally, he promised them protection from raiding Indians. Then he required all local officials who agreed to continue in office to take the oath of allegiance to the United States, after which all common citizens likewise were made to swear.

These ceremonies over, the march continued to the village of Tecolote, where similar oaths were extracted, as again at San Miguel on august 16. At these villages Kearny paid for all corn his men took, and he issued strict orders to the Missourians to observe the property rights of New Mexicans. It was at San Miguel on August 16 that Captain Cooke rejoined the command to report on Magoffin's mission to Santa Fe. He brought with him an American merchant from the New Mexican capital. From them Kearny learned what had transpired with Armijo.

Cooke and Magoffin, with their small escort, had reached the New Mexican capital on the night of August 12 and immediately had gone into conference with Armijo and his chief military aide, Colonel Diego Archuleta. Magoffin had stressed—incorrectly—to the governor that resistance to the Americans would be useless, and he had pointed out that a transfer of the province to American control would raise the price of real estate, thereby enriching the already prosperous class of New Mexicans. And there was possibly a bribe, although Cooke did not report this with certainty. Certainly Armijo's known avarice, combined with his distaste for battle, made such an offer likely. Legends have persisted in New Mexico that a satchel of gold passed under the table to Armijo during this conference. Whatever transpired, the New Mexican governor never directly said what he intended to do.

With Colonel Archuleta, Magoffin used a different approach, saying that the Americans were coming only to take part of New Mexico, that part east of the Rio Grande. The rest of the province, he said, would thereby become available for an able military man to govern to his own advantage. Archuleta was sufficiently mollified by this prospect to offer no resistance to an American conquest of the eastern part of the province, and the conference thus adjourned on a happy note. The four men met again the next morning, August 13, for cups of chocolate, after which Magoffin prepared a sealed packet for Kearny that he entrusted to Captain Cooke for transmission. Cooke then took his leave and rode to report to Kearny.

Despite his assurances, Armijo did lead his ill-prepared army out of Santa Fe to take up a position at Apache Canyon on August 16. This canyon, or pass, was a narrow defile through which the Americans had to march in order to reach Santa Fe and could easily have been defended by a mere handful of men until hunger and thirst forced the Americans to surrender. Armijo marched out because the New Mexicans were demanding a show of strength from him —something to uphold local honor—and he seemingly gave in. Yet the soldiers' hearts were not in the fight. And leaders of the militia soon fell to quarreling with the commander of the three hundred regulars. The result, on August 17, was an abandonment of the position; Armijo ordered the militia home, the eight cannons spiked and hidden in the woods, and the presidial troops dismissed. He then retreated with his personal escort of ninety dragoons, to turn up three weeks later in Chihuahua. Thus on August 17, when the American army rode into the canyon prepared to fight, they were greeted by one fat alcalde who rode up at a gallop on a mule shouting, "Armijo and his troops have gone to hell and the Canyon is clear." The next day, August 18, the Americans marched through the pass, marveling that they had escaped a stiff fight at so strategic a location. "Had Armijo's heart been as stout as the walls of rock which nature gave him to aid in defense of his country," later wrote Franks S. Edwards, "we might have sought in vain to force a passage."

That same day of August 18, during rain, Kearny's General Order Thirteen was read to the troops. It declared that New Mexico east of the Rio Grande was annexed to the United States as part of Texas, and ordered the troops to respect persons and property. Then, although the men and horses were tired and supplies were short, the army rode on to make the twenty-nine miles to Santa Fe before dark. Soon after noon officials arrived from the lieutenant governor, Juan Bautista Vigil y Alared, with dispatches stating that the Americans would be welcomed in the city.

The Army of the West reached the little villa capital just before sunset. Kearny was in front with his dragoons, followed by the infantry, with Doniphan's regiment of Missourians coming last; pennants and flags fluttered as they marched smartly into town. At the central plaza Kearny and his staff paused to drink wine and brandy with the lieutenant governor while a detail of troops rigged a temporary flagpole. Then the Stars and Stripes was raised with a booming salute of thirteen shots from a howitzer. Kearny next addressed the citizens, stating that he had taken possession of New Mexico—with no mention of taking only the eastern part of the province—in the name of the United States, and he promised respect of persons and property, as well as to give protection against the Indians. Finally he urged submission without fighting. Afterward he was the guest at a dinner at the home of Lieutenant Governor Vigil—and spent the night sleeping on the floor of the governor's palace wrapped in his blankets. New Mexico had been taken without firing a shot.

The next morning, August 19, there was yet a more formal proclamation to the people of Santa Fe and New Mexico. At nine o'clock in the central plaza, Kearny declared himself governor of the province and repeated his assertions of the previous day. Then he administered the oath of office to local officials, whom he left in office. "Vivas" from the crowd at the end of this ceremony showed that the people were not greatly distressed at the changes. And the following day the chiefs of the Pueblo Indians came to take the oath of allegiance to the United States.

The first unease among New Mexicans came on August 22 when Kearny issued yet another proclamation, this one formally stating that all of New Mexico belonged to the United States. Soon reports were circulating that the residents of the Rio Abajo (literally, downriver) district would rise to fight the invaders with support from regular troops brought up from Chihuahua. Kearny left Doniphan as acting governor and on September 2, with 700 men, marched downstream to verify these rumors—only to be well received, and submissively, everywhere. Probably the paucity of fighting spirit downriver came from the tales told by Armijo as he had fled, tales of 6000 American invaders of overwhelming strength. Kearny returned to Santa Fe on September 11 content that all resistance to American authority had evaporated. In Santa Fe he completed work on a code of laws (which would bear the name Kearny Code), and a territorial constitution was drafted. This basis established for civil government, Kearny next named civil officials: Charles Bent became the first governor, along with a complement of civilian officials. Then the general perfected his plans for the rest of his campaign, dividing his troops into three groups. Three hundred dragoons he would lead to California to effect its conquest; Colonel Sterling Price and the Second Regiment of Missouri Mounted Volunteers, just arrived by way of the Santa Fe Trail, would remain in Santa Fe to garrison the captured province; and Doniphan was to lead his Missouri Mounted Volunteers southward into Chihuahua after subduing troublesme Indians in New Mexico.

Doniphan quickly stockpiled supplies and departed from Santa Fe, as did Kearny. Doniphan wanted to make a quick campaign against the Navajos, then move south rapidly, for

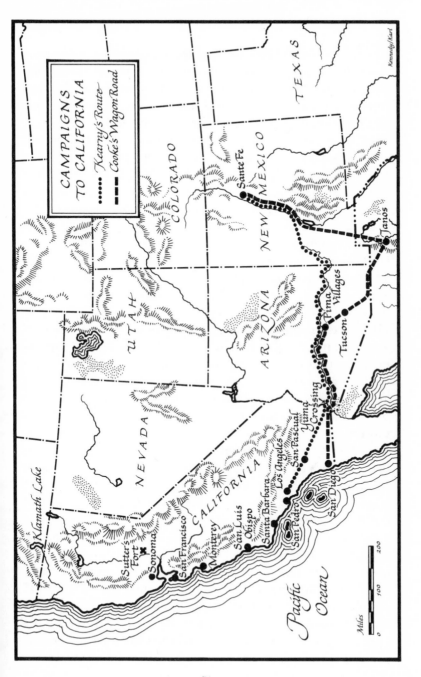

winter was coming on. To accomplish his task, the Missouri colonel divided his force into three columns, all to rendez-vous at Ojo Oso (Bear Spring, near present Gallup). His troops had not been paid, and most had no winter clothing, but they began marching without supply wagons. They suf-fered from exposure to heavy snowstorms, typhoid fever, and other vexations, and on November 21–22 held a peace con-ference with Navajo leaders at Ojo Oso. There Doniphan warned the Indians that the United States offered peace but would punish them if they continued to war against New Mexicans. He even invited young Navajos to journey to the United States to learn a trade. Then on November 22, a treaty was signed that stated, "A firm and lasting peace and amity shall henceforth exist between the American people and the Navajo tribe of Indians," and clearly stipulated that New Mexicans were included in the term "American peo-ple." This concluded, Doniphan sent most of his troops east-ward toward the Rio Grande, while he and a small detach-ment hurried west to meet with the Zuñi Indians. He held a conference with them on November 26, after which yet another treaty was signed similar in content with the earlier one. Then he and his men returned to the Rio Grande to re-unite with the main force; he found that those returning from Ojo Oso had suffered terribly, living on grizzly bear, deer, and various Navajo gifts of food. About December 1, Doniphan and his 856 followers, along with a caravan of 315 wagons of traders anxious to penetrate Chihuahua, started down the Rio Grande.

Back at Santa Fe, Sterling Price and his troops who re-mained behind felt cheated. They asserted that they had come to fight, not to be left behind for uninteresting garri-son duty. They drank, they gambled, they cursed the local population, they went after the local girls, and they soon were fighting with the local men. By December 1, Colonel Diego Archuleta found willing recruits for a revolt he was projecting; he was angry at what he felt to be an American double cross. He had been led to believe that he would be allowed to take control of western New Mexico and govern it, but the Americans had taken it all. Other conspirators felt that Mexican honor had been impugned by Armijo's failure to fight and his precipitous flight southward. In secret these conspirators gathered an army and weapons. At a meeting in Santa Fe early in December, the plans for an uprising were formulated: Governor Bent and Colonel Price were to be killed immediately, after which all American soldiers would be killed or else driven from the province. The date for the bloodletting was set for December 19, then put off until Christmas Eve. But American authorities learned of the plot, and some of the conspirators were arrested. Colonel Archuleta and other leaders escaped to flee to Chihuahua, thus ending the projected rebellion—or so Governor Bent thought. On January 5, 1847, he issued a proclamation describing what had transpired and asking the people to remain loyal to the new order.

Next Bent, thinking all danger past, decided to visit his family and friends in Taos. There on January 19 the uprising finally occurred. Actually the outbreak was a new rebellion plotted by Pablo Montoya, a self-styled "Santa Anna of the North," and Tomasito, an Indian; their followers mainly were residents of Taos Pueblo and some Mexican sympathizers unhappy with the new regime. Early on the morning of January 19 the insurgents killed and scalped Governor Bent. Five others in Taos, including the sheriff, the circuit attorney, and an army captain, were murdered. Seven more Americans were killed at Turley's Mill in the Arroyo Hondo, and a similar number died at the town of Mora. All northern New Mexico seemed threatened.

Colonel Price at Santa Fe heard of the outbreak the following day, January 20, and quickly he gathered an army to crush the rebels before the fighting spread. Marching 479 men northward through bitterly cold weather, he met the 1500 insurgents at La Cañada on January 24 and won a decisive victory. Five days later, another battle was fought, this one between Price's force and some 600 to 700 Mexican and

Indian rebels. They too were sent fleeing. On February 3 Price entered Taos, the center of the uprising, to find that the remaining rebels, about 700 of them, had taken refuge inside Taos Pueblo. The artillery was brought up, but the thick adobe walls refused to give way before the shells of the light pieces available to the Americans. Thereupon Price ordered a charge. Ladders and axes were employed, the walls were breached, and the Americans stormed inside. Seven of Price's men were killed and 45 wounded; approximately 150 rebels died before the fighting ceased. The 15 ringleaders of the revolt, including Montoya, were then tried and hanged by a makeshift court. A few skirmishes were fought in the next few days, including a battle that saw the destruction of Mora, but the victory at Taos effectively ended resistance to American authority in New Mexico.

Meanwhile Doniphan and his Missouri Volunteers were marching southward down the Rio Grande, half faint with hunger, subsisting for the most part on half-rations. Bivouacking on rock and sand, their buckskin and canvas apparel was torn to tattered shreds, and marching up to fifty miles in a single day ruined their footwear. Their camps were strewn with the bones of the animals they ate, the offal of the beasts they rode, and the refuse of the men themselves. George Ruxton, an English observer, termed them "listless and sickly-looking," and said they sat about "in groups playing cards, and swearing and cursing, even at the officers." Doniphan certainly did not set an example; he dressed in ragged clothes, pitched his own tent, cooked his own meals, and swore like the rest of the men.

Through the dreaded *Jornado del Muerto* of southern New Mexico, a sixty-mile stretch of burning desert, a three-day trek without water, they struggled before approaching El Paso del Norte (present Juárez). There they learned that Mexican defenders were ahead at a point known as El Brazito. Actually these Mexicans were extremely dispirited. In the El Paso district there were some 450 regulars and 700 militiamen under arms, but their colonel had become ill with what he believed was brain fever and fled to Chihuahua City. The second-in-command, a lieutenant colonel, also felt indisposed as the Americans approached, and so had delegated command to Captain, Brevet Lieutenant Colonel, Ponce de León, to whom was assigned 500 men and one two-pound howitzer. His was the force opposing the Americans at El Brazito (actually named Temascalitos) about thirty miles north of El Paso at three o'clock on Christmas afternoon.

In typical fashion Captain Ponce de León sent a lieutenant forward under flag of truce to demand that Colonel Doniphan surrender, else the Mexican said his force would charge and annihilate the Missourians. "Charge and be damned!" was Doniphan's laconic reply. Ponce de León was as good as his word, and the Mexicans soon were advancing —shooting ineffectively in the air. The Missourians calmly waited until the enemy was within range, then opened fire with devastating result. A flanking move toward the traders' wagons brought an equally withering fire from them, whereupon the Mexicans retreated in disorder. Seven Americans had been wounded slightly in this encounter, while the Mexicans lost about a hundred men and their howitzer. Ponce de León and his superiors at El Paso decided Chihuahua City was far more attractive than El Paso, and they abandoned it. A delegation of the town's leading citizens called on Doniphan to invite him into town. The colonel gladly accepted, and soon the Missourians were eating the lush fruit of the valley, feasting to make up for the rations they had missed, drinking the strong local brew, fighting Mexicans and each other in the streets, and dying of sickness as they had not died from Mexican bullets.

Doniphan at El Paso learned of the uprising at Taos, which cut him off from supplies, and he heard of preparations for battle by Mexicans at Chihuahua City. He determined to push forward, not knowing if he could retreat, but waited until February 5 for his artillery to reach him at El Paso. Then on February 8 the force began its 300-mile march southward with 924 effectives and approximately 300 traders and teamsters. They had 4 six-pounders, 2 twelve-pounders, and the captured Mexican two-pounder. Their road was filled with hardships and suffering: wintry cold at night, hot days, storms that battered down tents, deserts without water, even a grass fire. They advanced despite these hardships.

In Chihuahua City the officials knew of this advance and made preparations to meet it. There was some support for establishing a republic made up of several of the northern states, but this definitely was a minority view in Chihuahua, although probably not in the other northern states. In late August 1846 a weak governor, José María Irigoyen, was forced from office and Angel Trías Alvarez was installed. Trías, born in 1809 in Chihuahua City, had been educated in Europe and had entered state politics as a liberal in 1834 by securing the post of chief of police in the city of his birth. He had gained some military experience fighting the Apaches, and thus he made what local military experts considered to be good preparations for the coming battle with Doniphan and the Americans. About fifteen miles north of the city where the Sacramento River joined a dry canyon known as Arroyo Seco, he prepared to make a stand. By the time Doniphan approached, in late February 1847, Trías had gathered 1200 cavalry, 1500 infantry, and 1000 ranchers armed with machetes and lances. Strong breastworks had been erected facing the road over which the Americans would approach. In addition, Trías had found ten cannons, ranging from four-pounders to nine-pounders. Forced loans from the citizenry had paid for everything.

As the day of battle approached, Governor Trías proclaimed that Brigadier General José Antonio de Heredia would be in over-all military command, with Trías acting as second. Also heartening to the troops was the arrival of Brigadier Pedro García Conde, a professional military man serving as senator from Sonora but exiled from Mexico City and confined to Chihuahua by the government. Good leadership, numerical superiority, good breastworks, and an advantageous position for battle caused high morale among the Mexican troops. They were ready for the arrival of the gringos. The disaster of El Brazito was a forgotten bad dream and they began fashioning short ropes with which to tie up prisoners and quarreling about the distribution of the goods on the traders' wagons.

Doniphan and his men, along with the traders, arrived at El Sauz, a hacienda thirty miles north of Chihuahua City, on the evening of February 27. There Doniphan learned the exact detils of the Mexican preparations, but he knew that the next place he and his men could secure water was at the Sacramento River. They had to go forward. That evening, as the Missourians checked their powder and sharpened their swords, he said to them, "Cheer up boys. To-morrow evening I intend to have supper with the Mexicans on the banks of a beautiful spring." The next morning the Americans set out at daybreak. Doniphan and his staff rode in advance to reconnoiter. At the Sacramento, when they viewed the Mexican defenses, they chose not to fight head on. Instead, at noon, Doniphan ordered his troops while still a mile and a half away to cut sharply to the right and to cross the Arroyo Seco, gain the plateau, and thus face the Mexicans from a position not so stoutly defended. This maneuver proved brilliant, if very difficult for teamsters and wagons. The men sweated and swore in the choking dust, but they crossed the arroyo.

The Mexicans, thinking the Americans were trying to move around them and thereby continue down the road, charged with lances but halted suddenly when they saw the enemy turning toward them. This halt allowed Doniphan's artillery and infantry to catch up and get into position, thereby preventing a disaster. By this time it was three o'clock. Both sides moved artillery into place and opened fire. The Americans used solid shot, chain shot, and shells so effectively that the Mexican lancers broke and retreated. The Mexican powder was inferior to the Americans'; their shots reached the American lines only on the bounce and were easily seen and easily dodged. Throughout this cannonade Doniphan sat calmly on his horse and whittled, occasionally looking up to remark, "Well, they're giving us hell now, boys." The troops likewise were calm, even lightheartedly laughing, in the face of the poor Mexican shooting.

The artillery duel ended with the Mexicans dispirited. Doniphan ordered a charge. Across the intervening distance the Missourians moved, the artillerymen bringing their pieces forward as fast as the infantrymen—and using their pieces to good effect. One Mexican position after another came into American ownership. Trías and García Conde did manage to rally some lancers and make an effort to turn the tide of battle, but a few rounds of canister put an end to it. Then the Mexican lines were breeched: "With a whoop and a yell and a plunge we were over into their fort, man to man," later wrote one soldier. By five o'clock the shooting was practically over, and at dark a count of casualties was taken. Only one American had been killed and only 5 were wounded; approximately 300 Mexicans were killed and another 300 were wounded. The Americans had captured 40 Mexicans, along with almost all the Mexican animals, supplies, and ammunition. Governor Trías paused in the city only briefly, then fled all the way to Mexico City to ask for help. The next day Doniphan and his tired troops entered Chihuahua City without firing another shot.

Soon the Santa Fe traders who had accompanied the column were doing a brisk business, while the residents of Chihuahua City cried *"amigo"* to every American they saw. Again the Missourians debauched themselves: "Any form of manly dissipation was to their taste, as a rule; and they despised all carefulness, all order, and all restraint," wrote one observer. About 30 per cent of them soon were on sick report, most with venereal disease, all unfit for duty. As Doniphan considered his position, he realized the danger he was in. He was several hundred miles from Santa Fe, his men's twelve-month term of service was due to expire on May 31, and he could not abandon the traders. Thus he tried to negotiate with city and state officials, asking them to swear to remain neutral throughout the remainder of the war. This the Chihuahuans refused to do. Thereupon Doniphan dispatched a messenger, with a small escort, to find Taylor and ask for orders. This small party, with only their rifles for passports, reached Taylor at Saltillo and returned on April 23 with orders. The Missouri Mounted Volunteers were to join Taylor at Saltillo.

Late in April Doniphan led his men eastward in two sections, arriving at the city designated by Old Rough and Ready on May 21 after hardship and several fights with the Indians. There they learned that Taylor already had departed, but on May 22 General John E. Wool did review them. Their appearance at this time, according to their own officers, was "ragged." Following after Taylor, the Missourians found him at Monterrey—and he soon sent them down the Rio Grande to take ship for New Orleans. At the Crescent City they boarded steamboats that brought them back to Missouri, where they were mustered out of the service and where they were paid for the first time since they enlisted.

This army of Missourians had marched more than 6000 miles, had fought two major battles against armies superior in numbers to itself, had promoted commerce, had inflicted heavy casualties on the enemy, and had instilled a healthy respect for Americans among Mexicans in the northern states —all without uniforms, government supplies, commissary, or paymaster, a truly remarkable feat. And in the process they had aided in bringing New Mexico under the American flag.

But other battles remained to be fought and other territory to be conquered. And Brigadier General Stephen Watts Kearny was trying to accomplish both in the Far West. California was the next goal of American arms.

CHAPTER FOUR ❖

THE FAR WEST

CALIFORNIA in the spring of 1846 was uneasily Mexican territory. The population stood at some 5000, not counting the non-mission Indians but including some 680 foreign-born residents, principally Americans. Many of those American-born residents were recent arrivals who had not taken Mexican citizenship and thus were ineligible to receive land. That group constituted a discontented element with no stake in continued Mexican ownership of California. Many of them had congregated at the establishment officially known as New Helvetia, and more commonly called Sutter's Fort, for there they could find employment. John Augustus Sutter, the owner of this establishment, had been born in Kandern, Germany, in 1803, and had grown to manhood in Switzerland. He had immigrated to the United States in 1834, settling first in Missouri where he dabbled in the Santa Fe trade. In 1838 he moved to California, arriving there by way of Hawaii and Alaska. In California he received a land grant, to which he added by purchase, and thereby gained ownership of approximately 50,000 acres in the Sacramento Valley. On this property he erected a fortified post and engaged in wheat-growing, ranching, milling, mining, fur-trading, salmon-fishing, and shipping. He proved a genial, expansive host to Americans arriving in Mexican California.

Despite the element of discontented Americans congregated in northern California, the province did not have an American population "sufficiently large to play the Texas game," as Alfred Robinson wrote to the American consul at Monterey. Yet California was ripe for some type of dismemberment—or total swallowing—by a foreign power, for it was politically unstable and only tenuously connected to Mexico. A revolt in February 1845 had Centralist Governor Manuel Micheltorena expelled and Pío Pico replacing him as governor. Pico immediately moved the capital from Monterey to Los Angeles, thereby reviving the ancient feud between the southern and northern portions of the province. Colonel José Castro at Monterey, the military commander, gained control of the treasury during the revolt that ousted Micheltorena; he favored the northern part of the province and virtually governed it after Pico moved southward. These two men became so embroiled in their personal quarrel over who would govern the state that they were unable to present a united front during the crisis that was to come. Both men were native Californians, but both were more interested in personal enrichment than in securing protection and good government for the people. Thus by the spring of 1846 there was general discontent among the citizenry and growing talk of separation from Mexico.

California in the spring of 1846 had no postal system, practically no police or court system, no schools, no newspapers, few books, and little protection from Indian incursions from the interior. Even communication with Mexico was rare, more by chance than by design. Many Californians openly bespoke their desire to be annexed to the United

States. Some favored going under British ownership and a few wanted French control. Pico—fat, swarthy, and good natured, a farmer by occupation—led the pro-British party, while Castro—shrewdly intelligent and self-serving—favored independence with himself as dictator, although he concealed this ambitious scheme behind a pro-French façade. The only other Californian of major influence was Mariano G. Vallejo, a retired general living on his huge estate at Sonoma; probably the wealthiest man in the province, he was known for his pro-American sentiment.

President Polk was aware of the various political currents and aspirations in California, and to offset the British and French intrigue there he appointed Thomas O. Larkin a confidential agent for the United States on October 17, 1845. Larkin, born in 1802 at Charlestown, Massachusetts, had had a mercantile background in Wilmington, North Carolina, before moving to California in 1832. There he opened his own store to engage in the hide and tallow trade; he erected a flour mill; he traded with Mexico and Hawaii, dealing in flour, lumber, potatoes, furs, and horses; and he pioneered in land speculation in California. In 1844 friends in New England had secured him the position of American consul at Monterey, which office he continued to hold after Polk made him a confidential agent in 1845. His years in the province had convinced him that California should become American, and he strongly distrusted British and French intentions there. Polk's instructions to him in the letter naming him a confidential agent were in line with Larkin's beliefs: to warn Californians of any attempt to transfer jurisdiction of the province to England or to France and to encourage them in that love of liberty and independence so common among Americans. In short, he was to watch for an opportunity to promote a Texas-style revolution that would lead to annexation to the United States. And by April 1846 Larkin was quietly advising Americans, even all Californians, to think of independence, thereby earning his pay of $6 a day as confidential agent.

Besides naming Larkin a confidential agent, President Polk had two other plots afoot to acquire California should its ownership become a critical question—and should his efforts to purchase it fail. One of these was the overland expedition of John Charles Frémont. A Georgian by birth in 1813, Frémont had proven precocious in mathematics as a youth. Through a protector, Joel R. Poinsett, he had obtained a position aboard the *U.S.S. Natchez* in 1833 in a civilian capacity—reaching mathematics to midshipmen—during which he visited South America. After his return, he worked on several surveying projects until 1838 when, with Poinsett's aid, he was commissioned a lieutenant in the Corps of Topographical Engineers. Then came marriage to the daughter of Senator Thomas Hart Benton of Missouri, whereupon his powerful father-in-law secured for him leadership of several expeditions to the Rocky Mountains. With Kit Carson as guide, Frémont followed the trails of the mountain men, after which his wife, Jessie, wrote colorful reports under his name that were printed as government documents through Benton's influence—and gained him a reputation as the "Great Pathfinder."

In 1845 Polk sent Frémont westward with 62 armed men. Guided by Carson, the party arrived in California to be ordered out of the province early in 1846 by Colonel José Castro. After a brief show of fight, Frémont took his men north across the 42nd parallel into Oregon and encamped near Klamath Lake, to await developments and to be ready at a moment's notice should trouble develop in California.

Also ready to intervene in California was the Pacific Squadron of the United States Navy. Secretary of the Navy George Bancroft had issued standing orders to Commodore John Drake Sloat, commander of the Pacific Squadron, that in the event of war between the United States and Mexico he was to occupy such ports in California as would effect American control of the province. Although this fleet was small by most standards—consisting of two seventy-gun ships of the line and six lesser vessels—Sloat had sufficient strength to carry out those orders. He also had the experience necessary to his level of command. Born in 1781 in New York, he had entered the navy in 1800 briefly, then permanently in 1812, serving both in the Atlantic and Pacific before rising to the rank of captain in 1837. On August 27, 1844, he had been appointed commodore of the Pacific Squadron, and had arrived at Mazatlán, Mexico, to take the office on November 18, 1845. He had remained at Mazatlán for seven and a half months aboard his flagship, the *Savannah,* when the above-mentioned orders from Bancroft arrived.

Both Sloat and Frémont were aided by the quarrel between Castro and Pico, a quarrel that came to a head when Castro in the spring of 1846 decided to keep all revenue derived from the customs house at Monterey, between 80,000 and 100,000 pesos annually, for himself. Pico responded by calling for a general convention to meet at Santa Barbara on June 15 in order to avert what he labeled "external and internal disorders." Actually it was a plot to discredit Castro, declare independence, and ask for British protection. Castro responded by refusing to allow delegates from northern California to attend, proclaiming martial law, raising followers, and marching against Pico. Civil war was at hand—with California the prize for whichever party could muster the most strength.

At this important juncture came yet another development: United States Marine Corps Lieutenant Archibald H. Gillespie arrived with instructions from Washington. Gillespie had made his way to California through Mexico disguised as a merchant ostensibly seeking to regain lost health. Meeting with Larkin in Monterey, he revealed his true status and showed orders to Larkin from the president and the secretary of war. Then, aided by Larkin, he traveled north to meet Frémont, to whom on May 9, 1846, he delivered a packet of letters from Senator Benton and to whom he communicated instructions from the president. These instructions were verbal, not written, and their exact content has been the source of much historical controversy; Gillespie later asserted that Polk's message was "to watch over the interest of the United States, and counteract the influence of any foreign agents who might be in the country with objects prejudicial to the United States."

Whatever the content of Polk's message, Frémont acted with dispatch. He resigned his commission in the United States Army, paused to destroy a Klamath Indian village for attacking his camp, and then marched to California. On the way he heard rumors that Colonel Castro was gathering an army not only to fight Pico, but also to expel Frémont and his followers as well as all American non-citizens in the province. Frémont ordered these rumors widely circulated in order to gain adherents for his cause, while Castro aided in their circulation by establishing a military headquarters at Santa Clara and sending two lieutenants to the vicinity of Sonora (a village in northern California) to gather supplies and horses for his men.

This move by Castro led to wild fears on the part of resident Americans that they indeed were to be expelled from the province. A group of these men, anxious about Castro's intentions and emboldened by Frémont's re-entry, were moved to seize a herd of horses intended for Castro on June 10. They next offered command of their group to Frémont, but the Pathfinder declined, whereupon they decided to capture the town of Sonoma. Led by Ezekiel Merritt and William B. Ide, the insurgents arrived at their destination on Sunday morning, June 14, to surround the home of General Vallejo. The former *comandante-general* cordially invited them inside his home and produced bottles of aguardiente. Merritt and several others became befuddled by drink, but

Ide, a teetotaler, arranged the terms of capitulation. Vallejo then was sent to Sutter's Fort, where Frémont, who had taken command of the post, ill-advisedly locked the pro-American Vallejo in a bare cell and kept him there for two months. Meanwhile, at Sonoma, Ide and the others had seized the arms, ammunition, and one cannon they found there, had declared a republic, and had devised a flag decorated with the Lone Star of Texas, a stripe, and the crude resemblance of a grizzly bear. Thus began the "Bear Flag Revolt."

On hearing of this declaration, Colonel Castro immediately dispatched fifty men north under the command of Joaquín de la Torre to disperse the revolutionists. The two forces fought a skirmish on June 24 (later termed the "Battle of Olompali"), after which the Mexicans retreated. At this juncture Frémont assumed command of the Bear Flaggers. His first move was to march precipitously on the ungarrisoned fort at San Francisco; there on July 1 he spiked the ten guns (cast in Lima about 1625) and rendered them useless—despite the fact that they had been incapable of firing for forty years. Then he returned to Sonoma to address a gathering on July 4, advising his audience to declare independence and drive out Castro and his adherents. The next day he formally organized a "California Battalion" of volunteers with himself as their commander and Gillespie as his adjutant. But their glory was short-lived, for the United States Navy had arrived with a strong rumor that war had been declared between the United States and Mexico.

Commodore Sloat had been taking his ease at Mazatlán, Mexico, when on June 7, 1846, he heard unofficially that war had been declared. The following day he sailed northward aboard the *Savannah,* arriving at Monterey on July 2. Yet he did not sail in with guns blazing as Thomas a. C. Jones had done in 1842; he was anxious to avoid duplicating that blunder, and thus he contented himself with talking with Consul Larkin. The consul urged a delay, thinking he might achieve a quiet resolution with the native Californians who were upset with the imprisonment of Vallejo. Sloat restrained himself for four days, then acted. On July 6 he sent Captain John B. Montgomery, commanding the *Portsmouth,* to take San Francisco. The next day, July 7, Sloat ordered Captain William Mervine ashore at Monterey with 165 sailors and 85 marines. Mervine raised the American flag above the customs house to salutes fired from the *Savannah* and the three other American vessels at the port: the *Warren, Cyane,* and *Levant.* Next, Sloat's proclamation was read to the inhabitants. It stated that he came as a friend, that "henceforth California will be a portion of the United States," that its residents would be citizens and protected in their persons, property, and religion. Castro refused to accept this change, however, and stated that he would defend the province against all American forces with his utmost zeal.

Captain Montgomery nevertheless landed at San Francisco on July 9 with 70 men and took the village. And that same day the Stars and Stripes waved at Sonoma, and on July 11 it was raised at Sutter's Fort. Castro and his adherents retreated to the vicinity of Los Angeles. Sloat next issued orders to prevent looting, as well as to avoid quarrels between Americans and native Californians, and Frémont was asked to join the official American cause. The Bear Flag Republic had come to a quick end, lasting less than a month. And northern California was totally in American hands and just in time: on July 16 British Admiral Sir George E. Seymour arrived at Monterey aboard *H.M.S. Collingwood,* an eighty-gun warship, to be presented with an American fait accompli. Sailing away a week later, he reported to his superiors in England that there was nothing he could do. Obviously he had arrived to support the British cause but was too late.

At this juncture a new figure arrived on the stage of California history: Commodore Robert Field Stockton. Sloat had been in poor health for some time, and on July 23 he officially relinquished command of the Pacific Squadron to Stockton. A native of Princeton, New Jersey, born in 1795, Stockton had joined the navy in 1811 and fought in the War of 1812 with distinction, later against the Tripolitan pirates in the Mediterranean. He was active in the American Colonization Society and commanded the *Alligator,* which took Dr. Eli Ayres to Africa to secure the land that would become Liberia. Between 1828 and 1838 he was on furlough and leave of absence to manage his family property, then returned to active duty in 1838 as a captain. He was active in designing and building the first steam vessels for the navy. Then in October 1845 he sailed for the Pacific aboard the *Congress,* which took him to Monterey and command of the Pacific Squadron on July 23, 1846. Energetic and politically ambitious, Stockton quickly took a liking to Frémont, and that same day of July 23 enrolled the California Battalion in the volunteer forces of the United States: Frémont was named major of the new unit and Gillespie the captain. Next Stockton issued his own proclamation wherein he repudiated Sloat's promises; he denounced the Mexican government as aggressive, censured Castro for his treatment of Frémont, and said lawlessness at San Francisco and Monterey necessitated martial law.

The volunteer forces commanded by Frémont then were loaded aboard the *Cyane* and taken to San Diego in order to attack the retreating Castro's troops from the rear. Stockton himself followed down the coast on the *Congress* to land sailor and marines at San Pedro (eighteen miles from Los Angeles, and its port at the time). Larkin went with him, still hoping to achieve a lasting settlement with Castro. This proved impossible owing to heavy demands made by Stockton, who insisted that no negotiations could even begin until Castro agreed that California belonged to the United States. With Frémont in command of San Diego and advancing on Los Angeles, and with Stockton advancing from San Pedro, Castro and Pico realized they had lost; on August 10, after issuing one last bombastic proclamation, they fled to Sonora, Mexico, whereupon all resistance to the Americans ceased. Larkin entered Los Angeles on August 12, followed the next day by Stockton, Frémont, and a brass band of sailors and marines.

On August 17 Stockton issued yet another proclamation that placed the entire province under martial law and said all who did not accept American ownership should quit the region. Some native California leaders were arrested, but all were paroled—and soon a period of peace descended. Stockton then divided California into two districts, a northern one and a southern one, with Frémont in charge of the area around Monterey and Gillespie the one in the south. Local elections were held in September, and the American regime quickly became popular. Thus Kit Carson was sent eastward with dispatches for officials in Washington telling what had transpired. On the way he met General Kearny moving west with his 300 dragoons.

That meeting occurred on October 6 at the little New Mexican village of Socorro some sixty miles south of Albuquerque on the Rio Grande. The general persuaded the mountain man that he should be allowed to read the dispatches. After he learned of the conquest of California, Kearny sent 200 of his dragoons back to Santa Fe—gladly— for he knew it would be difficult to feed 300 men while crossing the arid Southwest. Then he prevailed upon Carson to turn around and guide his remaining 100 troops to California. Carson, who had not seen his family for almost two years, reluctantly agreed. That Kearny would continue to California was never in doubt; his orders were specific: he was to take the province and assume the military governorship of it.

Kearny, his staff, and 100 dragoons set their faces south on the morning of October 7. Pack animals were employed to carry their supplies and the wagons abandoned. Down the Rio Grande they continued to the present site of Elephant's

Butte Dam; then they turned west to follow the ancient route to the copper mines of Santa Rita del Cobre (near the present Silver City); from there they went through the Continental Divide to the headwaters of the Gila River, which they would follow to the Colorado. Occasionally their camp was visited by wandering bands of Apaches, including the famed Mangas Coloradas and his Mimbres followers, but the presence of so many well-armed Americans caused them to be peaceful, if not friendly. They were able to obtain some mules from the Indians, but their beasts suffered incredibly, so that some of the dragoons were afoot part of the way. In central Arizona they came to the land of the Pima Indians, who were more than friendly; when Kit Carson tried to bargain with them for food, the Pima chief replied, "Bread is to eat, not to sell. Take what you want." They did hear from the Indians of a Mexican garrison at Tucson, some hundred miles to the south, but that offered no hindrance, and no attraction, and they continued down the Gila.

The first disquieting news was had on November 22 near the junction of the Gila and Colorado rivers. There a detail of fifteen dragoons, led by Lieutenant William H. Emory, captured four Mexicans in charge of a herd of horses. From the herders Kearny learned of a counter-revolution in California. Kearny discounted part of what he was told, but the news was too disconcerting to be disregarded totally. And soon afterward, Lieutenant Emory intercepted a messenger carrying dispatches from California southward to Colonel Castro; these dispatches confirmed the bad news. There had been a counter-revolution.

When Gillespie had been placed in charge of the southern half of California, with headquarters in Los Angeles, he had only 50 troops to enforce martial law. As the Mexicans gradually turned surly and resentful, Gillespie arrested suspicious persons, thereby further alienating the population. The outburst came on the night of September 22 when an insurgent group attacked Gillespie's garrison and besieged it.

A few days later a band of 25 Americans were forced to surrender at Chino, lending confidence to the Mexicans—and causing yet more Californians to join the rebellion. Soon some 400 local people were under arms. And on September 29 Gillespie surrendered under flag of truce and was permitted to march to San Pedro, there to embark on the merchant ship *Vandalia*. His departure allowed Captain José María Flores, leader of the insurgents, to take command of Los Angeles.

While still besieged at Los Angeles, Gillespie had managed to dispatch a courier to San Francisco. This rider traveled the four hundred miles to San Francisco in just five days to tell Stockton of the uprising. He responded by sending Captain Mervine and the *Savannah* to San Pedro; it arrived on October 7 with sailors and marines, but all on foot and with no artillery. Gillespie and his men also came ashore, and the united force set out for Los Angeles. About fifteen miles inland, at Domínguez Rancho, they were attacked by the insurgents, who were armed with lances and a four-pound cannon called the "Old Woman's Gun." The Americans suffered a dozen casualties in a futile effort to capture the cannon, then retreated to San Pedro and the protection of the *Savannah*'s guns. This "Battle of the Old Woman's Gun" further encouraged the Mexican insurgents, and yet more recruits flocked to their standard. Only San Diego and San Pedro remained in American hands in southern California, and those two ports only because of the guns aboard the warships.

The exultant Mexicans convened a legislature in Los Angeles, which named Flores governor and *comandante-general* and which proclaimed martial law. The spirit of rebellion had grown so strong that even the arrival of Commodore Stockton at San Pedro could not end it, and he sailed to San Diego late in October to rally resistance at that point, taking Gillespie and his troops with him. However, Flores found his position precarious, for he could raise but little money, few weapons, and little ammunition. Finally, on December 3, his followers revolted against his rule and imprisoned him. In short, the Mexican position had become almost impossible: Stockton was to the south and Frémont was coming from the north with his California Battalion. And then, early in December, came word of the arrival of Kearny and the grandiloquently named Army of the West.

Kearny indeed had arrived, but his army was in a sad state. He had pushed his men across the burning desert of the interior of southern California in a week of suffering almost beyond description, then had entered the last range of mountains to be met by fog and drizzling cold. One officer commented about the dragoons at this time: "Poor fellows. They are well-nigh naked—some of them barefooted—a sorry looking set." Exhausted and half-starved, the dragoons encamped near an Indian village named San Pascual (thirty-five miles northeast of San Diego) after having been joined by Gillespie, a four-pound cannon, and 38 men from San Diego. Kearny's scouts reported that a Mexican force of lancers was in the village and preparing an attack under the command of Andrés Pico, brother of the departed governor.

The American general consulted with Kit Carson, who assured Kearny that the Mexicans were cowardly and would not fight. Thus Kearny decided to attack despite the fact that the dampness had wet the powder of his dragoons, and he ordered a charge. The horses of his troops were so jaded that soon the dragoons were strung out in a lengthy column. At this point Pico wheeled his men about and attacked. Mexican lances were used with deadly precision as the Americans tried valiantly to ward off the thrusts with sabers. After ten minutes the Mexicans withdrew, leaving 22 Americans dead and 16 wounded, including Kearny and Gillespie. Enemy losses were trifling, but fortunately they did not follow up this initial advantage. Carson and Lieutenant Edward Fitzgerald Beale slipped through the enemy lines that night of December 6, reached San Diego, and informed

Stockton of the sad plight of the American force. Stockton sent aid, and Kearny thereby was able to break out of his encirclement on December 10 and reach San Diego two days later.

The combined American forces at San Diego felt sufficiently strong to march out of San Diego on December 29—with Stockton commanding and Kearny acting as executive officer. Flores, released from prison in Los Angeles, gathered a force of some 450 men, approximately the same number as Stockton had, and they joined battle on January 8 at Bartolo Ford on the San Gabriel River (twelve miles from Los Angeles). The Mexicans were short of powder and shot, and were forced to retreat after minor skirmishing. The following day Flores rallied 300 men for another stand, but it also proved ineffective—and Flores departed for Mexico. Thus the Americans re-entered Los Angeles on January 10 without opposition, again to raise the American flag in the central plaza.

Meanwhile, Frémont, now a brevet lieutenant colonel, was advancing southward from Sacramento with 400 mounted riflemen and three pieces of artillery. At San Luis Obispo he captured Jesús Pico, a cousin of Andrés and a parole violator; the pleas of Pico's wife and fourteen children moved Frémont to decide not to execute him by firing squad, the usual sentence of those who broke parole. Then, marching on southward and knowing that Stockton was in Los Angeles and that he had refused to grant a capitulation to the insurgents, Frémont entered the camp of Andrés Pico through the mediation of Jesús Pico. On January 13, 1847, he received the final surrender of the rebels under terms of the Capitulation of Cahuenga. By this agreement the rebels were allowed to return to their homes, were to be protected in their lives and property, were to enjoy the rights of American citizenship, and were not to be forced to bear arms against Mexico. Stockton reluctantly agreed to the generous terms Frémont had signed at Cahuenga, for he was anxious to return to his naval command and win yet more glory. He therefore willingly departed, leaving Kearny and Frémont to quarrel over the governorship of California.

Stockton's orders from the Department of the Navy had been vague about establishing a government in California. Yet he had proceeded to name Frémont governor of the territory before departing. Kearny had specific orders from the war department that he was to take and govern the province, and he resolutely refused to recognize the appointment of Frémont. In fact, he regarded the brevet lieutenant colonel as subject to his orders. Both men were politically ambitious, and Frémont flatly refused to relinquish the governorship despite repeated orders from Kearny to do so. Subsequently, in March 7, 1847, orders from Washington upheld Kearny's claim, whereupon the general arrested Frémont, charged him with mutiny and insubordination, and sent him to Washington to be court-martialed. With Senator Benton as his counsel, Frémont tried to impugn Kearny's conduct of the war, but the court found the Pathfinder guilty and sentenced him to dismissal from the army. President Polk approved the verdict but remitted the penalty, whereupon Frémont in anger resigned his commission. He returned to California to develop the estate he had acquired, the seventy-square-mile Mariposa grant, and to become a senator when California entered the Union (thereby beginning a political career that saw him nominated for the presidency in 1856 as the Republican party's first candidate). Californians, meanwhile, found Kearny's administration much to their liking, for he ended martial law, was conciliatory in his appointments, and promoted the welfare of the province. Old and respected settlers, such as Mariano G. Vallejo and John A. Sutter were brought into positions of authority (both as subagents to the Indians to secure peace), and he used army troops to enforce the decrees of local alcaldes. Then in April 1847, with the arrival of a regiment of New York volunteers commanded by Colonel Jonathan D. Stevenson, Kearny felt California was completely in American hands. Thus on May 31, he passed the military governorship to Colonel Richard B. Mason and departed for St. Louis. His task was completed.

While these events were transpiring in California, one column of the Army of the West—the Mormon Battalion—was yet making its weary way west. Shortly after Kearny had started westward from Santa Fe with 300 dragoons on September 25, 1846, he learned by courier that 500 Mormons, forming a special battalion, had arrived in Santa Fe. These were men enlisted at the request of Brigham Young, president of the Church of Jesus Christ of Latter Day Saints (also known as Mormons); their salaries were to be paid to the church to help finance the Mormons' epic trek from Illinois to the Great Salt Lake area, a plan approved by President Polk. When Kearny received news of the Mormon Battalion's arrival in Santa Fe, he paused to send Captain, Brevet Lieutenant Colonel, Philip St. George Cooke back to the New Mexican capital to take charge of it. Cooke's orders were to blaze a wagon road to California.

Cooke was a strong-willed commander, and only the fact that Brigham Young had enjoined members of the battalion to remain obedient prevented a mutiny. Cooke first weeded out the old and the unfit, thereby reducing his command to 397 effectives, before departing Santa Fe on October 19. He followed the Rio Grande southward to a point below Socorro, then turned southwest to Playas Lake (in what is now Hidalgo County). There he found the old Spanish-Mexican road that ran to Janos, Chihuahua; from that town he turned westward to San Bernardino, an abandoned ranch (near the point where Arizona and New Mexico join on the Mexican border). At this ranch the battalion encountered many wild cattle, abandoned years before because of Apache hostility, and, just to the west of it, they were attacked by wild bulls. One almost gored Cooke—and in his diary he referred to the incident as the "battle of bull run." Casualties in the encounter included a private who was wounded in the leg, a sergeant who received broken ribs, and Lieutenant George Stoneman (later a governor of California), who almost shot off his own thumb in the excitement.

On December 12 the guide for the battalion, Antoine Leroux, returned from a scout with information gained from Mexicans he had encountered making mescal; they had informed him that at Tucson some 200 Mexican soldiers were gathered to oppose the Americans. Two days later this report was confirmed when officers from the Tucson garrison came to Cooke's camp under flag of truce. Their message from José Antonio Comaduran, captain of the presidio at Tucson, was that the Americans would be opposed if they tried to march through the town but that they would not be impeded if they would quietly bypass it. Cooke's reply was a demand that Comaduran surrender and throw open Tucson for the refreshment of his troops; this the Mexican emissaries could not accept. Thus on the morning of December 16, when Cooke sighted the town, he ordered preparations for battle—only to be informed by shouting Mexicans coming from Tucson that Captain Comaduran and the garrison had fled southward. Cooke told the local citizens that he had not come to make war on Sonorans, much less to destroy an outpost of defense against raiding Indians. He did open the public stores of Tucson to his hungry battalion, and many of the Mormons gorged themselves sick.

The Mormon Battalion departed Tucson on December 18, moving north down the Santa Cruz River to the Gila, and thence down the Gila to Yuma Crossing. Once across on California soil, the Mormons labored across the burning deserts of the southern, inland portion of the province, going three days and two nights with no water and scant rations. Clothing was so shredded that the men used what little they had to cover their feet during the heat of the day and then their bodies during the cold of the night. Crossing the final range of mountains, the coastal sierra, the Mormons were disheartened to discover the pass was too narrow to allow their wagons passage; first they tried to widen the pass with shovels, but were forced to dismantle the wagons, move them through, and reassemble them on the far side. They arrived at San Diego on January 29, 1847. Cooke, in his final report, commented, ". . . Marching half naked and half fed, and living upon wild animals, we have discovered and made a road of great value to our country. . . ." And he could write with great pride, "History may be searched in vain for an equal march of infantry." Cooke's Wagon Road would become a principal route to the gold fields in just two years, bearing the name the Gila Trail.

The California conquest secure, Stockton began preparing for further naval victories. Already he had blockaded the major Mexican port in the Gulf of California: Guaymas, Sonora. Before he could launch any new moves, however, he was replaced on January 22, 1847, as commodore of the Pacific Squadron. In fact, two men arrived with such orders: James Biddle and William Branford Shubrick. As Biddle was senior in grade, Shubrick had to defer to him. Biddle, a sixty-four-old native of Philadelphia and a graduate of the University of Pennsylvania, had entered the navy in 1800 to fight the Tripolitan pirates; he fought in the War of 1812 and continued in service for the thirty years of peace that followed. In 1846 he was commanding the East Indian Squadron, in which capacity he had negotiated the first treaty between the United States and China; he arrived in California in January 1847 but did not officially assume command of the Pacific Squadron until March. He departed for the eastern part of the United States on July 19.

Shubrick thus exercised command of the Pacific Squadron from January to March 1847, and from July 19 until relieved the following year. Born in 1790 at Bull's Island, South Carolina, Shubrick had entered the navy in 1806 after one year at Harvard, had fought in the War of 1812, and had stayed with the navy, reaching the rank of captain in 1831. In the fall of 1846 he was sent aboard the *Independence* to assume command of the Pacific Squadron, but had to defer to Biddle; yet for all practical purposes he controlled the fleet off the California coast, for Biddle was elderly and ready for retirement.

When Shubrick arrived, he found seven fighting ships and two supply vessels. These he supplemented by commandeering commercial ships; the captains of these vessels did not hesitate to agree to work with him, or to file claims, many of them exorbitant, for services rendered their country. Shubrick's first plan was the conquest of Mazatlán, Mexico's most important commercial port on the Pacific coast; he wanted to take it in order to gain control of the customs house there, declare a high tariff, and use the revenue collected to aid in defraying the costs of the Pacific Squadron. Ships of that day could not carry sufficient supplies to remain at sea for long periods of time; nor did the commodore of such squadrons carry sufficient funds to purchase all that was needed (or even to find merchants willing to cash treasury drafts). Secretary of the Navy John Y. Mason hoped to defray such costs through the collection of Mexican customs revenues, and thus Shubrick planned to take Mazatlán. However, he was unable to effect this plan during the spring and summer, even well into the fall of 1847, because adverse weather conditions made it virtually impossible for sailing vessels to operate.

Despite such weather, the navy was able to occupy parts of Baja California. On orders from Commodore Biddle, Commander John B. Montgomery aboard the *Portsmouth* sailed to San José (at the tip of the peninsula) and occupied it with a landing party of 140 men on March 30, 1847, without resistance. Similarly a landing party occupied Cabo San Lucas, and 90 sailors and marines took La Paz on April 14; there they confiscated $11,950 worth of cigars, the disposition of which was vague. That spring and summer the American ships did blockade Mazatlán, Guaymas, and San Blas despite the adverse weather. Then, after Shubrick officially assumed command of the Squadron on July 19, he reported to the secretary of the navy that he intended to occupy the major ports and blockade the minor ones—a policy quickly put into effect.

Soon landing parties went ashore to pacify them, even at the minor ports such as at Mulejé, Baja California, on September 30, 1847. Then a major operation was launched against Guaymas on October 17; Captain E. A. F. Lavallette, who commanded the operation, employed the *Portsmouth, Independence,* and *Congress* in a battle that lasted several days, saw one person killed (an Englishman), and some property damaged. The American flag was raised on October 20 after the town surrendered, whereupon all small arms and ammunition that could be found in the hands of the local populace was collected aboard the *Portsmouh.* Then on November 17, 1847, the *Dale* landed 65 marines and sailors to retake the town from 350 local Mexican troops who had moved into it. And a garrison remained there and at Cochori (a nearby village) until June 24, 1848, when news of the conclusion of the war reached the area.

Mazatlán was the major prize for Shubrick, however—and a tough one to take, for it was garrisoned by approximately 1200 troops under Colonel Rafael Telles. Shubrick personally commanded the operation, arriving off the port on November 10 with the *Congress, Independence,* and *Cyane.* During the dark of night, he sailed his fleet through the narrow entrance to the harbor and presented the town with his guns the following morning. Captain Lavallette went ashore under flag of truce on the morning of November 11 to ask for a peaceful surrender. Colonel Telles refused, although the town's civil officials wished to comply with the American demand. At noon that day Shubrick ordered 750 men ashore, Telles withdrew, and the city was occupied without resistance. This operation proved the most precise naval maneuver of the Pacific Squadron during the war, perhaps the best for the entire United States Navy during the two years of fighting.

Even more humiliating for the Mexicans than the surrender of these two towns was the American occupation of San Blas, site of a Mexican naval yard and port. In September 1846 Lieutenant Stephen C. Rowan and a detachment of men from the *Cyane* had slipped ashore to spike the 24 guns of the shore battery; thus on January 12, 1848, even a landing party from the supply ship *Lexington* was able to go ashore and occupy the port without resistance.

The remainder of the war for the Pacific Squadron consisted of suppressing local insurrections against American control in a few towns, as at La Paz, Baja California, in November 1847; there also were skirmishes at San José, Baja California, lasting from November 1847 to April 1848. And these ports were held long after the Treaty of Guadalupe Hidalgo was signed. In fact Mazatlán was ocupied until May 1848. By that time Commodore Thomas a. C. Jones had resumed command of the Pacific Squadron on May 7, thereby completing the humiliation of the Mexicans.

The Pacific Squadron thus had almost two years of constant warfare—from July 1846 to May 1848—during which time it was the decisive factor in the conquest of California, and it had occupied the principal Pacific port cities of Mexico. Sailors and marines on these ships had fought battles on sea and land while short of personnel and supplies and out of communication with the government. The Mexican Navy had been unprepared to offer stout resistance, contenting itself with saving national honor rather than seriously challenging the Americans. Shubrick's final report to the secretary of the navy noted proudly that his squadron had occupied twelve major cities and had destroyed or confiscated 40 enemy ships, mostly coastal vessels. And at no time did Shubrick have more than 10 ships involved. His indeed was a stirring accomplishment. But it had been overshadowed by events in the Gulf of Mexico and by fighting ashore in central Mexico, where the war actually was resolved.

CHAPTER FIVE

THE DECISIVE CAMPAIGN

THE UNITED STATES NAVY at the outbreak of the Mexican War was woefully ill-prepared, suffering from inadequate equipment, poor communications, constant shortages of supplies, and long lines of supply. Nor was it popular with prospective recruits; the London *Times* on June 29, 1846, reported, "The United States government has authorized recruiting officers to offer a bounty of $20.00 and three months' advanced wages to all able bodied men who will re-enter the service. New recruits are offered $15.00 bounty and three months' advanced wages." Since the War of 1812 there had been little opportunity in a naval career and, in fact, little need to promote an efficient navy. However, the Home Squadron, as the fleet in the Gulf of Mexico was known, did have many ships available; by 1848 it numbered seven steamers, three frigates, six sloops, one schooner, five brigs, seven gun boats, and four bomb vessels. Of these the largest was the fifty-gun *Raritan*. Pensacola, Florida, was the supply depot for this Squadron—nine hundred miles and one-month's sailing from the scene of action. And when a ship arrived at Pensacola, there was no guarantee that the supplies it needed would be available. In addition, the Home Squadron had to contend with vicious winter gales in the gulf known as "northers." Finally, disease, principally yellow fever, was the scourge of the sailors on this duty station.

When Zachary Taylor's troops were attacked on April 24, 1846, the Home Squadron was at the mouth of the Rio Grande using the port of Brazos Santiago. It supported Old Rough and Ready, even contributing a landing force of 500 sailors and marines to aid in the combat. Commanding the squadron at this time was Commodore David Conner, a man of long experience. Born in 1792 in Harrisburg, Pennsylvania, Conner had entered the navy in 1809 as a midshipman and had fought aboard the famed *Hornet* in the War of 1812, receiving two congressional medals for his efforts. He was promoted to captain on March 3, 1835, became commissioner in 1841, and was named to command the Home Squadron in December 1843, a position normally held for three years.

Shortly after the outbreak of the war Conner was given two major objectives by the secretary of the navy: to blockade the Mexican east coast ports and to wage war on privateers, and to assist the land forces of the United States. Conner quickly effected a blockade of Mexican ports in the gulf, but at first this effort was hampered because of his shortage of ships, especially small steamers capable of working close to shore. He did erect a partial blockade immediately.

Yet to make this blockade truly effective, Conner knew he had to capture the principal Mexican port cities. And, these captured, he could collect the customs to purchase supplies for his squadron. Thus on June 8, 1846, a preliminary expedition attacked Tampico (it would be occupied permanently on November 10 that year). Next, on August 7, came an assault on Alvarado, some thirty miles southeast of Vera Cruz and site of the major fleet anchorage Antón Lizardo.

Alvarado was bombarded but not taken. Then in September, when Conner was notified by the Bureau of the Navy that the administration wanted something done for the newspapers to make a "noise about," he ordered another attempt on Alvarado. This was done on October 15, but again was unsuccessful. However, on October 16 Connor's second-in-command, Captain Matthew C. Perry, departed with eight vessels to take Frontera, a port at the mouth of the Tobasco River and an important source of cattle; Perry was successful on October 23 and even sent men seventy-two miles upriver to attack San Juan Bautista, the capital of the state of Tobasco.

Then on November 14 the major city of Tampico was occupied by a fleet of 11 ships, and an expeditionary force of 32 men went upriver to Panuco where they destroyed a large store of Mexican supplies, including guns and ammunition. Colonel William Gates and 500 soldiers moved ashore to garrison Tampico, and it remained in American hands until the end of the war. This successful operation gave Polk his desired "victory news" to make "noise" about. Tampico thereafter was used as a supply base for the movement against Vera Cruz. Conner also was responsible for obtaining the neutrality of the Mexican state of Yucatán during the conflict. Yucatán long had been in rebellion against Mexico, even had offered itself for annexation to the United States at one time, but officials in Washington doubted its neuutrality and wanted its several important ports occupied. Conner sent Captain Perry with four ships to the town of Carmen; Perry arrived there on December 2, 1846, and occupied it without resistance.

Finally, Conner performed most important and vital service to the war effort by transporting General Winfield Scott and more than 12,000 troops to land at Vera Cruz in February 1847. This move came as much because of politics as because of strategy. By late 1846 Polk and his political advisers were disturbed by Taylor's growing popularity in the

United States and the increasing mention of his name as a Whig candidate for the presidency in 1848. Thus Polk decided to halt Taylor at Monterrey, to withdraw most of his troops, and to send an expedition to land at Vera Cruz. The man he chose to head this new offensive was the commanding general of the army, Winfield Scott.

Born near Petersburg, Virginia, in 1786, Scott had attended William and Mary College but had quit because he disapproved of the irreligious attitude of the students. After reading law he was admitted to the Virginia bar in 1806 and practiced this profession until 1808, when he was appointed captain in the army. Sent to New Orleans, the six-foot, five-inch, 230-pound officer was soon in trouble, for he openly said that the commanding general of the department, James Wilkinson, was as great a traitor as Aaron Burr; for this he was court-martialed and suspended from office for a year. At the outbreak of the War of 1812, he was yet a captain but soon distinguished himself at the battles of Queenston Heights, Fort George, Chippewa, and Lundy's Lane. Several times wounded, he showed such judgment and courage that he was promoted to brigadier and brevet major general, was voted the thanks of Congress and a gold medal, and was offered but declined the office of secretary of war in the Madison administration.

After the war ended, he twice visited Europe (1815 and 1829) to study foreign military tactics, wrote military manuals for the army which would remain standard for half a century, and conducted military institutes for the officers of his command, the Eastern Division, which was headquartered at New York City. In 1828 he participated in the Black Hawk War, and four years later commanded the troops in South Carolina during the heated Nullification Controversy. In 1835 he went to fight the Seminoles in Florida, for which he was praised for his "energy, steadiness and ability." President Van Buren sent him in 1837 to bring peace to the Niagara region, where refugees from Canada and the abortive uprising of 1837 were trying to precipitate a war with England. Then in 1838 Scott persuaded 16,000 outraged Cherokees to move peacefully to the Indian Territory from Tennessee and South Carolina, and it was his tact and skill as a negotiator that brought peace in the "Lumberjack War" over the boundary between Maine and New Brunswick in 1839. His reward for such services was to be named general-in-chief of the army in 1841, a position he would hold for twenty years.

Scott once ordered that any soldier found intoxicated had to dig a grave his own size and then contemplate it, for he soon would fill it if he persisted in drinking. His arguments on alcoholic beverages led to the founding of the first temperance societies in the United States. He was too aristocratic to have general public appeal and his rhetoric was too fancy to make a good speech. Despite such idiosyncrasies, even despite his undisputed military genius, his name had been prominently mentioned for the Whig nomination for the presidency in 1839 and again in 1844; thus in 1846 at the outbreak of the war with Mexico, Polk chose to place Zachary Taylor in command of the troops doing the fighting. But when Taylor became too prominent, with attendant political overtones, Polk decided to send Scott to complete the campaign. Thus on November 18, 1846, the president named Old Fuss and Feathers (as the troops called Scott) to lead an invasion of Mexico at Vera Cruz.

Well might Scott draw this assignment, for he had been arguing since the outbreak of the conflict that the Mexicans could be conquered only by the occupation of their capital, something that he said would never be accomplished by an invasion across the great deserts of the north. Instead he had urged the Polk administration to follow the route of Hernán Cortés in his conquest of the Aztecs: a thrust from Vera Cruz to Mexico City. By mid-November of 1846 Polk and his advisers finally realized that Scott was correct. Thus he received orders, first from the president on November 18 and then in writing from Secretary of War William L. Marcy on November 23. Rarely have orders of such import been so vague: "The President, several days since," wrote Marcy, "communicated in person to you his orders to repair to Mexico, to take the command of the forces there assembled, and particularly to organize and set on foot an expedition to operate on the Gulf coast, if, on arriving at the theater of action, you shall deem it practicable." All responsibility for success thus was placed on Scott, as was any responsibility for failure.

Scott sailed to New Orleans and from there to Brazos Santiago at the mouth of the Rio Grande. Hardly had he departed the capital of the United States when intrigues began in the Democratic administration to name Senator Thomas Hart Benton of Missouri a lieutenant general (thereby outranking Major General Scott), and to place him in over-all command of the war. Fortunately the scheme failed to win congressional approval, but Polk could content his partisan heart by refusing to give Scott adequate financial and logistic support.

At Brazos Santiago, Scott sent a messenger with a request for a personal meeting with Taylor, to take place at Camargo (upriver from the mouth of the Rio Grande). This messenger missed Taylor, who was off on a raid by land against Tampico, and then was killed when pursuing him by Mexican irregulars; Scott's message, containing an outline of his projected campaign, eventually was taken to Santa Anna and thereby led to the Battle of Buena Vista. And Scott and Taylor never had their personal meeting, but Scott did take most of Old Rough and Ready's troops, mainly the regulars. These men were gathered at Brazos Santiago, along with the soldiers brought by Scott, and all prepared to sail to Vera Cruz.

This army of invasion was delayed at Brazos Santiago by Polk's failure to send the necessary vessels for transport. And when the ships did arrive, they mainly were sailing vessels although Polk had promised they would be powered by steam. Yet the army embarked during the second week in February, stopping at Tampico on February 20, and then moved on down the coast. At the Lobos Islands the convoy made a rendezvous with yet more transports from New Orleans, and there Scott was able to drill his army briefly. Then the army sailed for Antón Lizardo, the final staging ground for the assault on Vera Cruz, arriving there on March 7. By this time Scott's army numbered approximately 12,000, but time was short; the yellow-fever season was drawing near, and Vera Cruz was a stoutly defended city. To the landward side its defenses were few, the main protection a wall; but toward the sea was a massive wall overlooked at one end by Fort Santiago and at the other by Fort Concepción. And on Gallega Reef in the bay, three-quarters of a mile from Fort Concepción, was the fortress of San Juan de Ulloa, imposing in its walls, batteries, and 2500 men.

The *comandante-general* of Vera Cruz was Ignacio Mora y Villamil, a competent military engineer who had been born in Mexico City in 1791. Mora had served in the Mexican Congress in 1825–26, had been secretary of war and marine briefly in 1837, and had been commanding general of the Army Corps of Engineers, as well as the author of manuals on fortifications and the attacking and defense of plazas. Mora had been expecting an American attack at Vera Cruz since the failure of the Slidell mission, and with the aid of his second-in-command, Lieutenant Colonel Manuel Robles, had tried valiantly to repair the city's fortifications. His elaborate plans to effect the needed repairs had been approved by his government, but it had never sent money to implement them. His unpaid soldiers thus had been reduced to stealing their own gunpowder and selling it in order to live. Santa Anna, on his passage through the city in August 1846, had ordered Mora to fight to the death to hold Vera Cruz; the central government had seconded these orders and again had promised funds, as well as men, to accomplish this end.

But by March 7, 1847, neither had arrived and Mora was growing desperate in his requests for aid. None came because the government was in chaos.

Nevertheless his position was strong. San Juan de Ulloa was a formidable fortress commanding the harbor; in it and in the city itself were some 300 serviceable cannons and mortars, large numbers of muskets, and huge quanities of ammunition. Streets and homes were sandbagged, barricades were erected, and traps were rigged outside the city walls with pikes, cacti, and swords. The governor of the state of Vera Cruz, Juan Soto, promised help from the 20,000-man state militia, while General Juan Morales had 3800 men in the city and 1200 in San Juan de Ulloa. Most of the citizenry had fled to the hills, but some 3000 had remained. Yet morale was high, and the troops talked laughingly of a coming victory.

Scott, meanwhile, was making a critical study of his problems and consulting with his senior officers. He knew he had to take Vera Cruz in order to penetrate the interior, for he could not leave a fortified position astride his line of supply and communication; also, he had to accomplish such conquest before the yellow fever season set in. His staff advised a frontal assault—a dashing, gallant, deadly attack that would win public admiration at home. Scott, however, felt that such an attack would so reduce his ranks that he could not advance further into Mexico, for the slaughter would be tremendous. Nor could he rely on siege to accomplish his goal, for starvation would take so long that the yellow fever season would arrive before the Mexicans surrendered. His final decision, therefore, was to put his men ashore at the beach of Collado about three miles southeast of Vera Cruz, thereby bypassing the fortress of San Juan de Ulloa and the other defenses. Thus he and Commodore Conner met to arrange an elaborate flag system of communication between the army and the navy.

On March 9 the fleet of approximately 100 ships, naval

vessels and army transports, assembled off Vera Cruz. In these vessels were 12,603 soldiers as well as horses and equipment. At sunrise they approached Collado beach to begin the operation. From sunrise to eleven o'clock that morning the soldiers were transferred to the naval vessels, which were better suited to landing operations than the cumbersome army transports; then from two until six o'clock the troops were loaded into 67 whale boats which Scott had ordered for this purpose. Each whale boat carried from 50 to 80 men. The first wave of troops, 4500 of them, went ashore at six, and by ten o'clock that evening more than 10,000 had been put ashore with their equipment and supplies and were in position to defend themselves. The entire operation had taken sixteen hours, was completed without a casualty, and comprised the first American amphibious landing.

The following day the remaining men and equipment were brought ashore, and by March 15 the town of Vera Cruz was surrounded on land, as well as blockaded by sea. Sand hills and needle-sharp chaparral made life miserable for the toiling soldiers and sailors ashore, who were acting as draft animals to pull the artillery pieces into place. Mexican irregulars, cavalry and infantry, harassed the Americans, but soon the batteries were ready to begin operations, the troops eager to hear what they called the "sweet music of those faithful bull dogs."

On March 21, just as the battle was ready to be joined, Commodore Conner transferred command of the Home Squadron to Matthew C. Perry, a fifty-two-year-old native of Newport, Rhode Island, who had been in the navy since 1809 and was a brother of the famed Oliver Hazzard Perry. The new commodore loaned Scott some of his siege guns manned by navy crews: 3 sixty-eight-pounders and 1 thirty-two-pounder. After Scott exercised the futile formality of asking the town to surrender, the cannonade began on March 22. At first there was little result. Gradually, however, the guns were moved closer and began to breach the walls, whereupon the Mexicans realized they were in serious trouble. Also, the naval vessels in the harbor were contributing to the uproar with their guns.

With no help from the interior in sight, General Juan Morales began considering surrender, for the damage to the city was growing steadily until hardly a house was without scar. The foreign consuls in Vera Cruz sent messages to Scott on March 26 asking him to have mercy, to which he replied he gladly would extend it when the city surrendered. He did halt the deadly fire on March 27 to notify the *comandante-general* that a surrender was necessary by six o'clock the following morning, else the storming would begin. Formal articles of capitulation were signed on March 28, for Morales knew his troops' morale had evaporated with the firing of the big guns. These articles were generous: the Mexicans were allowed the honors of war and were paroled on their word not to fight again until exchanged (a stipulation most Mexicans soon ignored), property was to be respected, and freedom of religion would be allowed.

The articles signed, the Americans moved into the city on March 29, and Commodore Conner sailed for Washington with word of this astounding victory. Scott had taken the city with only 19 Americans killed and 63 wounded, and the Stars and Stripes had been raised over the city while Mexican soldiers marched out, to the rousing cheers of American soldiers and sailors and to the booming of cannon salutes from ship and shore.

When word of this disaster reached Mexico City, there was little real fright. Mexican generals thought it would be months before the American army could move inland, by which time—as usually happened to foreign invading armies —heat, fatigue, and yellow fever would decimate the troops. Not so. Scott wasted no time. First he gathered supplies, for which he paid with drafts on the treasury of the United States and which he forced foreign merchants in Vera Cruz to accept at face value. Next he created the Military Department of Vera Cruz and detailed a small garrison to hold it. Then on April 8 he sent Brigadier General David Twiggs and the 1st division of regulars marching toward the highlands of the central plateau. Finally he addressed a proclamation to the local citizenry: "Mexicans, I am advancing at the head of a powerul army. . . . Americans are not your enemies." Then he also departed for the interior.

In this movement he was bothered by problems of transport, for the supplies he had ordered had not arrived from the United States. Polk was not yet ready to give him the needed support. Yet with his 8500 soldiers, half of them volunteers, and his cannon, Scott took the road inland. A few miles from Vera Cruz, Twiggs encountered the first Mexican resistance, a charge by lancers. This was easily beaten off, as were a few other sorties against them. During those first few days, however, there was not general threat, for Santa Anna had chosen to make his stand fifty miles inland at a narrow defile in the road, the pass of Cerro Gordo.

At Cerro Gordo Santa Anna gathered troops, and there he made his plea to the nation: "Mexicans, do not hesitate between death and slavery. . . . Awake! A sepulchre opens at your feet; let it at least be covered with laurels!" At his chosen site of battle he first conducted an inspection. Cerro Gordo was a small village, five miles beyond which was the Plan del Río; in between these two points the road twisted through a narrow opening around which there was no other known pass. And he knew that to defeat the Americans at this point would hold them in the low, hot country subject to the dreaded yellow fever. Scott had to move through the defile, thought Santa Anna, for he had artillery that had to follow the road. These considerations prompted the Mexican commander to implant his 25 pieces of artillery so that they could fire on the road, along with 3800 seasoned troops. And on El Telégrafo, a summit commanding the area, he located 4 four-pounders and 100 men. At the village of Cerro Gordo he had his reserve troops and guns.

The Mexican troops at Cerro Gordo were not raw conscripts. They were crack troops totaling 12,000 men—the
Grenadiers of the Republican Guard, the Libertad Battalion, the Atlixco Actives, the Zacapoastla Actives; the 3rd,
5th, and 6th of the Line; the National Guards of Jalapa,
Coátepec, Teusitlán, Matamoros, and Tepeaca. In reserve
were the 1st, 2nd, 3rd, and 4th Light Battalions of the Line;
and the 4th and 11th of the Line. Far behind them were the
Hussars of the Guard, the 5th and 9th Cavalry of the Line;
and the Lancers of Orizaba, Jalapa, and Chalchicomula.
Santa Anna felt secure with these troops at his command.
But in reality his men were restive from insect bites, inadequate water supplies, sickness, even an attack of cholera;
worse, the troops were whispering that the Americans were
invincible. To lift morale, Santa Anna ordered every de-
serter shot, and he made blustering speeches that not even a
rabbit could get through the pass at Cerro Gordo. He was
ready.

The first element of Scott's force, commanded by Twiggs,
arrived at the pass on April 12. Twiggs was not an excep-
tionally brilliant general; in fact, Scott declared he was not
really qualified to command "in the presence or in the absence of an enemy." That morning of April 12 Twiggs mustered what heat and fever had left him of his 2600 men into
normal marching formation, disregarding the warning given
by his scouts that Santa Anna was ahead. Only Mexican ov-
ereagerness saved the command. They opened fire before
Twiggs's division was entirely within the pass, and thus he
was able to extricate his men and supply train. Scouts then
made a reconnaissance and informed Twiggs of the magni-
tude of the opposition, but Twiggs nevertheless was prepared to order a charge the next morning, a dash straight
into the muzzles of the Mexican guns. Happily his staff officers persuaded him to give the troops a day of rest on the
thirteenth—and Scott arrived the next day to take field command. Twiggs's soldiers loudly cheered Scott's arrival.

Old Fuss and Feathers first wanted extremely detailed information. To get it he sent two engineering officers into the ravines on each side: Captain Robert E. Lee to one side and Lieutenant George H. Derby to the other. They found a trail around the flank of the Mexicans, and under cover of darkness a detachment hacked a path through dense woods and across deep ravines, taking with them the heavy twenty-four-pound howitzers. To cover this movement, Scott sent Twiggs on a diversionary movement against El Telégrafo; despite Mexican opposition, his troops occupied La Atalaya, a small peak, with 4 mountain howitzers, 4 six-pounders, and 2 twelve-pounders. "Charge 'em to hell!" was Twiggs's enthusiastic order to his men, and they moved down La Atalaya and began an ascent of El Telégrafo. However, they were forced to withdraw.

The major attack was mounted on the morning of April 18. The guns on La Atalaya opened fire, as did the big twenty-four-pound howitzers. The Mexicans were astonished, for they had not realized the big guns were in place, or even that they could get through by any route except the road. Then Colonel Bennett Riley of Twiggs's command moved out with the 2nd Infantry and 4th Artillery (fighting as infantry) to cross the ravine between La Atalaya and El Telégrafo; this brigade charged up the hill, some dying, some wounded. On they came despite heavy Mexican resistance. Grape and canister raked the valley, fired by the Mexican guns, but the American officers continued to shout "Charge!" and the men to cheer and shout. Over the top they went despite Mexican reinforcements by Santa Anna. Using bayonets, pistols, and muskets as clubs, they drove the Mexicans from the summit and raised the Stars and Stripes. And Captain John Bankhead Magruder turned the captured Mexican artillery on the retreating foe, while Riley and his troops poured down the hill after them.

Just as Santa Anna was preparing another stand at the base of the hill, Brigadier General James Shields arrived

with 300 men after a forced march of two miles around the
north side of the Mexicans. He had only volunteers and no
artillery, but his sudden appearance out of the chaparral dis-
concerted the Mexicans, who had no idea a force had encir-
cled them, and they fled in disorder. "Everyone for himself!"
was the Mexican cry. Riley's men used the momentary confusion to shoot the Mexican artillerymen at that point and
to turn their guns against their recent owners, further add-
ing to the disorder. Santa Anna, his staff, his officers, and his
troops rushed headlong to escape the insane Yankees. By ten
o'clock that morning of April 18 the battle was over. Scott
could not mount effective pursuit of the retreating foe because he had too few cavalrymen, but his infantry and artillerymen were ordered to march forward—with only two
days' rations in their knapsacks.

The Americans halted about four miles from the next
city, Jalapa, but the fleeing Mexican army did not pause at
that city. And at the next town, La Hoya, General Gregorio
Gómez, who commanded the defenses there, heard of the
disaster and fled toward Mexico City with his garrison. A
final tally of the Battle of Cerro Gordo showed Mexican casualties at more than 1000, while lost weapons numbered
4000 muskets and 40 cannons; American losses were 64 dead
and 353 wounded. Scott's army entered Jalapa at nine
o'clock on the morning of April 19, to be welcomed by the
ringing of bells, even to laughter at the soldiers' unkempt
appearance, but not by hostility. There, and as they marched
further into the central plateau, they did begin to suffer
from the vagaries of Mexican weather. They had departed
Vera Cruz to march through burning, sandy, desolate, water-
less, chaparral-infested desert; already without greatcoats and
blankets, their clothing in tatters, they had further lightened
themselves by discarding excess clothing, along with medical
supplies, salt, horseshoes, coffee, commissary stores, even ammunition. During the burning hours of daytime, in the hope
of enjoying a few hours of comfort, they had thrown away

their heavy clothing; but once they reached Jalapa and beyond, in the more temperate altitude, the temperature dropped at night to such chilling degrees that at least two blankets per man were needed, and not available. Those who became ill had to fall by the wayside, often to suffer a terrible fate at the hands of roving guerrilla bands of Mexicans. Yet even the knowledge of possible mutilation could not deter the fatigued and ill from straggling.

Scott tried to send the ill back to Vera Cruz, but this proved no boon. There the yellow fever season was raging, killing those left behind as well as those returning from the interior with great suddenness. The quartermaster troops in the port city tried to avoid yellow fever by moving to the wharf area, but hundreds of them still became ill and died of the dread disease, or of dysentery, or at the hands of secret Mexican patriots. By June 4 Scott was reporting to Secretary of War Marcy that 1000 were bedridden at Vera Cruz and another 1000 were ill at Jalapa.

The problem of irregulars cutting the highway from Vera Cruz to the interior, Scott's lifeline for securing supplies and reinforcements, became so serious that the American general proposed to the secretary of war that the road be abandoned altogether, that his army cut its line of communication and subsist entirely on its own. However, he did rely on Captain Samuel H. Walker to do what he could to keep the road open. Walker, already famed for his contribution in designing the revolver bearing the designation the Walker-Colt, which was widely used by the Texas Rangers, had served with Taylor as a Ranger, then had joined the Regular Army and was with Scott as a captain. Scott commissioned him and a band of men to scout the road east from Perote, which the advancing army reached on May 25. Scott specifically wanted the Rangers to halt the activities of Mexican guerrillas, who were increasing in numbers and in hostile activities. With the breakdown of Mexican governmental authority in the provinces, bands of irregulars were devastating the countryside while claiming to be partisans; but in reality they were bandits; they were particularly active in catching American stragglers, couriers, and small detachments and torturing or murdering them. Mutilated American bodies found along the road bore ample testimony to the ferocity of these irregulars, and to their daily toll of Scott's soldiers.

Walker and his hand-picked men gave the guerrillas a taste of their own medicine. J. J. Oswandel wrote, "Should Capt. Walker come across the guerrillas God help them, for he seldom takes prisoners. The Captain and most all of his men are very prejudiced and embittered against every guerilla in the country." The Rangers shot first and questioned later, with the result that some innocent Mexicans were killed in the process. Guerrilla activities did diminish somewhat. Walker unfortunately was killed on October 9 in a battle against irregulars at Huamantla.

President Polk and the secretary of war chose not to allow the Vera Cruz-Mexico City road to be abandoned by Scott. Instead, on July 16 they chose to order a detachment of Texas Rangers to Vera Cruz for this purpose. John Coffee Hays and his regiment were selected. Hays, already a legendary leader of this famed band of men, received the president's orders at the mouth of the Rio Grande. He and his regiment boarded ship at Brazos Santiago and were taken to the Mexican port city to begin patrolling on October 4. Major General Robert Patterson, the commanding officer at Vera Cruz, did not believe they could contain the Mexican partisans, for the Rangers were of non-imposing appearance —blue and black coats, slouch felt hats, black leather vests, long beards—rode horses that were range animals, and each carried a rifle and four pistols, a short knife, ropes, and whatever else caught his fancy. Yet soon the Mexicans were crying *"Los Diablos Tejanos"* and *"Los Tejanos Sangrietes"* ("Those Texas Devils" and "Those Bloody Texans") at their appearance—and avoiding the road from Vera Cruz to Mexico City. When on one occasion Hays's Rangers brought in a prisoner, Oswandel confided to his diary that the event was considered "one of the seven wonders."

During the late spring and early summer, Scott advanced slowly by stages into the interior. After the Battle of Cerro Gordo the Americans had moved forward to Jalapa. From that point Scott had hurried General William J. Worth and a division after the retreating Mexicans. Marching in the shadows of Orizaba peak, Worth ascended through the undefended pass of La Hoya to Perote Castle, once a fortified military position but in use as a prison prior to the war (especially for Texans captured during the decade of the Republic of Texas). Worth occupied the castle without opposition on April 22, finding 50 cannons there along with 25,000 balls and shells and some 500 muskets. He halted to await further orders from Scott rather than continue the advance.

Scott had waited at Jalapa to make his plans. He had to be certain he had sufficient food and clothing, as well as ammunition, on hand before sending the entire army forward. Moreover, many of his volunteers' enlistments were ending about the middle of June. When attempts to get the volunteers to re-enlist failed (only enough to make one company out of 3700), he sent them to the coast for shipment home, leaving him with 7113 men. Yet even then he chose to advance. The first week in May he sent General J. A. Quitman of Mississippi forward with his remaining volunteers, whose enlistments were to end in November, and on May 6 he sent orders to Worth to advance on Puebla.

The force he would face at Puebla had been gathered by Santa Anna during his retreat from Cerro Gordo toward the capital. The Mexican general had found the Brigade of Antonio de León, 1000 men, at the village of Orizaba; these he employed in rounding up fugitives, irregulars, and conscripts. By early May he was claiming an army of 4000 men under his banner (and actually had about 2500). But the troops were restive, and the populace was muttering against him. The nation had learned at last that Buena Vista had been a defeat, and the disaster at Cerro Gordo caused yet more resentment. Soon there even were rumors circulating that Santa Anna secretly was in collusion with the Americans, and some officers were calling for him to be court-martialed. He might have struck at Scott's rear with his new army with telling effect, but he learned that a national election had been called for May 15. He knew he could not afford to be absent from the capital when that occurred, so he moved his army to Puebla, arriving there on May 11 to find a sullen greeting.

Often before in his revolutionary schemes, Santa Anna had visited Puebla to gather men, arms, and money—all never to be seen again. And his arrival at Puebla in May 1847 meant to the townspeople that a battle probably would be fought there. Unknown to Santa Anna, the clergy in Puebla already had decided to open their town to Scott; they, along with the town's leading citizens, had heard that when Scott arrived the hated Mexican taxes were abolished, that the American troops respected persons and property, that trade became brisk, and that religion and churches were left in peace. Thus the clergy had been preaching non-resistance at Puebla before Santa Anna's arrival, while the governor and *comandante-general* had determined not to fight and had sent their arms and ammunition away. Finally, they already had sent word to the approaching General Worth that the city would be open to him.

Santa Anna's sudden arrival on May 11 upset the townspeople's plans. The general ranted at them, he raved, he seized horses, he conscripted men into the army, he demanded cash—even, according to rumor, took gold ornaments from the church to fill his coffers. Then, as Worth and Quitman approached on May 14, he rode out to attack them with 2000 cavalry. The Americans were prepared for the clash and easily fought it off, whereupon Santa Anna saw some of his men desert under cover of battle, while the remainder fled—as he did—toward Mexico City. Worth and Quitman thus were able to march into Puebla unopposed at ten o'clock on the morning of May 15. The troops stacked arms in the central plaza, drank the local water, and ate their fill of the local food. By June 4, Scott was reporting 1014 of them sick at Puebla, where he had arrived on May 28. The death march played almost every morning for men who had come to fight, who in fact had survived battle, but who had died of diarrhea, fever, or chills.

The American commander decided to wait for reinforcements at Puebla, and gradually they arrived. Six hundred troops left Vera Cruz for the interior on June 4, another 500 on June 11, almost 2000 on June 18, all to arrive at Puebla by July 3, raising Scott's strength to 8061 effectives and 2215 sick. Then on July 15 Brigadier General Franklin Pierce departed Vera Cruz with another 2500 men, arriving at Scott's headquarters on August 6. These additions brought Scott's army to 14,000 men, of whom 2500 were ill and another 600 were convalescent (and unable to perform their duties). During the period of this wait, Scott had seen to the purchase or manufacture of clothing, food had been accumulated, and the local population was friendly. Morale was high despite the troops having received only two months' pay since February. The time to advance on the Mexican capital had arrived.

Meanwhile, as Santa Anna retreated from Puebla toward the capital, confusion reigned and intrigue was the order of the day. Even on the pressing question of the defense of the city there was no agreement, and ill-advised plan followed equally absurd plan. Nicolás Bravo finally was picked to command the defenses of the city only because he posed no real threat to any faction. There was talk of securing a loan of 20,000,000 pesos from the states, but state leaders did not deliver. There even were plans to appeal to the Irish troops of Scott through their Catholicism to persuade them to fight for Mexico; broadsides to this effect were printed and enough of the Irish Catholics did desert the American cause to join a few other American deserters in the Batallón de San Patricio. However, this battalion could not protect the capital. The moderates next placed the Federal District under martial law and sent quotas for troops—32,000 of them—to the states to be met. But everywhere in the capital and in the states there was pessimism; Mexicans for too many years had seen too many military, economic, and political promises broken to respond yet again. Men failed to arrive, just as funds did not pour into the national treasury.

Into this deteriorating situation on May 19 came Santa Anna with some 3000 men. The following day he met with Acting President Anaya and a council of generals to announce that, despite his own wishes to the contrary, he would reassume the presidency. Few of the populace rallied behind him, however. In a move designed to win wide support, Santa Anna then restored freedom of the press, only to see it used against him with bitter and telling effect. On May 28 he responded by announcing his resignation in the belief that the feuding congress would rally behind him. Then, when it appeared his resignation would be accepted, he withdrew it on June 2 and locked up his political opponents, including the venerable Juan N. Almonte. Even freedom of the press was choked off, and Santa Anna had become a virtual dictator—with no popular support, even from the clergy, while the states withheld almost all aid.

Despite this opposition, the general-president began preparing the defense of the capital. Cannons were cast from melted bells, muskets were confiscated from the citizenry or purchased from foreigners, gunpowder was manufactured, while private contractors were put to work forging bayonets and other items of war. Santa Anna even managed to get some of these items paid for by the United States. He sent word to Scott at Puebla that he was anxious for peace but needed $10,000 to effect it immediately. Scott sent the money.

As to troops, Santa Anna had brought about 3000 with him into the capital. These he united with the 2000 regulars and 8000 militia in the city, along with 500 men who arrived from Querétaro, the 200 American deserters forming the Batallón de San Patricio, and all the able-bodied men he could conscript, thus bringing his total strength to approximately 25,000 men. And at San Luis Potosí to the north was the remainder of the "Army of Victory," about 4000 men and 22 cannons; but Santa Anna could not trust its commanding general to be loyal and wanted them to stay away from the capital, much as he needed them for its defense.

Santa Anna's strategy was defensive: he would concentrate his troops at the capital where, en masse, they would fight. The perimeter of the city would be rimmed with fortifications guarded by the militia, while the regulars were to be rushed to any threatened point. And Juan Alvarez, commanding the Army of the South (outside the capital), was ordered to move behind Scott, to harass his advance, and to be ready to destroy him when he retreated. Santa Anna's plans were considered eminently sound by so distinguished a military strategist as the Duke of Wellington, who in England was closely following Scott's campaign. "Scott is lost," he commented that summer. "He cannot capture the city and he cannot fall back upon his base."

His plans complete, Santa Anna put them into effect with ruthless despotism. Entire villages were depopulated, laborers were conscripted, and prisons were emptied. All fortifications, decreed the frenzied president, must be completed in only eight days. Soon breastworks, parapets, gun emplacements, trenches filled with water, and stockades commanded the road that Scott had to follow into the city. Morale among the Mexican troops increased in direct proportion to the growing number of fortifications. By August 9 all was in readiness as the Americans approached, and Santa Anna could boast in a proclamation: "Blinded by pride the enemy have set out for the capital. For this, Mexicans, I congratulate myself and you."

Scott began the march for Mexico City on August 7 at Puebla, Twiggs's division again in the lead. Day by day other divisions departed until all his men not on garrison duty or sick were marching for Mexico City: 10,738 men and officers. "We had to throw away the scabbard," he wrote, "and to advance with the naked blade in hand." The road they followed passed through beautiful countryside and picturesque villages, all with a backdrop of mountains scattered like crumpled pieces of paper. Even the Mexican citizenry was friendly. Thirty-six miles out of Puebla, and an equal distance from Mexico City, the road crested at 10,500 feet above sea level. A few more miles and the valley of Mexico lay before the Americans' eyes, never captured by a foreign enemy since Hernán Cortés. The army paused to look and then advanced again.

On August 9 the march halted at Ayotla, fifteen miles away from Mexico City. Twiggs, Quitman, Worth, all waited for Scott to arrive and plan the strategy. Scott at Ayotla studied his maps and listened to his scouts' reports, then chose to swing his army to the south of Lake Chalco and make his assault on the city from the village of San Agustín, ten miles to the south of Mexico City on the Acapulco road. This move got under way on August 15 over a route reconnoitered by engineering officers Robert E. Lee and Pierre G. T. Beauregard. General W. S. Harney's cavalry was in the lead, with Worth's division behind it; Pillow's and Quitman's divisions came next, with Twiggs left behind to hold Ayotla and, it was hoped, to deceive the Mexicans about the real approach. Santa Anna had left the route to San Agustín unguarded, for it consisted of cold lava flows (called *pedregals*) and waste land thought impassable. Thus with light skirmishing, the objective was reached and secured.

Santa Anna countered this threat by hurrying troops to

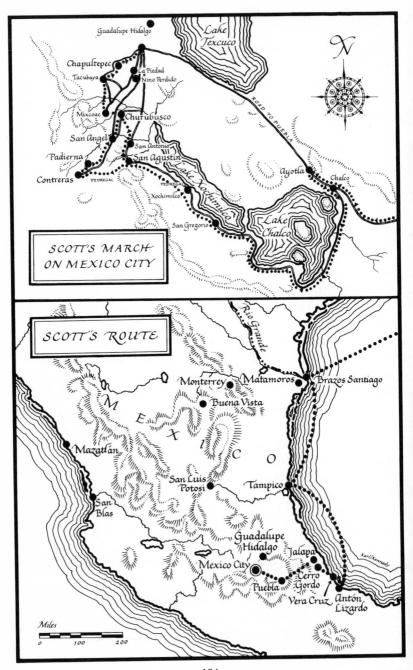

SCOTT'S MARCH
ON MEXICO CITY

SCOTT'S ROUTE

Lake
Texcuco

Guadalupe Hidalgo

Chapultepec
Tacubaya
La Piedad
Niño Perdido

ROAD TO PUEBLA

Mixcoac
Churubusco

San Angel
San Antonio

Padierna
San Agustín

Contreras
PEDREGAL
PEDREGAL
Lake Xochimilco

Ayotla
Chalco

Xochimilco

San Gregorio

Lake
Chalco

Rio Grande

Monterrey
Matamoros
Brazos Santiago

Buena Vista

M
E
X
I
C
O

Mazatlán

San Luis
Potosí

Tampico

San
Blas

Guadalupe
Hidalgo
Jalapa

Mexico City
Cerro
Gordo

Puebla
Vera Cruz
Antón
Lizardo

Karl/Kennedy

Miles

0   100   200

124

take up a position between San Agustín and Mexico City, troops commanded by General Gabriel Valencia, who had been to the north at the village of Guadalupe Hidalgo. Yet by this single movement, Scott had undermined Mexican morale, for it had rendered many of Santa Anna's strong fortifications useless. However, there still were stout defensive positions remaining before the Americans could reach their goal: the hill of El Peñón Cuahtitla where Valencia's veteran Army of the North was located, a bridgehead and convent at Churubusco, and the fortified hill of Chapultepec. All might not be lost as yet.

Scott could not tarry, however; he had only four days' rations on hand. He had but two choices: to follow the major road from San Agustín through to the village of San Antonio and on to Mexico City, or to make a further crossing of the pedregal and approach by a southwestern route from the villages of San Gerónimo and San Angel. He chose the latter, but left Worth, Quitman, his artillery, and baggage at San Agustín. Again the men crossed the cold lava flows and waste land, advancing to the village of Padierna, just north of Contreras at a point facing Valencia's troops. Unknowingly, they were caught between Valencia's army and one that Santa Anna personally had marched out from the city to San Angel. Then on the afternoon of August 19, Twiggs and Pillow advanced their troops to engage Valencia for six hours, while Santa Anna moved forward to San Gerónimo to a position menacing for the Americans. That night, however, a violent storm occurred, during which Santa Anna's troops withdrew to San Angel for protection. The Americans then slipped out of their camp at three o'clock in the morning of August 20 and three hours later fell on the unprepared Valencia. In just seventeen minutes the Battle of Contreras was over. Mexican losses were approximately 700, with the panic-stricken survivors fleeing toward the capital, to be joined by Santa Anna's troops. American losses were 60 dead and wounded, and the road toward the city was further opened.

Santa Anna confronted the retreating Mexicans, lashing out with his whip at them where he waited near San Angel. With what troops he could rally, he moved to the convent of Churubusco, ranting that Valencia was a traitor and to be shot on sight. He then ordered General Manuel Rincón, seconded by former president Anaya, to hold this convent against the Americans and thereby to protect the retreat of the San Antonio garrison. Churubusco was a natural fortress: it had stout walls, a parapeted roof, outer bastions, breastworks to the south and west, 4 eight-pound cannons, three smaller artillery pieces, and about 1500 men (including the Batallón de San Patricio). Rincón's chances of success seemed great.

Scott, meanwhile, had arrived amid cheering troops to take personal command from Twiggs and Pillow. He knew he had to capture the town of San Antonio and thus reunite his total army, else Worth, Quitman, his artillery, and baggage left behind at San Agustín would be exposed to the full brunt of the Mexican army. Therefore at eleven o'clock he sent Twiggs's and Pillow's troops forward. Poor scouting information led the advancing Americans to believe resistance would be light at San Antonio. Rincón contributed to the deception by holding his artillery fire until the Americans were within musket range. When the Mexicans did open fire, it was with deadly precision and the advance halted. Then Worth arrived on the scene with reinforcements, and his order to the 6th Infantry was to charge. Even this crack unit recoiled twice from the Mexican fire. For a time there was panic in the American ranks at meeting such unexpected resistance, but courage on an individual and squad level started an advance again. Finally the parapet was reached with the aid of a battery of artillery commanded by Captain James Duncan, which had been hurried forward, and the Mexicans inside Churubusco surrendered. Mexican

losses when finally tabulated (for the most part they were estimated) reached 4297 killed or wounded, 2637 prisoners that included eight generals; also they had lost great stores of ammunition, 32 cannons, and thousands of men through deser-
tion. American losses for the day were 131 killed, 865
wounded, and 40 missing. One of Scott's first orders was to
execute members of the Batallón de San Patricio who were
among the Mexican captives.

Old Fuss and Feathers called a halt after the day's activities to allow his exhausted army to rest. Also he knew that
the Mexican capital was in ferment and wished for a peaceful surrender. Thus he immediately wrote a note calling for
such, only to be met by a Mexican request for an armistice.
To this he agreed, and General Mora y Villamil joined Quitman and Twiggs on August 24 through the mediation of the
Spanish and British ambassadors to draft an agreement. This
called for a period of peace during which a treaty was to be
concluded. Scott used the days that followed to reprovision
his army; he paid for these provisions by cashing drafts on
the government of the United States with merchants from
Mexico City. And his troops cleaned their weapons, washed
themselves, and tended the sick.

Santa Anna also used the period of peace to good advantage: he collected an army and prepared further defenses of
the city. Thus when negotiations broke down over unrealis-
tic Mexican demands, he was ready to continue the fight,
which began the first week in September. On September 7
Santa Anna took personal command of troops half a mile
west of Chapultepec at stone buildings a quarter of a mile
long known as El Molino del Rey (The King's Mill). Inside
it was the largest iron foundry in Mexico. Spies had reported
to Scott that cannons were being cast inside and that gunpowder was being manufactured there, to be stored 500 yards
away in a powder magazine called Casa Mata. The next day,
September 8, Scott ordered General Worth to take both.
After the briefest cannonade, Worth sent 500 hand-picked

Americans to storm the mill. They were almost cut to pieces before reinforcements arrived. They finally stormed inside both the mill and the powder magazine to find no evidence of cannon-casting. American losses in this Battle of Molino del Rey totaled 117 killed, 658 wounded, and 18 missing from a total of 3447 who had been engaged. Mexican casualties were estimated at approximately 2700. An American colonel who participated in the assault, Ethan Allen Hitchcock, wrote in his diary that the storming was "a sad mistake." Yet it had contributed to a further undermining of Mexican confidence in Santa Anna and opened the way to the final and decisive battle at Chapultepec.

Had Scott chosen to continue the advance that afternoon of September 8, he would have found Mexican defenses in a poor state. However, he knew there was a strong Mexican force on his flank, and he chose to let his troops have breathing space. Also, his losses at Molino del Rey required him to exercise great caution; he knew the Mexican army yet to be fought greatly outnumbered his army. Not until September 11 did he counsel with his staff about proceeding; they met at La Piedad knowing that a powerful Mexican army numbering 15,000 was ahead of them. Carefully Scott explained the various approaches to the city and what might be met at each; finally he stated his desire to fight at Chapultepec and enter the city through the western gate. Then he asked for opinions. Robert E. Lee, in his capacity as an engineering officer, argued for the southern approach, as did three other engineers and four officers. The other engineer present, Pierre G. T. Beauregard, along with Generals Twiggs and Riley, prefered the western route through the fortress of Chapultepec. After everyone had a say, Scott announced his decision: "Gentlemen, we will attack by the western gates." Pillow and Quitman were sent to make a feint at the eastern gates as a diversion, but were to abandon that position during the night of September 12.

The Mexicans had gradually been fortifying Chapultepec

castle since the previous May, but work had progressed rapidly in September to ready it for any assault. However, there were the usual shortages of money and supplies to hamper the preparations. Still it was a formidable obstacle, as its commander, General Nicolás Bravo, knew. His major difficulty proved to be Santa Anna's conviction that the main assault on the city would come at the eastern gate of Niño Perdido, and thus most of the available troops had been sent there.

The bombardment of Chapultepec began on September 12. Lieutenant George P. Andrews had fired rounds of canister down the road and flat areas around the castle to clear it and thereby allow the artillery to be emplaced closely on the night of September 11. The next morning the cannonading of the fortress by twenty-four-, sixteen-, twelve , and eight-pounders, as well as howitzers and mortars, began, to continue all that day and into the next morning from just 1000 yards away. General Bravo had his artillery return the fire, but not with such telling effect, for his powder, as usual, was poor. Then two Mexican guns were silenced by the American artillery. And the pounding of the building continued. Gradually his troops began to lose heart, whereupon Bravo sent a message to Santa Anna asking for fresh troops. These were promised but only at the critical moment.

The American artillery opened fire on the morning of September 13 at five thirty and continued to fire until eight o'clock that morning. When it halted, the infantry under Twiggs and Pillow advanced; both these generals had strong reservations about the outcome, and even Scott was worried. But the troops advanced, clothed in the courage of battle fury, and inside the fortress they poured. Bravo did not receive the promised reinforcements, and thus he had to fight hand to hand mainly with military students, cowering infantry, and despondent artillerymen. Each fallen American seemed to fill the others with additional fighting ardor. After just ninety minutes of combat General Bravo surrendered his sword, and the Stars and Stripes replaced the Mexican tricolor at the mast. The battle was over. American losses numbered slightly under 500, while Mexican dead, wounded, and captured totaled approximately 1800.

This time Scott did not hesitate after his victory. Leaving a few men behind to hold the castle and guard the prisoners, he sent Quitman's division hurrying along the Belén causeway toward the city. They met occasional resistance, but when such was encountered the artillery was hurried forward to fire a few rounds and the advance continued. Santa Anna was half mad with fury and tried to rally resistance, but the demoralized Mexican troops would not stand against the deadly artillery fire. They fled—as did many of their officers and even most of their generals. By 1:20 p.m. the American flag was flying at the city wall. Then Worth's troops entered the city by the Verónica causeway; individual acts of courage were too numerous to be noticed, and just before nightfall Mexican resistance collapsed. Thus Worth also gained the city wall. Retreating Mexican soldiers swept away both Santa Anna and the troops he was hurrying forward to fight the invaders. Then night descended, and the fighting gradually came to a halt.

During the night Santa Anna tried to rally yet more defenders. Inside the Citadel, a fortified position, he had 5000 infantry and 15 cannons, and an additional 7000 men in the city itself. But even he grew discouraged, and at one o'clock on the morning of September 14 he ordered the city evacuated, declaring that honor had been satisfied, that Mexico City was indefensible. He marched the remainder of his army north to the town of Guadalupe Hidalgo, leaving the city open to the Americans. Three hours later, members of the capital's city council tried to negotiate a surrender with Scott, but he refused; however, he did give quiet assurances of good conduct by his soldiers. Thus just after dawn on September 14 the American troops under General Quitman marched into the *Zócalo* (the grand plaza) of Mexico, to be followed by the marines and the other army divisions. Crowds of silent Mexicans watched as the American flag was raised before the Palacio Nacional, home of the viceroys of old and of Mexican presidents, dictators, and emperors; the Stars and Stripes was greeted on that ascent by the music of an American band and the cheering of the troops. Finally General Scott arrived in full-dress uniform. Then, as marines patrolled the "Halls of Montezuma," Scott named Quitman governor of the city.

The fighting had ended. The time for negotiation had arrived, for neither Scott nor Santa Anna was ready to commit his cause to battle. But much remained for Scott to do. Inside the city there was much resentment against Americans, especially by lower-class residents. Within hours, shots were being fired from ambush at the gringos, and indignant Americans responded by destroying the property from which the attacks were made. Looting by the troops followed, and then conduct toward Mexican women degenerated rapidly. A "state of terror" lasted several days before Scott could control his men and the Mexicans lapsed into sullen acquiescence of the occupation. Still there remained sections of the city where Americans were unsafe, where knifings were common, and where the prudent did not go. Then the Texas Rangers arrived to change that.

Colonel John C. Hays rode into the capital more than a month after its conquest. When the Rangers arrived at the Zócalo, a *lépero* (the name given the lowest class of Mexican robbers, murderers, and thieves) threw a rock and knocked off Hays's hat. The captain calmly pulled his six-shooter and killed the man, thereby serving notice that *Los Tejanos Sangrietes* had arrived. While Hays was inside the capitol seeking a billet for his men, another protesting Mexican was shot by a Ranger. Within hours the *léperos* learned that the Texans' reprisals were deadly. Even the theft of a handkerchief from a Ranger's hip-pocket was considered justification for instant execution by six-shooter; in fact, some of the Texans sewed a corner of their handkerchiefs in their pockets as a temptation to would-be thieves and then shot without question when the handkerchief was tugged. This message was driven home even more forcefully a few days later when a Ranger named Adam Allsens innocently rode into the district known as "cutthroat" and was cut to pieces. That night the Texans rode into the district seeking revenge. The next morning the Mexican police discovered more than eighty bodies of *léperos.* This affair largely ended the murdering of Americans in the city, but Scott thought it best to billet the trigger-happy Texans outside the capital thereafter. They spent their remaining months in Mexico patrolling the road to Vera Cruz and pursuing raiding groups of bandits parading as patriots. In fact, Scott so enforced order in the areas under his command (using both Rangers and troops) that a delegation of leading Mexican citizens asked him to become dictator of Mexico. He refused.

Thus Winfield Scott in just over five months had brought the fighting part of the United States-Mexican war to an end. The Duke of Wellington, when he learned of Scott's victory in Mexico City, urged young English officers to study the campaign, and he declared, "His campaign was unsurpassed in military annals. He is the greatest living soldier." Unfortunately for Scott the Democratic administration in Washington did not want a military hero, especially one who was a Whig. Thus they chose to accept the petty charges filed against him by the quarrelsome generals Worth and Pillow, and on February 18, 1848, Old Fuss and Feathers had to submit to a court of inquiry. Polk finally realized that such charges would not help and withdrew them, especially after Congress again voted Scott its thanks and yet another of its gold medals. Scott would remain in Mexico awaiting the outcome of negotiations for peace. His task was completed, and magnificently.

CHAPTER SIX ❖

NATIONS DIVIDED

INTERNAL DISSENSION racked both Mexico and the United States during the war, as it had before hostilities began and would for years afterward. In the north of Mexico Federalists threatened revolt, and many talked of joining Taylor's invading army. Throughout the United States, but especially in the north, there were strenuous objections to the war—most of it from Whigs and abolitionists, but some from within the Democratic party.

These objections became particularly pronounced in the debates in Congress over Polk's war message. The basic Whig-abolitionist position was that a conspiracy of Southern slaveowners had caused the Texas revolution and had stolen Texas from Mexico; that the annexation of Texas was immoral and an act of aggression against Mexico; that Taylor's occupation of the territory south of the Nueces River was an unnecessary provocation; and that Polk and the southern Democrats were causing a war in order to gain additional slave territory, especially California. "They just want this

Californy so's to lug new slave states in," chanted poet James Russell Lowell.

The objection that got the most discussion was the so-called Nueces boundary violation. After all, even the most avid abolitionists were sufficiently realistic to accept that the Texas Revolution had passed into history and that annexation was an accomplished fact. And the California question was a relatively new one, all tangled with the Oregon question and the issue of British intervention on the West Coast. So the antiwar element rang the changes on the theme of the Nueces. "American blood has been shed on American soil," Polk had said in closing his war message. "American blood has been shed in a Mexican corn field," sneered back the opposition. Abraham Lincoln, then serving his only term in the House of Representatives and already a stout abolitionist, spoke bitterly against the occupation of the "disputed" territory. (It will be remembered from the first chapter that this dispute took place entirely in the United States; the unvarying Mexican position was that all of Texas still belonged to Mexico and the Sabine was the boundary.) Another peace man in Congress said, "The river Nueces is the true western boundary of Texas. . . . It is our own President who began this war." Another declared, ". . . It is grievous to know that when we pray 'God defend the right' our prayers are not for our own country." Nor was it only Whigs and abolitionists who harped on the Nueces question. Even expansionist-minded Thomas Hart Benton opposed the move to the Rio Grande and once referred to the war as an "aggressive war in Mexico." John C. Calhoun offered constitutional objections to Polk's war message.

The truth was that the president had dodged the issue by asking for a declaration of war. A state of hostilities existed, American troops were under attack, and he asked for a war bill which would appropriate $10,000,000 and authorize him to issue a call for 50,000 volunteers. To this strategy was added a preamble in the House which served in the place of a declaration of war. Calhoun maintained that war could not exist until Congress declared it. The preamble carried in the House 123 to 67; 17 Whigs finally voted for it, 14 Democrats against it. Then the war bill itself passed 174 to 14, with 20 abstaining. The 14 nays were from northern Whigs.

In the Senate there was some danger that it might not pass, at least as it stood. Polk's friends went to work. Benton was brought around, and Calhoun was persuaded to abstain. On Monday afternoon, May 11, the bill was split between two committees, and the Senate pretended it had other business to attend to. Imagine the politicking that night and the next morning. A caucus of Democratic leaders met and the vote was a tie. Senator Edward A. Hannegan of Indiana was sent for, and he broke the tie in favor of the war bill. Late Tuesday the bill, with a few minor word changes, passed 40 to 2, 3 abstaining, including Calhoun. The House was reconvened Tuesday night to accept the changes.

There is an interesting story about Senator Hannegan, who cast the decisive vote in the caucus, although it is only problematical whether this would have made much difference in the long run. Hannegan's election to the Senate turned on the vote of a single farm hand from DeKalb County, Indiana, in the election of 1842. The vote that year for the legislative representative from DeKalb and Steuben counties was tied at 360 for Madison Marsh and 360 for Enos Beall. Marsh contested, claiming that the ballot of one Henry Shoemaker had been illegally rejected. The ballot was ultimately allowed, and Marsh entered the Indiana legislature, where he voted for Hannegan for the United States Senate. A man named Smith was one vote short of the necessary majority on the first ballot; Hannegan received only three votes. But, after much jockeying, on the sixth ballot Hannegan got a bare majority through Marsh's vote and went to Washington to represent the people of Indiana (and Henry Shoemaker). There a few years later he seems to have determined (in part) the course of the United States Senate on the war bill. Quite a string of decisive single votes.

The war bill carried, and Polk issued the call for volunteers. The response was almost overwhelming from every part of the country. Despite political problems in Congress, there can be little question that a decided majority of the nation supported Polk and the war. Now committed to the war in Mexico whether he liked it or not—and there is good reason to believe that he did not like it, despite the castigations of detractors from 1846 to the present—Polk turned to face what loomed as an equally pressing problem. Fifty-four forty or fight! What could be done about the British? Would they settle the Oregon question amicably? Would they support Mexico in the war? Would they refrain from intervention in California or from establishing a protectorate there?

It is worth a moment's speculation to consider whether the outcome in Oregon might have been different if war had not come on the Rio Grande. Polk and Buchanan had little option now but to placate Britain. That the British Foreign Office and large segments of the British population were unfriendly to the United States is amply evidenced, and some historians have laid a large share of the responsibility for the war with Mexico on the activities of British agents. The American minister in London put his finger upon the problem: the purpose of official Britain was to keep United States's affairs with Mexico so unsettled that the United States government would accede to a reasonable settlement in Oregon. And, of course, this is exactly what Polk had to do.

In December 1845 he had staunchly reasserted the American claim to 54°40, the line agreed upon by Russia (then in Alaska), asking Congress to annul the joint occupation agreement with Britain. Congress had quickly agreed, and it appeared at that time that the Polk administration would adopt a hard line in the Northwest. Noting not only the tempo of diplomatic affairs but also the rapid insurgence of American furriers, the Hudson's Bay Company had moved its Columbia River station to Vancouver Island in 1845. But the mounting tension with Mexico reshaped United States policy in Oregon. Secretary of State Buchanan sought out Britain's representative in Washington, and Polk Democrats revived an 1842 suggestion of Daniel Webster's that the 49th parallel be extended to the Pacific. The British Foreign Office, which at the time of the Webster-Ashburton negotiations had wanted the 49th only as far as the Columbia River, thence down it to the Pacific (which would have taken in about half of the present state of Washington), now acceded to the proposal, save that Vancouver Island would remain British. Polk gave this proposition to the Senate without recommendation, and the Senate passed a resolution favoring it. Hastily a treaty was thrown together in June 1846 establishing the present boundary between the United States and Canada in the northwest.

Although some historians assert that the 49th parallel was the utmost American diplomats had ever hoped to obtain, this does not square fully with the posture of the administration—until after the total breakdown of negotiations in Mexico following the Paredes coup. This whole situation deserves more intensive study, but it is interesting to note that after war with Mexico began, and especially after the surprising victories at Palo Alto and Resaca de la Palma, the British attitude seems to have shifted.

If British attitudes softened toward the United States, they hardened toward Mexico. Paredes found that British support became an illusion and that French aid had been nothing but a dream. After the loss of Palo Alto and Resaca de la Palma (Resaca de la Guerrero in Mexico), Mexico was thrown into turmoil. Public opinion welled up over the defeat and there were a rash of pamphlets published "explaining" the actions of the Mexican commanders. Arista himself was placed under arrest and later court-martialed. Meanwhile Taylor moved across the Rio Grande and occupied Matamoros. The Paredes government then was confronted with something more devastating than the loss of possible European support, for a revolution was building in northern

Mexico. Polk's problems with Whigs, abolitionists, and other peace supporters were nothing compared to Paredes's troubles with Federalists and latent separatists.

The separatist movement in northern Mexico dated from Santa Anna's 1835 abrogation of the Constitution of 1824. Finding encouragement in the success of the Texas Revolution, Federalists organized the Republic of the Rio Grande in 1839. Conspiracy, intrigue, and double-dealing ended its aspirations for independence but did not quell Federalist ideals. Northern Mexico's dissatisfaction with the various Centralist governments is a well-established though not well-known fact. Indeed, this Federalist revolution against the Mexican government, as well as the earlier Paredes revolution against Herrera, has been entirely ignored in most of the recent interpretations of the war.

Shortly after Taylor arrived at Corpus Christi, he began receiving messages from Federalists in Tamaulipas, Nuevo León, and Coahuila, some surreptitious, some forthright. As early as September 1845 he was told that should war occur, those three states would announce for independence and support the United States. Much of the supplies for his Army of Occupation were furnished by merchants in Matamoros. In February 1846 José Carbajal visited Taylor at Corpus bearing dispatches from Antonio Canales, leader of the erstwhile Republic of the Rio Grande. In a letter addressed to Taylor on January 29, 1846, Canales wrote: "It has been the will of providence to permit the people of my unhappy country to pass through the ordeal of military oppression, internal turmoil, and unprecedented misrule. . . . You will doubtless have heard of the conspiracy of General Paredes and his army against the constituted authorities and laws of his country: . . . falsely he pretends to act for and with the consent of the nation. . . . We are resolved to destroy the degenerate and immoral army . . . and establish a constitution based upon the just rights of man. Should it not be possible . . . these Northern States will separate forever from Mexico." He hoped for Taylor's assistance but urged him not to divert the attention of Mexican patriots from the "tyrant" by a precipitate invasion.

Orally, Carbajal told Taylor that he had full power from Canales to conduct negotiations. Carbajal introduced several proposals, which Taylor dutifully relayed to his government: that the United States furnish arms and ammunition to the Federalists; that Taylor remain on the Nueces until the Paredes government was overthrown and a boundary settlement could be negotiated: and that then the new Federalist governent would promptly pay the American claims. In a written memorandum Carbajal added: ". . . The whole mass of the nation is hostile to his [Paredes's] usurpation. It should also be noted that our social compact being broken, *we* are the rightful owners [of the land]." On March 1, 1846, Canales issued a proclamation to the northern states calling for revolution. Carbajal, who had returned to Camargo, wrote Taylor: ". . . You may depend upon it *we will soon drive all the votaries of Paredes beyond the mountains.*"

Taylor completed his move to the Rio Grande, the opening battles of the war were fought, and Americans occupied Matamoros. During this time Canales's troops did not join Taylor, but neither did they fight with the regular Mexican forces. As a matter of fact, among the charges leveled at Mejía, Ampudia, and Arista for the Mexican losses was that they had at one time been associated with the Federalists. American forces in Matamoros encouraged the dissension, not unnaturally, and a Texan, Hugh McLeod, established a Spanish-English newspaper which exhorted the Federalists to rebel. Throughout northern Mexico, from Zacatecas to Coahuila and from Monterrey to Tampico, the threat of uprising was in the air. The town of Reynosa made proposals to Taylor; Camargo pronounced for revolution; Tampico tried to get American naval aid; an incipient rebellion broke out in Victoria, capital of Tamaulipas; a meeting of *alcaldes* from more than a score of towns declared that the states of Tamaulipas, Nuevo León, and Coahuila should take separate action from the rest of Mexico; and elsewhere rumblings were heard. To some observers the Republic of the Rio Grande seemed, at last, about to materialize.

It is by no means improbable that if the United States had guaranteed the independence of the Republic of the Rio Grande, the entire history of the war would have been different, but all Taylor was authorized to do was ensure protection of the northern states during the war. Federalists could not accept this because of the inevitable consequences after the war. So the Republic of the Rio Grande never came into full existence, and there was never any outright military co-operation with the United States. But from almost every account, friendly relations generally existed between American troops and Mexican civilians, and trade, branded "smuggling" by some, flourished. However, the threat that the Federalists *might* join Taylor was always present during the summer of 1846. They used the threat, the war, the invading American army as a lever against Paredes to force the restoration of constitutional government.

Everywhere Paredes looked that summer there were insurmountable obstacles. After the defeat on the Rio Grande he called a congress into session and asked for the support of the Mexican people. Congress obediently elected him president of Mexico on June 12, 1846. Later that month, deciding that his April proclamation of defensive war had not adequately unified the Mexican people, he asked for a formal declaration of war. It was voted on July 1 and proclaimed on July 6, but it did not elicit any greater support from dissenters. Paredes proposed personally to lead an attack against Taylor, but rather than to unify Mexico, this served to alarm Federalists who felt that the president's real purpose was to suppress rebellion.

By the end of July uprisings against the Mexican government had become general. Most were Federalist in nature, but some were personally directed against Paredes, and some were the machinations of ambitious leaders. It is really impossible to analyze the turbulent political-military picture which day by day turned like a kaleidoscope into different patterns. In a public statement from Havana on February 20, 1846, Santa Anna had vehemently declared against the alleged monarchical schemes of Paredes; this had won him the support of his former vice president, Gómez Farías, who was the leader of a radical group of Federalists. Almonte, now disenchanted with Paredes and eager to support his old master despite Gómez Farías's Federalism, joined the movement, and an uprising was planned at Vera Cruz. Outbreaks also occurred at Acapulco, Guadalajara, and lesser places. Paredes announced he was leaving Mexico City to take personal command of the army (although he actually remained secreted in the city) and turned the government over to his vice president, Nicolás Bravo, on July 28.

On August 3, 1846, Bravo proclaimed the restoration of constitutional government, but this did not appease the Federalists, for it was the inadequate document that had replaced the *Siete Leyes*. That same day the garrison at Vera Cruz announced in favor of Santa Anna. On August 4, in Mexico City, General José Mariano Salas, commander of troops there, also announced for Santa Anna and Federalism. Two days later Bravo resigned. It was clear that Centralism had fallen; it was not clear what had replaced it. On August 22 Salas, guided by Gómez Farías and other Federalists, solemnly restored the long-defunct Constitution of 1824. In the midst of these tumultuous August days, Santa Anna slipped back into Mexico, as enigmatic, ambivalent, and opportunistic as ever.

He had sensed the dissatisfaction with Paredes in February and had begun his schemes to return. To the American consul at Havana he had proposed that, if he were permitted to come through the American naval blockade, he would unite the various factions in Mexico and conclude an imme-

diate peace with the United States. Even the consul had little respect for the idea, but it was a possibility of bringing
the war to an early conclusion, and Polk approved. On August 16, Santa Anna landed at Vera Cruz and read a patriotic
proclamation addressed to the people of Mexico. Once again
his public image, though slightly tarnished, was that of
champion of the people. Once again he declared his support
of Federalism, and incredibly advised the restoration of the
Constitution of 1824 (which he himself had destroyed in
1835). Shortly thereafter he left to take command of the
troops who would soon confront Taylor at Buena Vista.

Under the restored constitution a national election was
held in November to choose deputies to Congress who
would select a new president. After much maneuvering, on
December 22, 1846, the radical Federalist, Gómez Farías,
was elected, and he was to take office two days later. As before, in his reforming zeal, it took him only a few months to
bring constitutional government down about his ears, although his zeal was not entirely to blame. Two strong factions existed in the Federalist camp, the *puros,* who wanted
"pure" reform, and the moderates, who tended toward con-
servatism in politics and religion. The new president was a
radical *puro* and anti-Church. It was over the issue of financing the war that these factions clashed and constitutional
government fell.

The administration was in desperate financial plight.
The million pesos that Paredes had raised with much difficulty to conduct the war had disappeared along with his government amid much talk of corruption in high places. Efforts to levy taxes proved futile, as did attempts to borrow
money from merchants in Mexico City, although one forced
loan had been made to help Santa Anna finance his Buena
Vista campaign. Since the Church had the greatest wealth in
Mexico, the anti-Church *puros* in Gómez Farías's congress
began discussions of ways and means to pry some of it loose
to support the war. The anticlerical president encouraged

this approach. After heated debates, on January 11, 1847, a law was passed authorizing the president to raise money on Church lands by pledging them if he could find lenders, by selling them if he could not borrow. The moderates objected, and a fury of protest broke out all over Mexico; ministers of state were even threatened with excommunication if they dared implement the law. Then this law was revised and strengthened on February 4, but as Gómez Farías's desperation grew, the opposition to him increased. The militia of Mexico City turned against him, as did the Regular Army units shortly thereafter. By the end of February, revolution once more was mounted, the government was in a shambles, the deputies were afraid to assemble in Congress, and Gómez Farías was forced out of power.

At this moment, returning from his defeat at Buena Vista, came Santa Anna, traveling south well ahead of his dejected and dispirited troops. Suddenly, to his astonishment, he found himself the man of the hour: *puros,* moderates, monarchists, clerics—all now welcomed him as the savior of Mexico. On March 23, 1847, principally with support from the moderates, he formally assumed the presidency, to the celebration of the nation and a vote of thanks from Congress for his "victory" at Buena Vista. Still, his position was precarious. The *puros,* who had earlier supported him, were in national disfavor because of the anticlerical laws; the moderates, who had brought him to power, distrusted his motives; Scott was about to invade Vera Cruz; and the national financial crisis was unsolved. His shaky political support was later to desert him; Scott was to be successful at Vera Cruz; and the immediate problem was financial. Santa Anna quickly milked 2,000,000 pesos from the Church in return for an annulment of the laws of January 11 and February 4. The Church, its hierarchy and its wealth, was without doubt the only stable institution in Mexico—and without doubt the strongest.

A problem of lesser import plagued Mexico during the

war—that of Yucatán. Yucatán had rebelled against Central-ism in 1839 and had established its independence in 1842. Because of its geographical position, no serious attempt at re-conquest had been made. Thus at the outbreak of the war the Paredes government was faced with what was an essen-tially hostile government on its southern boundary. Yucatán proclaimed its neutrality, and when the United States laid its naval blockade on the Mexican coast, this was respected. However, in November 1846, the Mexican government, then under Federalist domination, offered Yucatán such conces-sions that it voted to rejoin the Mexican Republic under the restored Constitution of 1824.

When this occurred, United States naval forces promptly occupied several key ports in Yucatán. A rebellion was taking place at the same time, and the insurgents emerged victorious early in January 1847. They immediately sent an emissary to Washington requesting that Yucatán's neutrality be re-established, to which Buchanan agreed. There was a discussion with the secretary of state over whether the United States would entertain a proposal of an-nexation, but Buchanan said such was an impossibility. Yu-catán's troubles were not over; an Indian uprising threw the country into turmoil, and in September, Justo Sierra O'Reilly, son of the chief executive, was sent to Washington to seek aid. He was courteously received by Buchanan, but an answer to his request was delayed for months. If Mexico City had not been occupied by that time and the war ended for all practical purposes, it is possible that Buchanan's reac-tion to Yucatán's proposals might have been different. In any event, it is worth noting that the neutrality of Yucatán and its hostility toward Mexican Centralism was a minor fac-tor in Mexico's weakness during the war.

During these exhausting trials of the various Mexican governments, the Polk administration was not free of tribu-lations. Dissension and antiwar sentiment in the United

States were more vocal but not as violent. There was no dictatorship to be overthrown and no constitution to be restored, and the opponents to the war could not muster anything close to a majority, as the Federalists had done by temporary coalition. Yet abolitionist objections continued to be pressed, in and out of Congress, and to these were added the dissonant voices of various other peace groups. Furthermore, like the Mexican governments during the war, the American government faced financial problems, albeit not as ruinous, religious problems, and jealousy among military authorities.

The basic objections of the abolitionists did not change, but they expanded their position to emphasize their opposition to the extension of slavery. In the famous Wilmot Proviso they were given a dramatic sounding board. David Wilmot was elected to congress from Pennsylvania in 1844 as a Polk Democrat. As such, he supported the administration and voted for the Walker Tariff in 1846. By doing so he fell under heavy criticism from his constituents, who opposed the reduction in protective duties. It was partially to remedy this political misstep and partially from heart-felt conviction that he introduced an amendment (actually drafted by an abolitionist congressman from Ohio) to a war appropriation bill in August 1846. Called the Wilmot Proviso, it provided that no form of involuntary servitude, specifically slavery, should ever exist in any territory acquired as a result of the war with Mexico. This had twofold significance: first, it indicated the generally accepted conclusion that territory would be acquired from Mexico (in addition to Texas, which was already a slave state); and second, it threw down the glove to proslavery men in Congress. An ancillary significance was that it moved Wilmot from the Democratic fold. He served in the House until 1851, generally voting thereafter with the Whigs; he became an outspoken abolitionist and later helped to organize the Republican party; he threw his political support behind Lincoln in 1860, entered the Senate in 1861, and was rewarded with an appointment to the United States Court of Claims.

The debates on Wilmot's amendment were explosive and vituperative. Questions of constitutionality were raised, never to be fully resolved until 1865, and peace men found another opportunity to interject sermons on the immorality of the war. The amendment passed the House and went to the Senate just before the adjournment of the first session of Congress. It was reintroduced in the next session and passed the House, again after hot debate, by a vote of 115 to 106. Curiously, both the Whig and Democratic parties were split on the measure: nearly 40 per cent of the Democrats voted in favor of it, and over 30 per cent of the Whigs opposed it. The favorable Democratic vote came from Northerners such as Wilmot; the Whig opposition came partially from Southern Whigs and partially from a variety of constitutional objections.

In the Senate the proviso provoked renewed debate. One senator (John Berrien of Georgia) went so far as to offer a resolution that no territory at all be acquired from Mexico and, despite the passage of Polk's war bill, that the objectives of the conflict be limited to the settlement of the claims and of the Texas boundary. Calhoun introduced a series of five resolutions that in effect outlined a revised Southern position on the extension of slavery. The chief element of these was a constitutional theory that Congress had no power to legislate on or control the status of slavery. It was a concept that Chief Justice Roger B. Taney later extrapolated from in the Dred Scott case. None of these resolutions passed, and the proviso was defeated, 31 to 21. As in the House, the party vote was split. Eight Democrats from Northern and border states voted for it; twenty-one, mostly from Southern states, voted against it. Ten Southern Whigs were also against it, and thirteen Northern Whigs voted aye.

Although the proviso did not carry, its immediate effect

was to delay much-needed war appropriations for nearly six months. Thereafter, the House attached it to numerous measures; Lincoln remarked later that he believed he had voted for the Wilmot Proviso at least forty times. Always it was defeated in the Senate, and always it slowed the passage of wartime legislation. Perhaps more important, it increased the tempo of sectional controversy. Its initial introduction had also provided one of the issues in the congressional elections in the fall of 1846.

It is not unusual in American political history for the party of the man in the White House to lose congressional seats in off-year elections, and the Democrats might have expected it. Many of Polk's policies were unpopular, especially in the North, although by no means wholly so. The Walker Tariff was disliked by manufacturing interests; the Oregon settlement was objected to by radical expansionists; the war bill was considered by some to have been political sleight-of-hand; and the war itself was at a low in public approbation that fall. The Whigs made good use of all of these, although the party itself was divided into somewhat amorphous and overlapping factions. Southern Whigs supported the war but at least superficially opposed the acquisition of territory from Mexico; Northern Whigs vaguely opposed the war and firmly opposed the extension of slavery, an incongruous acceptance of territorial expansion; "conscience" Whigs opposed the war but were vague on what its results should be, and some of them later supported the tenuous movement to annex all of Mexico. Despite these differences, the Whigs won control of the House.

When the new congress assembled as the year 1847 began, the United States was nearly as divided as Mexico. Revolution, of course, was not to be expected, although there was some talk of secession by radicals. It probably was the Whig desire for the presidency in the 1848 elections that prevented conditions from becoming almost as chaotic as those in Mexico. Whig leaders smelled electoral victory, talked of military heroes such as Taylor and Scott as popular candidates, and when pressed supported the war. This created an anamoly for the administration. Neither Taylor nor Scott could be allowed to develop heroic public images. Both generals, especially Scott, accused the administration of failure to support them adequately, and there is, sadly, some truth in these charges, as has been seen in previous chapters. Yet at the same time, the administration had to press the war to a successful conclusion. It was this factor which led Polk and Marcy to take most of Taylor's troops from him and to give Scott command of the Vera Cruz invasion. It was also this same factor which led Polk, almost in desperation, to attempt to conclude an early peace, despite the fact that it was unlikely he would succeed. Thus, throughout the remainder of the war, President Polk had to contend with a fundamentally obstructionist congress, the forthcoming election in 1848, and a heterogeneous variety of objections to the war among the American citizenry.

No simple analysis of the opposition to the war is possible. Much of it was purely politically motivated; a very substantial portion came from coagulating antislavery forces; some was basically religiously oriented; a small bit was an idealistic precursor of twentieth-century internationalism; and most of it was a combination of two or more of these. A few examples might serve to illustrate these elements.

In December 1845 a group of citizens from New York of various political persuasions signed a petition to Congress proposing what has been called the first United Nations organization: ". . . Deeply impressed with the evils of war, and believing it possible to supersede its necessity by providing another method of settling national disputes, respectfully petition your honorable bodies to provide . . . a proposal to other governments that a Congress of Nations may be assembled, to form a code of international law, by which their varying interests may be determined."

Peace movements in the United States—that is, those

that were not squarely based on antislavery sentiment—had their roots in the reactions to the War of 1812 and the Napoleonic wars in Europe. Most had religious overtones, and many developed abolitionist undercurrents. An idealistic peace society was established in Massachusetts in 1815, and its example was soon followed in a number of other states. In 1828 the American Peace Society was founded by William Ladd, who sought to combine the state societies into one organization. Two years later the American Peace Society unequivocally announced that its purpose was the abolition of war. After a fruitless attempt to capture control of the society, abolitionist William Lloyd Garrison and others founded the Non-Resistant Peace Society. With the outbreak of the war in 1846, other peace societies sprang up rapidly, some being splinter groups and others simply local in nature. All concentrated on harsh criticism of Polk and his administration and on demands for an end to the war.

As a generalization, all religious sects and denominations had difficulty resolving the twin virtues of patriotism and pacifism during the war. The Methodist Church was particularly torn. Strongest in the South and in the frontier regions, according to W. W. Sweet, it was one of the most evangelical Protestant institutions. Consequently, its leaders were interested in expansion. In 1847 a delegation of a hundred Methodist ministers visited the White House and assured President Polk of their support of the war, but this was not an official attitude. The New England Conference of the Methodist Church passed at least two resolutions against the war, and this was not a gestalt representation. A Methodist minister in Louisiana secured a leave of absence "to lick the Mexicans," and a captain's commission in the army. Other ministers rushed to volunteer as chaplains. A Northern pastor told a volunteer company that a principal feature of Christianity was to fight and die for one's country.

Southern Baptists were possibly more prowar than the Methodists. A Nashville church organ, perhaps typical, her-

alded the war as the beginning of religious and political freedom in Mexico. The most moderate of Southern Baptists appeared only to urge a speedy return of peace. Northern
Baptists did not take an official position, but two New York
missionary societies viewed the moral effects of the war as
disastrous. A Boston Baptist minister called the war one for
the purpose of extending slave territory. Some elements of
the Presbyterian Church saw the war as a blessing in dis-
guise; it would open Catholic Mexico to Protestant prosely-
tism. One minister pled that his congregation prepare to put
a Bible in every home in Mexico. Where the Methodists
seemed to be interested in growth in acquired territory, the
Presbyterians appeared to be interested in evangelical activities in Catholic Mexico. However, some Presbyterians
openly opposed the war, including two synods in Pennsylvania and Ohio. Episcopalians accepted the war with a kind
of phlegmatic resignation. Lutherans tried to ignore it, although two small synods condemned it. A Dutch Reformed
minister declared that it was an honor to die in a war for
such "just causes and desirable ends," but he probably represented a minority sentiment of that denomination. Only one
official statement came from the Disciples of Christ: the war
was "one of the greatest crimes in our modern history."

The most open and unequivocal opposition came from
Quakers, Unitarians, and Congregationalists. The Congregationalists were strongest in New England, and their opposition was both moralistic and antislavery. A nonsectarian (but
primarily abolitionist) peace organization stated that Unitarians led all denominations in the cause of peace. A prowar
newspaper in Massachusetts accused Unitarian clergymen of
using Whig arguments against the war, "spicing the whole
occasionally, with a few grains of affected piety." Theodore
Parker, one of the most eloquent of all peace advocates, condemned the war as aggressive and urged all Christians to refuse to pay taxes in support of it or to participate in the
manufacture of war materials. The Society of Friends felt no

need to harangue its membership on the evils of war. It concentrated on bombarding members of Congress and the administration. One antiwar petition to Congress contained 9000 names. Also the Quakers tried to deluge the general public with propaganda directed against the war.

Roman Catholics in the United States faced a peculiarly trying dilemma. Mexico was Catholic, yet an underlying tenet of the Church called for patriotic support of the State. Furthermore, Catholicism was plagued by a mid-nineteenth-century upsurge of anti-Catholicism, which was given impetus not only by the war itself but by the defalcation of the Irish Catholic unit known as the San Patricio Battalion. Both the Irish in America, most of whom were Catholic, and the Catholic Church suffered castigation. Much has been written to defend them as patriots, and there is little indication that either group contained many advocates of peace. Their course, naturally, was a defensive one, for some militants went so far as to dub the war a "Protestant Crusade."

Anti-Catholic sentiments were frequently expressed in the United States. A Baptist editor cried that if Mexico gained victory "the yoke of papal oppression would be placed upon every state of this Republic." Other Baptist propaganda declared that a nun in Mexico seduced an American soldier in order to secure his help in removing the body of a priest from her cell. A Presbyterian paper solemnly stated that God "has his own purposes to accomplish upon the wicked treacherous and idolatrous people of Mexico and He is making the United States . . . the rod of his anger. . . ." Ray Billington has amply demonstrated the propensity of mid-nineteenth-century evangelists for fostering anti-Catholic prejudice. Playing into such hands and hoping to add to the anti-Catholic foment, Mexican officers occasionally published broadside appeals to Catholics in the United States Army to desert to the side of Mexico.

Such appeals to American Catholics had, if anything, a reverse effect, but anti-Catholic sentiment occasioned two concerns to the administration: the war should not take on any religious overtones that could be prevented, and neither the Mexican people nor the Mexican Church, especially the powerful hierarchy, should be deluded into believing that American soldiers were Protestant ogres. Almost immediately after the passage of the war bill Polk took the first step to correct any such impression. After conferring with prominent Catholic bishops, the president requested that they select two members of the Catholic clergy to serve as chaplains in the army. Actually, at the time, there was no such post as chaplain, and the two selected were appointed special employees, as were other Protestant ministers. It was hoped that this move would also ease any feeling by Mexican Catholics that the United States Army was anti-Catholic. Polk also asked Bishop John Hughes of New York to go to Mexico for the purpose of relieving any prejudice against the United States because of a feared anti-Catholic bias. The bishop was forced to refuse the mission, not because he disapproved but because Polk at that time could give him no official standing.

Although there was a small flare of resentment among some radical Protestant sectarians in the United States at the news of the appointment of Catholic chaplains, most people agreed with a New Orleans newspaper of the time that there was no reason why the selection of a Roman Catholic should be any more objectionable than that of an Episcopalian or any other Protestant. Religious toleration had become a viable asset of the American character by the mid-nineteenth century, and the rantings of zealots did little to disturb it. Internally the real emotional issue in the country was not religion but slavery and the extension of slavery.

Abolitionist forces bombarded the war and Polk's war aims continually, sometimes through the peace societies, sometimes through the churches, especially the Congregational and Unitarian, and often in outright and undisguised attack. Occasionally these were aberrant anti-American propaganda, but usually they took the form of protests to the war and the possible extension of slavery. Opposition to the extension of slavery had been evident since the Missouri Compromise of 1820 and became especially pronounced over the Texas question. Jackson had delayed Texas recognition in deference to it; Congress had passed the "gag rule" in 1838 to quell further discussion of Texas annexation (as a slave state); and antislavery forces had defeated the Annexation Treaty of 1844 because of their firm commitment against the extension of slavery. Later the antislavery position was made perfectly clear in the Wilmot Provisio. Among the most effective of this propaganda was the *Biglow Papers* by James Russell Lowell, which called the war "a national crime committed in behoof of slavery." His attack was all the more effective because it was based upon ridicule, both in poetry and prose. Other New England intellectuals joined in opposition to the war, such as Ralph Waldo Emerson and Henry David Thoreau.

All of this variegated opposition to the war might have been mustered by Whig leaders into a serious threat to Polk and the administration policies had the Whigs not fixed their eyes so determinedly on the presidency in 1848. But, even so, Polk constantly ran into obstacles in Congress. And there his biggest problem was financing the war. There were two aspects to the financing of the war: one was to persuade Congress to pass appropriations bills; the other was to persuade Congress to pass bills to bring the funds into the treasury to meet the appropriations. Both gave the administration great annoyance.

Although the nation began the fiscal year 1845–46 with a surplus in the treasury of over $7,000,000, receipts had been less than Robert J. Walker, secretary of the treasury, had anticipated, and expenditures were greater. Consequently when the war began the surplus had evaporated. Government financing in those days was much more simple than it is today. In order to meet the war appropriations, the first of which was the $10,000,000 attached to the war bill, it was necessary to get the money into the treasury.

Two approaches to raising the funds could be taken: increase taxes, and borrow through bonds and treasury notes. Traditionally the two principal sources of revenue had been the sale of the public domain and the customs duties. But the Democrats were too fully committed to lowering the tariff of 1842 to back off. The Walker Tariff of 1846 was passed, lowering the rate, to go into effect in December 1846. Revenue from customs dwindled almost to nothing in the first two quarters of the fiscal year 1846–47 as importers held back awaiting the lower schedule in December. Senator Benton, Walker, and the general land commissioner worked out a scheme for grading the public domain and offering some of it at lower prices, hoping thereby to increase sales. But Congress would have none of it. With revenues off and war expenses skyrocketing, the government had no choice except to borrow.

The public credit was not good, especially in Europe, where investors held nearly $200,000,000 in securities of the various states. And the war depressed it further. The month that war was declared a London newspaper predicted that no British investor could then be persuaded to buy any form of American security. In June 1846 Walker estimated that the treasury deficit at the end of the forthcoming fiscal year would be over $12,000,000. Congress authorized a $10,-000,000 loan in treasury notes and bonds. Walker found it exceedingly difficult to persuade investors to purchase, especially during the fall and winter. In December 1846 Walker was forced to up his estimate of the deficit to $23,000,000. After some haggling, Congress authorized a $23,000,000 loan. Though the prospects then looked bleak, a turnaround came in 1847. The war news was better, and unexpected circumstances caused the European market for American agricultural products to expand. By mid-1847 a surprising prosperity existed, imports increased, and even the lower duties of the Walker Tariff yielded greater incomes than had been anticipated.

Further financial relief was found in the plan to collect American customs in the occupied Mexican ports. There was no objection to this from Mexican merchants because the American duties were substantially lower than Mexico's. This actually resulted in an upsurge in the Mexican economy by the end of the war. A few other military measures were taken toward the end of the war. Assessments were levied on some of the occupied towns, $150,000 on Mexico City, for example. In November 1847 Scott ordered that the American occupation forces would cease paying rent on houses and other buildings except where contracts existed. In December the American military government began collecting taxes previously paid to the Mexican government— perfectly appropriate since the United States Army had restored law and order and was for all practical purposes the only central government in Mexico at the time.

All in all, the war was less expensive than some pessimists had predicted. At war's end the public debt stood at $66,000,000.

Sentiments of the business community during the war varied. A near panic swept down Wall Street when the war bill was passed. Some predicted a return to the dark days of 1837. A large portion of the private economy rested upon European trade: exports of American staples, imports of European, especially British, manufactured goods. Furthermore, a great many American merchants operated on annual credit advanced by British factors. War, it was believed, threatened this. Far more alarming in May 1846 was the fear that Britain might support Mexico in the war and thus lower economic sanctions on the United States, or worse, cut off trade entirely. And if the British navy should blockade major American ports, what then but disaster? No wonder Wall Street panicked. Although its worst fears were not realized, there is no doubt that the nation's businessmen joined the various peace groups, first in opposing the war, then in clamoring for an early peace. The prosperity of 1847 relieved the pressure on the administration from this quarter, but the business community, perhaps eyeing the mounting national debt, never became a proponent of the war.

Because the war was not popular in so many segments of the population, because peace groups kept up a constant barrage on Congress and the administration, and because Polk himself was not happy with war for a variety of reasons (personal religious convictions, the creation of political figures from military leaders, the strengthening of the Whig party, etc.), the president very early began making attempts to secure peace. Had he been fully aware of the internal turmoil in Mexico he would have realized the futility of these attempts.

The earliest of these was a discussion with Bishop Hughes in May 1846 of the possibility that Hughes might be able to influence the Catholic Church in Mexico to aid in the restoration of peace. There was an offer of British mediation that the Paredes government spurned. In July 1846 Buchanan sent dispatches to Mexico suggesting negotiations for peace which would ignore the causes of the war, thinking this might be acceptable. These arrived as the Paredes government was crumbling and were hotly rejected by General Salas. Then came the scheme to return Santa Anna, but it backfired.

Next was a rather unusual venture. Moses Yale Beach, editor of the New York *Sun* and a prominent Catholic layman, went to Vera Cruz with his wife and his secretary in January 1847, traveling on British passports. Beach was armed with letters that gave him immediate standing with the highest Catholic prelates in Mexico. He also carried with him a scheme to build a canal across the Isthmus of Tehuántepec for his own personal enrichment and that of anyone in Mexico who would join with him. Beach was conniving and secretive; his secretary was perhaps the most unusual and mysterious woman in nineteenth-century America. Mrs. Jane McManus Storm, born in New York, had been involved in Aaron Burr's divorce case, had brought a shipload of European immigrants to Texas in the 1830's, had remained in Texas for a few years on friendliest terms with the most important men of the time, and had returned to New York a few years before the outbreak of war to write features for the *Sun*. In Matagorda, Texas, a duel was fought for her honor; Mireabeau B. Lamar dedicated a book of poems to her; the editor of the Louisville *Courier* said in his memoirs that she had more to do with starting and ending the Mexican War than any other one person, but he did not explain himself. She later remarried, returned to Texas to help her husband establish the frontier town of Eagle Pass, followed him on diplomatic assignments to the Dominican Republic, contracted with William Walker to furnish a thousand colonists to Nicaragua, aided her husband in a venture to colonize former slaves on Santo Domingo, and with him established a large plantation in Jamaica, where she died in 1878. She was a natural diplomat and secret agent, a born adventurer, and as one man wrote of her, "God made and equipped her for a filibuster."

What she and Beach did in Mexico is shrouded in the mystery that surrounded every element of her life. Santa Anna, avaricious and desperate for funds, fell in, at least temporarily, with the Tehuántepec proposal. Through his Church connections Beach seems to have been important if not instrumental in causing the prelates to resist the levy laws of January 11 and February 4 and to bring the downfall of Gómez Farías. Beach and Mrs. Storm narrowly escaped Mexico with their lives, crossing the mountains to Tampico. Both later filed reports with the state department and were apparently confidential agents in Mexico. While not exactly peace negotiators, their objective was to hasten the end of the war.

Even while Beach moved about his secret affairs, another

peace mission was projected. A former minion of Santa Anna's arrived in January 1847 suggesting his intimate familiarity with high Mexican officials and implying that he was on a secret peace mission. Buchanan agreed to a proposal that a joint Mexican-American peace commission meet in Havana to discuss terms for peace. The intriguing Mexican was sent to Mexico with dispatches for the Mexican government. The overture was ill-conceived and refused, out of hand, by Mexico; the agent was expelled from the country. By the time he returned to Washington in April 1847, the battles of Cerro Gordo and Churubusco had been fought and Scott had occupied Jalapa. The time seemed ripe for another peace overture.

CHAPTER SEVEN

END OF WAR

THE UNPOPULARITY of the war in the winter of 1846–47 and the reluctance of congressional co-operation caused Polk to make a major effort to effect peace with Mexico. After consultations with his cabinet, especially Buchanan, a plan was evolved to send a commissioner to Mexico with broad powers of negotiation. With an eye on the 1848 elections, Polk desired to appoint a man who was not likely to make political capital out of the mission. Buchanan suggested Nicholas P. Trist, chief clerk of the state department, and Polk's cabinet gave unanimous approval.

Trist was born in Virginia in 1800, received a good education, became proficient in both the French and Spanish languages, married a member of the Jefferson family, and was a staunch member of the Democratic party. As a matter of fact, as early as the election of 1828 he had supported Andrew Jackson vigorously in the columns of a newspaper he owned, and thus may be considered one of the first of the Jacksonian Democratic Republicans, the initial divergence from Jeffersonian Republicanism. From obscure motives, Henry Clay, then John Quincy Adams's secretary of state, gave Trist a post in the state department. After Jackson's inauguration he was continued in public service with a position in the treasury department. Later he served for a brief time as Jackson's private secretary, and in 1833 he was appointed American consul to Havana. He filled this post with success and honor until 1841. He was replaced by the Whig administration of William Henry Harrison but was given the office of chief clerk of the state department by fellow Virginian Abel Upshur after Daniel Webster resigned as secretary of state. At this time, this post was second in authority to the secretary, and Trist served as acting secretary of state whenever Buchanan was absent from Washington.

By every logical measure, Trist should have been the ideal man to serve as peace commissioner to Mexico. He was an experienced diplomat with an excellent knowledge of Spanish and Spanish tradition. He was a party man but without personal political ambitions. And he was privy to the entire background of the war. Because of the inherent difficulties of his mission, his role in Mexico has become a controversial point. He has been variously characterized as a "diplomat with ideals" and as a man whose vanity led him virtually to sell out the administration and forfeit American objectives. Whichever the case, he seems to have had some ability, a penchant for writing very long letters, and a sensitivity about his personal honor that amounted to little less than egotism. And it was he, and he alone, who negotiated the treaty that ended the war—a treaty that was contrary to his instructions and that he signed after he had been removed from his post.

Trist was furnished his instructions and the proposals for a treaty, if he could arrange one, on April 15, 1847. If he could obtain a meeting with a properly qualified Mexican official, Trist was to turn over to him the treaty proposal. However, the American diplomat was authorized to make a number of changes in the proposal if necessary—in other words, to bargain. He could offer up to $30,000,000 in indemnities if Mexico would cede Upper and Lower California, New Mexico, and right of transit across the Isthmus of Tehuántepec. Various alterations, scaled down from the maximum, were included in the instructions, but the cession of Upper California and New Mexico was unalterable, as was an outlet on the Gulf of California. Trist was given dispatches for General Scott, but the entire project was to be kept secret from the public.

The negotiator slipped out of Washington quietly, traveling overland to New Orleans where he registered under an assumed name. However, there had been a leak, and news of his journey filtered into the papers, though the details of his instructions remained unknown. Trist arrived in Vera Cruz on May 6 and delayed there to await an escort to Scott's headquarters in Jalapa. Filled with an unnecessary sense of urgency, he maladroitly forwarded to Scott by courier a letter, a dispatch from the war department, and the sealed proposal for the treaty. Had he had the good sense to wait and deliver the dispatch in person, had Secretary of War Marcy's instructions been less ambiguous, or had Scott been less sensitive about the mistreatment he believed he was receiving from Washington, several weeks of ridiculous and costly delay would have been averted.

Marcy's instructions included a statement that if Trist notified Scott that a certain "contingency" had occurred, Scott was to cease all military operations. To the General this was tantamount to placing him and the entire war effort under the command of a state department clerk. If Trist had presented these instructions personally, he could easily have explained that the "contingency" was nothing more or less than the ratification of the treaty Trist was to negotiate. Scott fired off an indignant note to Trist, acknowledging receipt of the material and giving notice that he would refuse to obey the armistice instruction. Trist shot back a somewhat conceited letter, the tone of which further angered the general, in which he informed him that the order regarding the armistice came directly from the president.

When Trist arrived in Jalapa, Scott had quarters provided for him but refused to call on him. Consequently, and again showing poor judgment, Trist in his turn refused to call on the general. Like piqued school girls the two then barraged each other, the state department, and the war department with angry letters, while the entire effort of the United States government in Mexico virtually ground to a halt. When Scott finally understood the intent of the instructions, he was too far committed to indignation to be able gracefully to meet with Trist. But in his own way, he made an overture. Trist had become ill; Scott sent him a jar of marmalade; Trist accepted the peace offering graciously. By the end of July, the quarrel was over, and the relations of the two men did a complete about-face. They became the fastest of friends. But, as President Polk wrote: "because of the personal controversy between these two self-important personages, the golden moment for concluding a peace with Mexico may have passed."

Actually, this was not quite so, and in point of fact there was never to be a "golden moment" for negotiating with Mexico because of the increasing instability of the government. Following the uprising against Gómez Farías, Santa Anna had assumed the presidency, Temporarily and precariously unifying the major factions. After less than two weeks, on April 2, he named Pedro María Anaya, a moderate, acting president, and left to take command of the troops confronting Scott. He was disastrously out maneuvered at Cerro Gordo on April 18, regrouped his forces at Puebla, near Mexico City, and was forced to flee from there to the capital on May 15. He then seized the presidency from Anaya, who, though he aspired to quit the presidency because he feared revolution, resented Santa Anna's high-handed tactics. The Mexican government now was close to anarchy. Santa Anna called himself president but was trusted by none and held the office only because he held the army. A new congress, elected on June 15, assembled, but day after day failed to obtain a quorum because the various factions feared the others might put something over on them. Santa Anna thus became a virtual dictator and ruthlessly prepared the defenses of Mexico City.

Meantime the dispatch of April 15 from the state department had been placed in the hands of the Mexican foreign minister but not answered. In July Charles Bankhead, the British minister, suggested the use of a bribe to lubricate the Mexican bureaucracy. Scott had funds available and agreed to the plan; Trist condoned it because it seemed the only possibility of achieving peace. However, the proposal was never put into effect.

Scott's army began its advance on August 7; Churubusco on the outskirts of Mexico City fell on August 20. That night the Mexican minister of foreign relations, José R. Pacheco, urgently requested Bankhead to ask for a truce for the purpose of answering the sealed dispatch of April 15, which he had received weeks earlier. Scott agreed, writing to Santa Anna the next morning. The wording of this note unfortunately was such that it appeared the American forces were exhausted and were suing for peace. Santa Anna used it to posture a Mexican victory, and his prestige in the city rose.

Then Trist bumbled into Santa Anna's hands by entering into negotiations with Mexican commissioners who at the time had no instructions from their government and were inferior to him in diplomatic rank. This too was taken as a sign of weakness, and the Mexican Congress passed an arrogant resolution that no peace could be considered until the American armies were withdrawn from Mexico and Mexico was indemnified for the entire cost of the war. The commissioners—Joaquín de Herrera, Ignacio Mora y Villamil, José Bernardo Couto, and Miguel Atristán—persuaded Congress to delete this from their instructions. Trist and the commissioners held meetings from August 27 through September 2, but the discussions were futile. Fundamentally the position of what passed for the Mexican government at that time was that it would be willing to abandon its pretentions in regard to Texas provided that the United States would pay for it. It was a face-saving posture, but a rather incongruous one, since a victorious American army was encamped just outside the capital, and the Mexican nation was in a state of anarchy, with a virtually illegal government in power in the capital.

Trist was in a frustrating position. He certainly could not make peace if he refused to negotiate over the absurd Mexican stand. On the other hand, if he did negotiate it would be taken for a further show of weakness. Trist therefore entered into discussions, and before the meetings were over had violated and exceeded his instructions. In essence, he permitted himself to be out-talked, but one cannot help but sympathize. A lack of realism had characterized all Mexican negotiations for a quarter of a century. Trist was not the first, nor would he be the last, to surrender in futility to "nonnegotiable demands." It would be needlessly fatiguing to trace the details of these negotiations and Trist's concessions, since after the conference broke down neither government accepted them.

On September 6 the Mexican commissioners submitted a counter-proposal. Mexico would accept the annexation of Texas if the United States paid for the territory. The Nueces would be its boundary, and a no-man's-land would be established between it and the Rio Grande. Mexico might be persuaded to part with a portion of Upper California provided the United States granted an endless number of conditions, including the assumption of the claims. "Mr. Trist has managed the negotiations very bunglingly," said Polk. "I thought he had more sagacity and common sense. . . ." On October 6 orders were issued recalling Trist in most definite terms and stating that Mexico must sue for peace before further negotiations would be considered. On October 21 the recall order was repeated.

Meantime Santa Anna had used the truce to gather his forces and perfect the defenses of the city. Aware of this duplicity and that the negotiations had broken down, Scott on September 6 canceled the truce. Fighting began again at Molino del Rey two days later, and on September 14, American forces took possession of the capital. Santa Anna slipped out of the city to his hacienda, where he resigned on September 22. Manuel de la Peña y Peña, a reasonable and moderate man who was serving as chief justice, assumed the presidency. Establishing himself first at Toluca outside Mexico City, he moved the seat of government to Querétero in October. Although questions were raised about the legality of his assumption of the office, many of the best men in Mexico came to his support, including Herrera. Soon the various states began to acknowledge him as acting president, as did a few of the foreign diplomats. Congress assembled and on November 11 named Anaya acting president. Peña y Peña became foreign minister. It seemed that a government of sorts had come into existence and that peace negotiations might be renewed.

In the United States the attitude toward peace had shifted. Polk had decided that Mexico must sue for peace; Trist had been recalled; and a movement to annex all of Mexico had begun to grow. Partially the "all-of-Mexico" movement was idealistic. Proponents of this idea argued that it would be beneficial to the people of Mexico to extend a stable, republican government to them. State by state Mexico could be trained in the processes of democracy and evolve through territorial stages into full statehood in the American union. The final result, enthused some, would be a grand United States of North America, embracing both Mexico and Canada. It was not a completely vainglorious dream, but, also, the all-of-Mexico movement was rapacious. Covetous eyes were cast at the mines of Guanajuato and northern Mexico. Others viewed the income from customs as a reward for conquest. A few envisioned the dismemberment of the vast landed estates, and some, of course, as always saw self-interested political advancement. Whatever the motives, the proposals to absorb all of Mexico hardened the stance of the Polk administration. But Polk and Buchanan were to be frustrated by the actions of Nicholas Trist.

Trist offered to reopen peace negotiations on October 20, and Peña y Peña assured him that commissioners would soon be appointed. It was nearly a month later before this was done. The new commissioners were Couto and Atristan (former peace commissioners), Manuel Rincón, and Luís Gonzaga Cuevas. On November 16 Trist belatedly received the recall order of October 6 and the rebuke of October 25. A few days later Peña y Peña, at this time serving as foreign minister, received news of Trist's recall and rightly assessed that it was a blow to the peace party in Mexico. Polk's demand that Mexico must sue for peace might prove more than the national vanity could stomach. Trist pondered the question, and historians have since debated his decision. A treaty of peace based on his original instructions loomed in the offing if he ignored the recall. If he did not negotiate, the war might continue indefinitely. Yet it would not really be a war; Scott had already established a military government and made plans to support it from Mexican revenues. But there would be guerrilla uprisings; the new, moderate government at Querétero would fall; and Mexico would again disintegrate into anarchy. Right or wrong Trist reached his decision on December 4.

On that day he notified the British minister that he proposed to enter negotiations with the new Mexican commission. Two days later he haughtily, in the words of Jack Nortrup, "set the government of the United States straight. . . . Since the facilities of the government were inferior to his private judgement, the chief clerk felt himself obligated to educate the President. [Neither Polk nor Buchanan knew] what was going on in Mexico." The peace party and the new government were "a group of apostles dedicated to the welfare of mankind." Perhaps Trist does not deserve quite such scathing scorn; yet, without doubt he had disobeyed orders as well as proceeded to negotiate a treaty which not only was contrary to his government's position but also contravened his original instructions. His motivation seems more egotistical than idealistic; he was unquestionably out-maneuvered by the Mexican peace commission; and, for all practical purposes, he gave away at the treaty table most of the advantage that had been won at a frightful cost in human lives and an enormous (for its time) expenditure of money. In defense of Trist's defiance of his government and his bungling of the negotiations lies only the speculation of what might have been had he not grasped time by the forelock. As he explained himself to Buchanan, "if the present opportunity be not seized *at once,* all chance of making a treaty *at all* will be lost for an indefinite period—probably forever."

Sixty days passed between the time of Trist's decision to remain in Mexico and the completion of the treaty negotiation—ample time for additional correspondence with his government, yet his sole communication was a coded postscript in a letter to his wife. Polk's cabinet was outraged. Polk believed that Trist was "arrogant, impudent, and very insulting." Unperturbedly, Trist plunged into the negotiations. He handed over the original treaty proposal to the Mexican commission and invited comment. The commission replaced it with a counter-proposal. Trist used this as a basis for working out the treaty. He abandoned the Tehuántepec right of way. He stipulated the impossible—that the United States would rescue any Mexican citizens held by such savage bands as the Comanche and Apache and that his government would forcibly restrain such tribes from entering Mexico. He overlooked his instructions to obtain a favorable railroad route to the West Coast in the Gila Valley and instead agreed that no railroad should be built without the mutual consent of both nations. He absolutely ignored his orders to obtain an outlet on the Gulf of California and accepted the Gila and Colorado rivers as the boundary. He also ignored his orders not to recognize land grants made in the ceded territory after the declaration of war. And finally, he not only agreed to an indemnity of $15,000,000 but also agreed to assume the payment of the claims owed by Mexico to American citizens.

On the positive side, he did negotiate a treaty with the only existing government in Mexico. He did obtain the major demands of the Democratic administration: the Rio Grande boundary, New Mexico, and California. (It might be borne in mind, however, that the lower Rio Grande had been the accepted boundary since 1835, that New Mexico had welcomed American armies without firing a shot, and that California had been a prey to foreign occupation since the overthrow of Micheltorena.) Trist did settle the claims question, although both territory and claims were charged to the long-suffering American taxpayer. This total obligation amounted to $22,140,053. He did hold firm at $15,000,000 for the cession against demands for $30,000,000, and he did refuse a stipend to the Mexican government to put down revolutions that were already breaking out. Later, under his fatuous assumption of responsibility for actions committed by Indian tribes prior to the treaty, Mexican claims against the United States came to $31,000,000.

The basic terms of the Treaty of Guadalupe Hidalgo are well known. The United States paid Mexico the $15,000,000 (plus interest), assumed the claims, and assumed responsibility for Indian damages. Mexico ceded New Mexico and California and accepted the Rio Grande as the boundary of Texas. A line was drawn on an inaccurate map to indicate the remainder of the boundary. The United States honored all land grants in the ceded area, even some rather questionable last-minute alienations. Mexicans residing in the cession were offered United States citizenship. Trist and the Mexican commission signed the treaty on February 2, 1848.

There was a furor over ratification in both countries. In Mexico an outbreak of indignation over the cession of so much territory flooded the newspapers. Dozens of vituperative pamphlets were published castigating the efforts of the commission. Anaya, Peña y Peña, and the peace men stood staunch. The honor of Mexico was saved. It had not been necessary to beg for terms. Fifteen million dollars in specie would restore the destitute treasury. The ceded territory was already lost. New national elections were held and a new congress convened. In the phraseology of Justin Smith, "a quorum of shaking legislators" ratified the treaty.

In the United States, dissension continued. The treaty arrived speedily in Washington on February 19. The cabinet was divided, but with a surprising show of logic ignored the question of Trist's malfeasance. Here was a treaty: should it be accepted or rejected? On February 23 it was submitted to the United States Senate. It was met with jeers: A mere scrap of paper! An agreement between a discredited clerk and an illegal government! Such terms as Mexico might have imposed if she had won the war!

In the midst of the discussion the venerable John Quincy Adams fell, unconscious, at his desk in the House. He died two days later, and a somber influence pervaded the debates. The tide ebbed. Soon the comment became "What better can we do?" On March 10, by a vote of 38 to 14—several, including Senator Sam Houston of Texas, not voting—the treaty secured the two-thirds majority needed for ratification. A few minor amendments were made, which the Mexican government approved in its ratification.

On March 17, 1848, Nicholas Trist was placed under arrest. He was escorted under guard out of Mexico but never put on trial. His position in the state department was forfeited. His contribution to his country's welfare is a matter of debate. Not until shortly before his death in 1874 did the American government compensate him for his expenses in Mexico. But willy-nilly, the treaty he negotiated had become the law of the land, remade the map of the New World, and reshaped the destinies of thousands of North Americans.

On the afternoon of May 25, 1848, a carriage approached the village of Querétaro, the temporary capital of the Mexican republic. Inside the carriage were Nathan Clifford, attorney general of the United States, and Ambrose H. Sevier, senator from Ohio and chairman of the Senate Foreign Relations Committee; they were the commissioners designated to exchange ratifications of the Treaty of Guadalupe Hidalgo. Some ten miles outside the village they were met by Luís de la Rosa, Mexican secretary of state and relations, who accompanied them into town—to cries from the local citizens of *"Viva la Guerra! Abajo la Paz!"* (Hurray for War! Down with Peace!) The next day, May 26, Clifford met Acting President Manuel de la Peña y Peña to present his credentials. Then five days were consumed in conference, with some delay owing to slowness in preparing a Mexican copy of the agreements necessary to put the treaty into effect.

The formal exchange of ratifications of the treaty took place on May 30. At that time Secretary Rosa asked that the American army of occupation remain in Mexico City until Mexican authorities could take precautions to avoid disorders during the transfer of authority. Such arrangements were soon completed, and at six o'clock on the morning of June 12 the Stars and Stripes was replaced above the National Palace by the Mexican tricolor. Customary honors were rendered both standards, while the crowd of people on the *Zócalo* remained silent. That same day the American troops began withdrawing to Vera Cruz for embarkation. The deadliest war in American history, in terms of total deaths per thousand who served per year, at last was over. Of the 100,182 soldiers, sailors, and marines who participated, only 1548 were killed in action, but 10,970 died from disease and exposure. Thus the mortality rate was 110 per 1000 per annum (as compared with a Civil War rate of 65; a Spanish-American War rate of 27.79; and a World War I rate of 16. In World War II the death rate was about 3 per cent of the total strength of the armed forces). And the death rate was appallingly high in relation to the length of actual combat, for the conflict with Mexico lasted just twenty-two months (with only seventeen months of actual combat). Nor were the deaths directly attributed to combat and disease during those twenty-two months the true total of those who died as a result of the war; Americans would continue to succumb to diseases contracted in Mexico for the next several decades. J. J. Oswandel, a veteran of the war, wrote in 1885, "After the close of the war we returned home with impaired health . . . with a disease, contracted in a strange climate, which, in a few years after the war had taken from their homes more than half of those who returned."

A special messenger delivered the signed copy of the Treaty of Guadalupe Hidalgo to President Polk in Washington on the morning of July 4. Immediately he instructed the secretary of state to prepare the necessary papers so that it could be proclaimed on the American anniversary of independence. Such was the case. However, that proclamation by the president, which formally brought the war to a close and seemingly ended all differences between the two republics, was not a "Treaty of Peace, Friendship, Limits and Settlement." Great questions had arisen from the ashes of the old questions that had been settled in battle. The new questions were even more grave than the old. They would bring the United States to the very brink of civil war, would threaten yet another contest of arms with Mexico, and would leave lingering hatreds on both sides of the international boundary for years.

To the Texans of 1848, however, there was no question but that the war had settled something: their western boundary. Even before the Treaty of Guadalupe Hidalgo had been ratified, the Texas legislature on March 14, 1848, created Santa Fe County, which included almost all of New Mexico east of the Rio Grande. And Judge Spruce M. Baird was sent to organize it, but upon his arrival at Santa Fe he found his mission had become embroiled in the larger question of abolition and slavery. Military and civil officials in New Mexico were anxious to prevent the region from coming under Texas's jurisdiction. The military commander, Colonel John M. Washington, informed Baird that he would not allow Texas to exercise control, that he would support the government established in New Mexico by General Kearny until ordered to desist by the federal government— an order he already had received from President Polk, but which he chose to disregard. Baird finally grew discouraged and left New Mexico without accomplishing his goal. Texans were highly indignant. How, they wondered, could the Mexican War have begun with American blood shed on American soil in the Rio Grande Valley except on the basis of the Texan claim to the Rio Grande as its boundary; and if the Rio Grande was the Texan boundary in the south, then why not to the north and west? Then came the election of 1848 and the inauguration of a new president.

In June 1846 Zachary Taylor had written that he would decline the presidency even "if proferred and I could reach it without opposition." In August 1847 he stated, "I do not care a fig about the office." Yet by that fall he was warming to the idea and writing his views on political issues; he said the Bank of the United States was a dead issue, that he favored internal improvements, and that he would use the veto to protect the constitution. His political backers in the United States were appalled that he could write such statements from Mexico, preferring him to keep his views unknown.

By late fall in 1847 Taylor had come to believe he would be nominated by both political parties and that he would be elected by acclamation—as had his hero George Washington. Taylor liked to have his sycophants make favorable comparisons between himself and the "Father of our Country." And the Whigs did nominate him on their fourth ballot on June 7 at their convention at Philadelphia, with Millard Fillmore of New York as his running mate. But the Democrats did not select him, as he had anticipated; instead at their convention in Baltimore on May 22, they had chosen Lewis Cass of Michigan and William O. Butler of Kentucky as their standard-bearers. There also was a third-party candidate, Martin Van Buren, who headed the slate of the Free-Soil party of radical abolitionists. On Election Day, Taylor won by a narrow margin, carrying seven northern states and eight southern; he won only because the Free-Soilers split the vote so badly in New York that Taylor carried it. The vote in the electoral college was Taylor 163, Cass 127, and Van Buren none.

Old Rough and Ready was forthright in his statements regarding the Texan claim to New Mexico. Despite his ownership of slaves, he supported the provisions of the Wilmot Provisio and issued orders to the army to prevent county organization of New Mexico by the Texans. He also sent word to New Mexicans to organize their own government, write a constitution, and apply for admission to the Union as a free state. He followed the same course with California, where the gold rush of 1848–49 had brought so many thousands of people that it also was asking for statehood and an end to military government. Finally, on the question of Utah, settled in 1847–49 by the Mormons who were petitioning for statehood under the name "Deseret," Taylor looked with disfavor because of the Mormon practice of polygamy.

Yet of all these questions, the most volatile was the Texas boundary problem and the future of New Mexico. Southerners became so incensed that they were threatening to join the Lone Star State in secession if New Mexico east of the Rio Grande was not given to Texas. Governor Peter H. Bell of Texas convened the legislature there in special session in August 1850 to hear a report about the second attempt to organize Santa Fe County; Robert S. Neighbors had traveled to the region in 1849 but was rebuffed by military authorities (although he did organize El Paso County). Governor Bell told the Texan legislators that they must meet the federal impediment "boldly, and fearlessly and determined. Not by further supplications or discussions . . . ; not by renewed appeals to their generosity and sympathy; not by a longer reliance on the delusive hope, that justice will yet be extended to us; but by action . . . *at all hazards and to the last extremity.*" This attitude was seconded by other Southerners; Alexander Stephens of Georgia declared in a speech before the House of Representatives that the first federal gun fired on Texas officials would be a signal for "free men" from the Delaware to the Rio Grande to rise up against the Union. Taylor remained adamant, however; to such talk he crisply replied, "Disuion is treason."

Complicating progress of a settlement was the question of the Texas debt. During its years as a republic, Texas had incurred a public debt of approximately $10,000,000; this debt had been backed in part by the public land of the republic. And when Texas had entered the Union, it had retained its debt *and* its public land, the land to be used to pay the debt. To reduce the size of the state, Texans argued in 1850, would be to reduce the state's ability to pay its debt. Much of this debt had been bought cheaply by Eastern speculators, and they joined their voices to those of the Texans to urge the government to leave Texas its land. Furthermore, half of the debt had been backed by the customs revenue of the Republic of Texas. Since the United States now collected ths tariff, Texas argued that the federal government was responsible for that portion of the debt.

Fortunately for the nation the "Old Giants" were still active in Congress: Clay, Calhoun, Webster. Each of these men was a sectionalist. But each loved the Union more than section, and together they moved to stop dismemberment of the Union. Clay called for compromise in a speech on January 29, 1850. California would enter as a free state; New Mexico would be given separate territorial status; Texas would be paid $10,000,000 for ceding its claim to New Mexico, thereby allowing it to pay its debts; and Utah would be given territorial status.

Clay's proposal met bitter debate, perhaps the most bitter in the history of Congress. On March 7, 1850, Daniel Webster addressed the Senate "not as a Massachusetts man, not as a Northern man, but as an American." Slavery, he said, was forever excluded from New Mexico and Utah by the laws of nature; the arid Southwest, he argued, would not admit a cotton culture. Thus, he aserted, there was no reason needlessly to anger the South.

Suddenly in the midst of this heated debate, President Taylor died. On July 4, 1850, Taylor attended the laying of the cornerstone of a monument to his hero, George Washington. Taylor sat too long in the hot sun, then when he returned to the White House, drank cold water and ate cold cherries, washed down with iced milk. That night he developed what his doctors diagnosed as "cholera morbus"— probably a heat stroke—for which they bled him. He died on July 9, to be succeeded by his vice president, Millard Fillmore, a moderate who favored compromise.

By September 5 all the measures proposed by Clay had been passed. Lumped together, these measures were called the Compromise of 1850. Without doubt they preserved the Union and postponed civil war for a decade. But they killed the Whig party; Northern and Southern branches of the party were so alienated that they could never unite again. And the compromise made civil war almost inevitable, for it upset the principles of the Missouri Compromise and led to the doctrine of popular sovereignty just four years later when the Kansas-Nebraska Act was passed. Popular (or squatter) sovereignty was a doctrine that would allow territories to be created with no designation as to slavery or non-slavery; that anyone could go to such territories with or without slaves; and that whenever these territories entered the Union, the people therein would vote on slavery or non-slavery. The Compromise of 1850 made "Bleeding Kansas" a reality, which in turn would lead to the Lincoln-Douglas debates, John Brown's Raid, the formation of the Republican party, the election of Abraham Lincoln, Southern secession, and war. Perhaps it was cold comfort to dismembered Mexico, but the "Mexican Cession" led in the next two decades to the death of a million gringos, as well as to sectional hatreds that persist to the present.

Another immediate problem arising out of the Treaty of Guadalupe Hidalgo was the necessity of surveying the new boundary that had been established. By the terms of the agreement, each nation was to appoint a commissioner and a surveyor whose acts, when signed by all four men, would be as binding as the treaty itself. Just before going out of office in March 1849, Polk named Democrat John B. Weller of Ohio the American commissioner and Andrew B. Gray of Texas the surveyor. These two men met with their Mexican counterparts at San Diego on July 6, 1849: General Pedro García Conde and José Salazar Larregui. They proceeded to survey the southern boundary of California without great difficulties.

By this time, however, the Whigs had taken office, and in a political maneuver Weller was fired as boundary commissioner in mid-February 1850. The position first was offered to the Pathfinder, John Charles Frémont, but he declined. Finally in August that year a new commissioner was named, a Rhode Island literary figure, John Russell Bartlett. The new commissioner met the Mexican survey commission in El Paso early in December, there to discover that the map used by the treaty-makers at Guadalupe Hidalgo (one by J. Disturnell of New York) was sadly in error. The Mexican commissioner used this error to get Bartlett's agreement to a boundary forty miles north of El Paso rather than the eight miles the map showed. The Bartlett-Conde Agreement, as this was known, thereby gave away 6000 square miles of territory to Mexico, territory rightly belonging to the United States and territory vitally necessary for a southern transcontinental railroad route. When Gray, the surveyor, protested this giveaway, the Whig administration in Washington fired him. Congress in 1852 responded by withholding funds for completing the survey, and the work in the field came to a halt.

This embroglio almost resulted in a second Mexican war. Governor William Carr Lane of New Mexico insisted that the land in dispute belonged to the United States and said he would exercise jurisdiction over it. Texans, anxious that the eastern terminus of a transcontinental railroad be in their state, rushed to join Lane's fight. In Chihuahua, Governor Angel Trías likewise claimed the land. He said the Bartlett-Conde Agreement was irreversible and proclaimed that he would exercise jurisdiction over the disputed 6000 square miles of territory. Both sides were amassing troops, and war clouds hung heavily over the Southwest early in 1853. By April that year Trías had a brigade at El Paso and his entire state militia under arms. And in Mexico City diplomatic officials were circulating a directive "to the Mexican diplomatic agents abroad with respect to securing aid of England, France, and Spain to 'restrain the ambitious designs of the United States'" and "to secure aid, direct or indirect, for Mexico in case of hostilities with the United States." Meanwhile, Lane had raised a volunteer force of New Mexican and Texan civilians and also was ready to fight.

Conditions in 1853 were vastly different from those of 1846, however, and neither the United States nor Mexico really wanted a second war. The election in November 1852 had returned the Democrats to power in Washington, and thereby had defeated another hero of the Mexican War, Winfield Scott. Southerners had found this candidate accept-

able but had repudiated the Whig platform; Northerners
had liked the platform but had repudiated the candidate.
The Democrats, meanwhile, had deadlocked between Lewis
Cass of Michigan and Stephen A. Douglas of Illinois and had
nominated instead a dark-horse candidate, Franklin Pierce
of New Hampshire. Too new to politics to have many enemies, Pierce was acceptable to all factions of the Democratic
party, and thus proceeded to win the election handily; he received 254 electoral votes to Scott's 42.

The Democratic administration that took office in March
1853 did not want another war. Pierce and other party leaders realized that the war of 1846–48 had cost their party an
election, and they failed to see how a second war could do
anything other than the same. Thus when the dispute in the
Southwest came to a head early in 1853, Pierce replaced
Governor Lane and instructed the new man to await developments at the national level rather than take local action.

The end of the war with the United States first had
brought a short period of stability in Mexico, as all realized
that internal bickering had cost victory in the late war and
that the quarreling had resulted in dismemberment of the
republic. The moderate José Joaquín de Herrera was placed
in office, to be succeeded peacefully on January 15, 1851, by
José Mariano Arista (whose failures at Palo Alto, Resaca de
la Palma, and Matamoros had been forgotten); these two
men gave Mexico its most honest government yet, reducing
army appropriations and consolidating the national debt.

Yet there was a growing liberal tendency evident during
these two regimes, a tendency that alarmed conservatives.
And on January 5, 1853, these conservatives overthrew the
Arista administration to install a military dictatorship and
talked longingly of a European monarchy. Juan Bautista Ce-
ballos held the presidency from January 5 to February 7,
1853, and then Manuel María Lombardini from February 7
to April 20, 1853, while the question of the form of government was discussed by the ruling junta. Its choice was Anto-

nio López de Santa Anna, who had been in exile in Vene-
zuela since 1848. The fifty-eight-year-old veteran returned by
invitation to be president for one year. By December 1853,
however, he had himself elected president for life with the
title of "Serene Highness" and the right to name his successor. He lived on such a vast scale that heavy infusions of
money were needed. Thus when James Gadsden arrived in
Mexico City, he found the government there willing to
make a sale; Santa Anna did not want war when he could get
money.

Both the United States and Mexico were anxious to
make an agreement. A treaty was soon concluded, and it was
signed on December 30, 1853. Generally known as the Gadsden Purchase Treaty, it drew the final boundary between
the United States and Mexico and called for payment of
$15,000,000 to Mexico in return for the territory ceded.
Certain American senators objected to the price, however,
one saying that as a private citizen he could have bought the
same land for only $7000. The senate reduced the amount of
the payment to $10,000,000, and the treaty became effective
on June 30, 1854. A new boundary commission was appointed
and had completed its task by mid-1855. (Ironically the sale
of this land, of which Santa Anna at first boasted, so angered
Mexicans that in March 1854 a counter-revolution began
against him that led to his resigning on August 9, 1855, and
fleeing into exile once again. Not until the amnesty at the
death of Benito Juárez in 1874 was he allowed to return
permanently, to die in obscurity and poverty in 1876.)

Even the addition of the Gadsden Purchase to American
ownership did not satisfy some residents north of the boundary. In the decade following the Treaty of Guadalupe Hidalgo, there were further attempts to wrest still more land
from Mexico, not in a spirit of Manifest Destiny so much as
from a restless spirit of adventurism principally in California. Disappointed argonauts there organized several filibustering expeditions, principally in Baja California and Son-

ora. The first of these came in 1851 under the leadership of Joseph C. Morehead, son of a former governor of Kentucky who was quartermaster-general of California at the time. Morehead early in 1851 had weapons, equipment, and funds at his disposal; these remained from an abortive expedition against the Yuma Indians. Instead of returning them to the state, he used them to raise an army of malcontents to invade Sonora to make it an independent republic "as Texas had been" or else to annex to the United States—the real purpose was obscure. During March and April 1851 several parties ranging in size from twenty-five to a hundred men left for Sonora. Yet when Morehead himself prepared to sail from San Diego aboard the *Josephine,* a bark he had purchased, American customs officials searched it thoroughly for weapons and ammunition but could find none. Nor could Mexican officials at Mazatlán, who swarmed aboard when the *Josephine* reached that port. At this point the filibuster collapsed, and Morehead returned to Kentucky to practice law and to die in the Civil War.

Mexican officials decided that the best defense against future invasions was to strengthen the defenses of their northwest. In Baja California geography would serve this purpose; Sonora they decided to populate with colonists recruited from among the French argonauts in California. The French were susceptible to Mexican offers of land and financial aid, for they were suffering from the foreign miners' tax and other forms of discrimination in California. In November 1851, 85 of them sailed to Guaymas under the command of Charles Pindray. They were settled near Cocóspera, Sonora, where their numbers increased to some 150. But the Apache Indians attacked them and the promised Mexican aid never materialized. Pindray was shot under mysterious circumstances, and the colony dissolved.

Many Frenchmen in California were still willing to emigrate to Mexico, however. Under a new leader, Count Gaston de Raousset-Boulbon, an impoverished, reckless French nobleman, expeditions left San Francisco in 1852 and 1854 to Guaymas and thence inland, ostensibly to mine. Friction soon developed between the volatile Frenchmen and the equally volatile Mexicans, leading to the capture of Hermosillo by Raousset-Boulbon during 1852. Raousset-Boulbon returned to San Francisco to recruit anew to make himself "Sultan of Sonora." Then in the spring of 1854 with 400 men he landed at Guaymas. His reception was unfriendly, however, and on July 13 the battle of Guaymas was fought. The French were defeated, and thirty days later the Count was executed.

Simultaneously, another filibuster was recruiting. William Walker, later called the "grey-eyed man of destiny" and himself an argonaut (from Tennessee), sailed from San Francisco in October 1853 with forty-five men aboard the brig *Caroline*. They landed at La Paz, Baja California, on November 3 to capture the local governor and proclaim Baja California a republic. Threatened by hostile Mexicans and prevented from receiving needed supplies and reinforcements by customs officials at San Francisco, Walker gradually retreated northward to Ensenada, just south of San Diego, where on January 18, 1854, he annexed Sonora to his republic by proclamation. In May, however, he ingloriously fled north across the border and was arrested and tried for violation of the neutrality laws. A sympathetic jury freed him, and the following year he left for incredible adventures in Central America that eventually would bring him the presidency of Nicaragua and later death by firing squad in Honduras on September 12, 1860.

Finally, in 1857, Henry Alexander Crabb would lead a final filibuster into Sonora. Crabb, failing to be elected to the United States Senate in 1856, chose to involve himself in his wife's family holdings in Sonora. There he met a would-be governor, Ygnacio Pesqueira, who invited him to raise an army of Americans to aid Pesqueria in winning the governorship; in return the Americans would get land and min-

ing concessions. Crabb returned to California to gather an
army of some 100 men, whom he marched overland to Sonora. But when they arrived, Pesqueira already was governor
and naturally had turned violently anti-American. At Ca-
borca, Sonora, on April 6, 1857, the Americans were induced
to surrender, partly by force and partly by treachery; the
next morning they were executed in small batches, Crabb
last; his head was preserved in vinegar for a time and exhibited to an exulting populace.

The Crabb expedition brought to a close almost a decade
of expansionist activities in the Southwest. Yet there were
those who continued to want Mexican territory. For example, Acting Governor Richard C. McCormick on December
6, 1865, told the second legislature of the Territory of Arizona that it should petition congress to acquire "the port of
Libertad, upon the Gulf of California. . . . Its acquisition,
with that part of Sonora which lies between it and our present line, would give new life and importance to the region
below the Gila River, and be largely beneficial to the whole
territory." McCormick doubtless was correct in believing
such an acquisition would benefit southern Arizona, but he
was too late. He should have informed Nicolas Trist of this
need in 1848, not the Arizona legislature in 1865. The time
for obtaining more Mexican territory had long since passed.

What then did the war between the United States and
Mexico really accomplish? For Mexico it reduced the nation
by approximately one-half of its nominal territory, and did
not produce a stable, constitutional government. Nor did it
fuse a sense of nationalism. More blood would have to be
shed in local revolutions, millions of pesos expended, foreign
aggressors battled, thirty years and more of tyrannical dictatorship endured, and the Revolution of 1910 fought before
these were accomplished. Mexico's search for modernity—
for liberty, equality, and justice—was not to be achieved by
grandiose promises of planting the Eagle and Serpent above
the White House, nor by demagogic pronouncements, nor

even by conscripting men and raising armies, but ultimately through a sense of national identity combined with creation of the means by which peasants and Indians could participate with the upper classes in governing the republic, as well as acquiring title to the land they worked.

For the United States the war seemingly brought a successful resolution. The Texas question was settled, the claims were paid (albeit by American taxpayers), the possibility of British intervention on the West Coast was ended, and a large amount of territory was added from which would come such mineral riches in the next three decades as to finance the industrial revolution in the country. (Even today a majority of American oil, sulphur, copper, and other minerals come from Texas, the Mexican Cession, and the Gadsden Purchase areas.) But also the war brought renewed political bitterness from abolitionists, a fearful struggle over extension of slavery, and congressional approval of the doctrine of Popular Sovereignty, all of which in turn would lead inevitably to that most bloody and tragic of conflicts, the Civil War. Simultaneously the war also trained most of the leaders of the Civil War, giving them combat and leadership experience that would prolong this brothers' war. And, even today, despite rather clear facts, the American mind yet appears burdened by a lingering sense of guilt.

Thus just as there is controversy as to the origins or the war, there also might well be controversy as to its results.

ANALYTICAL BIBLIOGRAPHY

THIS BIBLIOGRAPHY is an attempt at a comprehensive listing of books and pamphlets relating to the Mexican War and its origins. Brief analytical comments are made about the more significant or interesting works. To make the bibliography more useful, the entries are arranged in subject categories rather than alphabetically. An alphabetical list of the authors and main entries is provided at the end, and the items are numbered for identification purposes. Over 120 special subject headings, ranging from "Attitude of Americans at Home" to specific battles, are set down in alphabetical order, except for general histories of the war, which are listed first. Second and third subject references of a particular work are made by number. For example, David Lavender's *Climax at Buena Vista* is listed first under "Battles, Campaigns, and Military Operations" and then cross-referenced by number under "Buena Vista, Battle of." To conserve space in this rather lengthy bibliography, standard or easily recognizable abbreviations are used for names of journals and periodicals, and only the last or common names of publishing houses and presses are given. Standard library practices have been followed in capitalization, in italicizing, and in the main entries: author, if known, title, or corporate entity. Cross-references are given in the author list for pseudonyms or other confusing main entries.

Only representative samples of general histories of the period, of biographies, of general diplomatic histories, of college textbook "readings" or "problem" books, and of addresses, sermons, and abolitionist tracts are included.

Not included in the list are manuscript collections, federal documents, newspapers, broadsides, and poetry, fiction, and drama. In the case of manuscripts, the authors felt that most of the worthwhile manuscript material is now in print. Of course, there are a few exceptions, some known and, unquestionably, some unknown sleepers, such as the Chamberlain diary brought to light a few years ago by *Life* magazine and the Beauregard journal discovered by T. Harry Williams. But the assumption here has been that the valuable manuscripts are in print. Furthermore, with the ready availability of the *National Union Catalog of Manuscript Collections,* anyone interested specifically in unpublished material can locate it easily.

Similar reasons dictated the exclusion of federal documents. In the first place, they are so incredibly numerous as to make a comprehensive listing totally impractical. In the second place, they are fairly easily located through the use of guides and indexes to the federal documents. Particularly valuable in this respect are B. P. Poore, *Descriptive Catalogue of the Government Publications of the United States, 1774–1881,* Washington (G.P.O.), 1885; the indexes to the *Annals of Congress;* and Adelaide R. Hasse, *Index to United States Documents Relating to Foreign Affairs,* 3 vols., Washington (Carnegie Institution), 1914. To be found in this last index are over 1200 different entries relating to the war and diplomatic affairs associated with it.

Newspapers were not included for two major reasons. Nearly every newspaper published during the period carried some stories on the war; many of them had fairly extensive coverage; but over-all they tended to lift or adopt material from each other. The best newspaper accounts of the war appear in the New Orleans *Picayune,* whose unusual editor, George Wilkins Kendall, became the first modern war correspondent by following the troops in the two major campaigns. One of the finest, and certainly one of the rarest and most expensive, of Mexican War items is his book *The War Between the United States and Mexico,* with colored illustrations by Carl Nebel.

There is a group of newspapers that deserve special attention—those published by Americans in Mexico. The first of the "war" newspapers however, was the Corpus Christi *Gazette,* which came into being on January 1, 1846, primarily to serve Taylor's camp. It was established by Samuel Bangs with José de Alba, a Mexican-Texan, as editor. After Taylor moved south to the Rio Grande, the paper folded, and Bangs shortly moved his press to Matamoros. There he found that Hugh McLeod, a Texan, had beat him by a few weeks with the *Re-*

public of the Rio Grande, the first issue of which was dated June 1, 1846. The following month McLeod was succeeded by John N. Peeples and the name was changed to the *American Flag.* It was issued weekly until the end of the war and was then moved to Brownsville. Bangs attempted to establish another paper, but after a few months retired from the scene.

In Monterrey, Mexico, in February 1847 the *American Pioneer* was established and was apparently issued until the end of the war. For a short time, another paper, the *Gazette,* was also put out in that city. There was a short-lived sheet printed in Saltillo in 1847, and the *Eagle* was issued at Vera Cruz from April through June of 1847. Also, even before the American occupation of California, an English-language paper, the *Californian,* was established in Monterey, California, later moving to San Francisco.

The *American Star* was, by all odds, the most important of the "war papers." It was established on April 25, 1847, immediately after the occupation of Jalapa. In May it was moved to Puebla, and in September to Mexico City. By October it had grown into a full-fledged daily newspaper and served as a semi-official organ of the United States Army in Mexico. After the war it was re-established in Corpus Christi. There were a number of papers of lesser importance issued temporarily and sporadically in the wake of the American forces.

Most of these "war" newspapers can be considered fugitive items, with scattered issues in scores of repositories. There are several complete files of the *American Star,* including one in the Library of Congress, where there is also a file of the *Californian.*

Broadsides were not included in the bibliography because of their fugitive nature and because only a small percentage has actual value as historical sources. And most of those that do were incorporated in other publications. Specifically, much of the Mexican source material on the war first appeared in broadside form which later was incorporated in pamphlets. For this reason, a number of three- and four-page issues printed in Mexico have been included in the bibliography.

Finally, works of poetry, fiction, drama, and music were not listed because they contribute little to the historiography of the war. An exception was made in the case of James Russell Lowell's *Biglow Papers.* None of the other poetry found by the authors had either historical value or literary merit. A few pieces deserve mention more because of the effort that went into them than for any other reason. Shepard M. Ashe, *Monterey conquered: a fragment from la gran quivera,* New York (Shepard), 1852, is a 148-page poem of saga-like dimensions, Henry Barnes, *The guerilla bride,* Bellefontaine (the author), 1858, is

176 pages long. William F. Smith, *Guadaloupe: a tale of love and war*, Philadelphia (the author), rhymes for 156 pages. And *The rough and ready songster* . . . , New York (Naffs and Cornish), 1848, contains 250 pages of "songs without music."

Several music publishers were quick to capitalize on the war, but none of the works had durability. Perhaps the most interesting was "Buena Vista Quickstep" composed and published by William Cumming Peters in 1848. Peters was Stephen Foster's music teacher and published Foster's first compositions, including "O Susanna."

There are a couple of dozen or so works of fiction based on the war. Gustave Aimard wrote at least three; Mayne Reid's *War life; or the adventures of a light infantry officer*, New York (Townsend), 1849, was quite popular and passed as a first-hand account. His *Scouting expeditions of McCulloch's Texas Rangers* . . . is listed in the bibliography. At least one Ned Buntline (Edward Zane Carroll Judson) was based on the war; *The volunteer; or the maid of Monterey*, Boston (Elliott, Thomas & Talbot), 1863. This and, very curiously, approximately 40 per cent of the contemporary fiction examined revolved around women in the war. The plots of most dealt with women who disguised themselves as men and volunteered, usually in order to follow a lover who had enlisted because the girl's parents refused to accept him. All of these romances of course had happy endings.

A small handful of dramas have been based on the Mexican War, several of which, surprisingly, were written in the twentieth century. In 1938 a scenario was written for a movie, based on the heroic cadet defense of Chapultepec by Alfonso Teja Zabre, entitled "Murio por la patria: los niños heroes de Chapultepec."

Approximately 16 per cent of the works listed here are Mexican imprints; less than 2 per cent are European; the remainder were printed in the United States. Over the years there have been cycles of interest in the Mexican War or at least cycles of publication about it, with a renewed interest in it the past two decades.

Approximately 23 per cent of the works listed were published between 1845 and 1849; only 14 per cent between 1850 and 1899; 44 per cent between 1900 and 1949; and, a surprising 19 per cent in the last two decades. The peak decades after 1850 were 1910 to 1919 and 1950 to 1959, each with approximately 11 per cent of the publications, and the single year after 1850 having the largest number of publications was 1928, with nearly 4 per cent of all imprints.

Approximately 7 per cent of the works may be classified as general histories of the war, encompassing origins, campaigns, and results. About 40 per cent are specialized or topical studies of some aspect of the conflict, many of these being scholarly articles in journals. Reminiscences and memoirs account for 17 per cent of the publications, biographies for 13 per cent, and miscellaneous items for the remaining 15 per cent.

GENERAL ACCOUNTS OF THE WAR

1. Acevedo, Alvear. La guerra del 47. Mexico, 1969.
2. American Heritage. Texas and the war with Mexico. By the editors of American Heritage. Narrative by Fairfax Downey in consultation with Paul M. Angle. New York (American Heritage), 1961. American Heritage Junior Library.
3. Bill, Alfred Hoyt. Rehearsal for conflict: the war with Mexico, 1846–1848. New York (Knopf), 1947.
4. Bishop, Farnham. Our first war in Mexico. New York (Scribner), 1916.
5. Brooks, Nathan Covington. A complete history of the Mexican War: its causes, conduct, and consequences; comprising an account of the various military and naval operations from its commencement to the treaty of peace. Philadelphia (Griggs, Elliot), 1849. A judicious evaluation of the causes of the war. No mention of slavery, expansionism, or California. Says claims issue sufficient cause, but that Polk provoked war by ordering Taylor to the Rio Grande. Also says Texas annexation was not sufficient cause for Mexican belligerency. Translated into German by Carl Joseph Koch. Baltimore (Hutchinson and Seebold), 1849.
6. Castillo Negrete, Emelio del. Mexico en el siglo XIX: o sea su historia desde 1800 hasta la época presente. . . . 28 vols. Mexico (Santiago Sierra and others), 1877–83. Vols. 22–25 are entitled Invasión de los norte-americanos en Mexico. . . . Vol. 24 contains Gaxiola's La Invasión . . . en Sinaloa (q.v.).
7. Castor, Henry. The first book of the war with Mexico. New York (Watts), 1964. Juvenile.
8. Chidsey, Donald Barr. The war with Mexico. New York (Crown), 1968.
9. Complete history of the Mexican War: containing an authentic account of all the battles fought in that republic including the treaty of peace; with a list of the killed and wounded; together with a brief sketch of the lives of Generals Scott and Taylor . . . by an eye witness. New York (Dow), 1850.

10. Courmant, F. de. Des Etats-Unis, de la guerre du Mexique. . . . Paris, 1847. A contemporary French view of little or no value.

11. Dufour, Charles L. The Mexican War: a compact history. New York (Hawthorne), 1968. Popular treatment with emphasis on campaigns.

12. Frost, John. History of the Mexican War. . . . New Haven (Mansfield), 1859. A revised and expanded version was issued by Armond Hawkins in New Orleans, 1882. Frost, who graduated from Harvard in 1822, was one of the most prolific writers of non-fiction in nineteenth-century America. According to one account he published over 300 works, assisted by a corps of writers. His works range from a history of the world to a history of California.

13. ————. The Mexican War and its warriors. . . . New Haven (Mansfield), 1848. Also 1849 and 1850.

14. ————. Pictorial history of Mexico and the Mexican War. . . . Philadelphia (Thomas Cowperthwait), 1848. Other editions 1849 and 1862.

15. Gregory, Thomas B. Our Mexican conflicts. New York (Hearst), 1914.

16. Henry, Robert Selph. The story of the Mexican War. Indianapolis (Bobbs-Merrill), 1950. Often called the best modern work on the war—with good reason. It is thoroughly researched, carefully documented, and judiciously worded. It is now, however, a quarter of a century old, and much recent scholarship has gone into studies of the war.

17. History of the war between the United States and Mexico. Philadelphia (Zieber), 1847. Quotes extensively from contemporary newspaper accounts and war department orders and correspondence; finds Mexican refusal to negotiate the claims question as the primary cause of the war.

18. Jenkins, John Stilwell. History of the war between the United States and Mexico, from the commencement of hostilities to the ratification of the treaty of peace. Auburn (Derby & Miller), 1848. Many other printings. Thorough and well-written account of the war. One of the best contemporary histories and very popular at the time. Reviews the claims issue, the history of Texas, and the so-called Nueces boundary; finds that the hostility of Mexico over the annexation of Texas caused the war. Says nothing about Polk or expansionism.

19. McElroy, Robert McNutt. "The Mexican War," Met. Mag., XXV

(March 1907), 663–81; XXVI (April-September 1907), 59–71, 199–210, 331–41, 457–65, 551–660, 742–50; XXVII (October-November 1907), 66–73, 195–203.

20. ———. The winning of the far west: a history of the regaining of Texas, of the Mexican War. . . . New York (Putnam), 1914.

21. Neff, Jacob K. The army and navy of America . . . to the close of the Mexican War. . . . Lancaster, Pa. (Hills), 1849. An earlier edition (1845) did not include the Mexican War; a later edition (1866) carries Thomas H. Burrowes as joint author. There was also an 1851 edition. About seventy pages are given to a superficial discussion of the Mexican War.

22. Read, Benjamin Maurice. Guerra Mexico-Americana. Santa Fe (Impresora del N.M.), 1910. A New Mexican historian apologizes to Mexico for American expansionism.

23. Ripley, Roswell Sabine. The war with Mexico. 2 vols. New York (Harper), 1849. The earliest major history of the war and long the only thorough one. It is surprisingly detailed and accurate considering its early date. The major causes, i.e. claims, annexation, and Mexican refusal to negotiate, are mentioned objectively without discussion or interpretation, and Ripley does not attempt to affix blame or culpability on either nation. The author, a professional soldier and officer in Scott's command, was more interested in the military engagements, but perceptively discusses the effects of both U.S. and Mexican domestic politics on the course of the war. Justin Smith believed that the purpose of the work was to exalt Pillow over Scott. See also No. 242.

24. Rives, George Lockhart. The United States and Mexico, 1821–1848. 2 vols. New York (Scribner's), 1913. Although over half a century old, this is still the best study of the diplomacy of the period; it is also one of the best accounts of the Mexican War, which fills most of the second volume.

25. Roa Bárcena, José María. Recuerdos de la invasión norte-americana, 1846–1848, por un jóven de entónces. Mexico (Buxó), 1883. Reprinted Mexico (Editorial Porrúa), 1947. Bancroft praised the book saying it was the "result of study of both American and Mexican documents," and it has often been referred to as the standard work from the Mexican viewpoint. Most of the book deals with the military actions in which the author frequently goes out of his way to praise Mexican troops. The war was caused by American expansionism; the abrogation of the federal system in 1835 gave the Texans a pretext for in-

surrection; Texas became the pretext for U.S. aggression in Mexico. The unjustified claims provided another pretext. Smith found the work partisan and often unreliable.

26. Singletary, Otis A. The Mexican War. Chicago (U. Chi.), 1960.

27. Smith, Justin Harvey. The war with Mexico. 2 vols. New York (Macmillan), 1919. Reprinted Gloucester, Mass. (Peter Smith), 1963. DeVoto (1943), No. 501: "The research behind Professor Smith's book is certainly one of the most exhaustive ever made by an American historian, and if it came to an issue of fact I should perforce have to disregard my own findings and accept his. But it is frequently—very frequently—altogether impossible to understand how Smith's conclusions could exist in the presence of facts which he himself presents. If there is a more consistently wrongheaded book in our history, or one which so freely cites facts in support of judgements which those facts controvert, I have not encountered it." The first portion of the DeVoto quotation is probably an understatement. The authors of this present work consider it doubtful whether any book in American history has been so thoroughly researched. Anyone who studies Smith's *magnum opus* with any care, checking his citations and sources as we have done, cannot help but gain the deepest respect for such indefatigable scholarship. The use of Smith's citations and bibliography, however, is occasionally frustrating. He had so many and so varied sources that he resorted to abbreviated forms which make following his trail difficult and, at times, impossible. The twenty volumes of his typescript notes (each between 300 and 400 pages) in the Garcia Collection at the University of Texas are helpful. But some of the citations cannot be located today, either because his entry was too cryptic or, more often, because the material is no longer extant— especially true in the case of manuscripts in the numerous Mexican archives which he visited with a special pass from Porfirio Díaz. As to Smith's interpretations and conclusions, every man must be his own judge, but it would be unsound and unreasonable to contest any one of them without serious and thorough investigation. Some historians, blinded by bias, have taken views at odds with Smith's without the foundation of research to validate such deviation. Unfortunately, too, Smith's work has been glibly labeled chauvinistic (and therefore bad) by superficial students who have not studied nor perhaps even read it. All of which is not to say that the present authors have followed Smith slavishly. Since 1919 over half a century of research and publica-

tion has gone into studies of the Mexican War period. Reminiscences and ancillary studies have appeared in scores of state and local journals. Significant advances in the understanding of the mid-nineteenth century, especially politics in both Mexico and the United States, have been made. Unlike DeVoto, however, we do not believe that Smith was wrongheaded, and when we have departed from his interpretations we have done so with caution and, we hope, without bias. *The War with Mexico,* which won the Pulitzer Prize in 1920 and the Loubat Prize (best book in the English language in the preceding five years) in 1923, remains today a monument of historical scholarship.

28. Stephenson, Nathaniel Wright. Texas and the Mexican War: a chronicle of the winning of the Southwest. New Haven (Yale), 1919. This lively little book in the Yale Chronicles of America series views the annexation of Texas as imperialistic and as the cause of the war with Mexico, which was also a manifestation of American imperialism.

29. Vigil y Robles, Guillermo. La invasión de México por los Estados Unidos en los años de 1846, 1847, y 1848, Apuntes históricos anecdoticos y descriptivos. Mexico (Correcional), 1923.

30. The war and its warriors; comprising a history of all the operations of the American armies in Mexico; with biographical sketches and anecdotes of the most distinguished officers in the regular army and the volunteer force. Philadelphia (Hogan and Thompson), 1848. See No. 13.

31. The war with Mexico; containing a short account of the important events from the encampment on the Rio Grande to the surrender of Vera Cruz. . . . By an officer of the army. Rochester, N.Y. (Dewey), 1847.

32. Wilcox, Cadmus Marcellus. History of the Mexican war. Edited by Mary Rachel Wilcox. Washington (Church News), 1892. Wilcox was assigned to Taylor after his graduation from West Point in 1846 but shortly thereafter was transferred to Scott's command and participated in the campaign in central Mexico. One of the author's objects was to show that the war was just and unavoidable. The claims and the annexation of Texas were the principal causes, and Wilcox believed that the Mexican recalcitrance over the claims was sufficient by itself to provoke war. The greater part of this large tome (711 pages), however, is primarily concerned with military actions on which Wilcox, later a major general in the Confederate Army, was qualified to write.

33. Willard, (Mrs.) Emma Hart. Last leaves of American history; com-

prising histories of the Mexican War and California. New York (Putnam), 1849. Reprinted 1853 and 1856. Mrs. Willard was a prolific writer of history and a leading advocate of female education. Her textbook on American history went through many editions. This work on the Mexican War is an excellent one for its time.

34. Young, Philip. History of Mexico. . . . Cincinnati (James), 1850. To the capture of Vera Cruz by Young; continued to the treaty of peace by George C. Furber. See No. 80.

35. Zirckel, Otto. Tagebuch geschrieben während der Nordamerikanisch-mexikanschen Campagne. . . . Halle (Schmidt) 1849.

ABOLITIONIST LITERATURE; SEE ALSO SLAVERY

36. Allen, George. An appeal to the people of Massachusetts on the Texas question. Boston (Little, Brown), 1844. Vehement antislavery opposition to the annexation of Texas as a precursor of war.

37. [————]. The complaint of Mexico and conspiracy against liberty. Boston (Alden), 1843. Didactic abolitionist tract. Its pertinency to the Mexican War is its pretended Mexican view of the conspiracy of the slaveocracy as territorial aggrandizement.

38. De Witt, Charles J. "Crusading for peace in Syracuse during the war with Mexico," N.Y. Hist., XIV (1933), 100–112. Abolitionists in Garrison's Non-Resistant Peace Society, led in Syracuse by Samuel J. May, were probably not untypical of others around the country.

39. Discourse II. The consequences of convenant breaking. N.p., 1847. See also No. 53.

40. Going, C. B. David Wilmot, free soiler (1814–1868): a biography of the great advocate of the Wilmot Proviso. New York, 1924.

41. Jay, William. A review of the causes and consequences of the Mexican War. Boston (Mussey), 1849. Simultaneously published in Philadelphia and New York. This is the most significant abolitionist work on the war. It follows Benjamin Lundy's incredible rationalizations about the Texas Revolution resulting from a conspiracy of the slaveocracy. Then it makes a thoroughly deprecatory examination of the claims issue. It next debunks the Texas claim to the Rio Grande and touches lightly upon the desire for California. Several chapters then relate alleged atrocities by Americans in Mexico during the war. The final chapters are

a hodge-podge of vituperation against Polk, eulogy for J. Q. Adams, immorality of war, etc. Running throughout the book is a constant vilification of the actions of the American government in its relations with Mexico.

42. [——— and others]. Dedicatoria a los habitantes del Nuevo Mexico y California, sobre la omision del congresso en proveerlos con un gobierno territorial, y sobre los daños politicos y sociales de la esclavitud. Nueva York (Harned), 1850. An antislavery tract enjoining New Mexico and California to become free-soil and apologizing for American actions during and immediately after the war.

43. Livermore, Abiel Abbot. Revisión de la guerra entre Mexico y los Estados Unidos. Mexico, 1948. Translated and annotated by Francisco Castillo Nájara. Recent Spanish translation of well-known abolitionist tract.

44. ———. The war with Mexico reviewed. Boston, 1850. Awarded a $500 prize by the American Peace Society for "the best review of the Mexican war on the principles of Christianity and on enlightened statesmanship." Describes the horrors of war and argues the South's desire to acquire new slave territory.

45. [Lowell, James Russell]. The Biglow papers, edited, with an introduction, notes, glossary, and copious index, by Homer Wilbur, A. M. . . . Cambridge, Mass. (Nicholas), 1848. Numerous other printings and editions, one of the best of which is Boston (Houghton Mifflin), 1885. Both Hosea Biglow, the purported author, and Homer Wilbur are inventions of poet Lowell. The work is a satire in verse, with prose introductions and explanations for each "paper" castigating the Mexican War, the slaveocracy, and war in general. It was one of the most effective abolitionist writings. Of the nine papers, five originally appeared in the Boston *Courier* and four in the *Anti-slavery Standard*.

46. Lundy, Benjamin. Life, travels, and opinions. . . . Philadelphia (Parrish), 1847.

47. ———. War in Texas. . . . Philadelphia (Merrihew & Gunn), 1837. This preposterous work initiated on a nation-wide basis the idea that the Texas Revolution was the result of a conspiracy of the slaveocracy for the purpose of making Texas a slave state in the Union. Ergo, the Mexican War was fought for the same purpose. The preceding item (No. 46) is a reiteration of this in different form.

48. Moody, Loring. Facts for the people, showing the relations of the United States Government to slavery, embracing a history of the

Mexican War, its origin and objects. Boston (Anti-slavery press), 1847. Critical of the war as an instrument of aggressive slave-ocracy, but contains also, as did a number of the abolitionist tracts, the curious perversion of anti-Americanism as well. American atrocities toward Mexico are related with a gory relish that offsets the lack of factual basis.

49. Shackford, Charles Chauncy. A citizen's appeal in regard to the war with Mexico. Boston (Andrews & Prentiss), 1848. Primarily an antislavery polemic, but also violently antigovernment. Labels the war one of conquest.

50. Smith, Justin Harvey. "The Biglow papers as an argument against the Mexican War," Mass. Hist. Soc. Proc., XLV (1912), 602–11. See No. 45.

51. Stearns, Charles. Facts in the life of General Taylor, the Cuba blood-hound importer, the extensive slave holder, and the hero of the Mexican War. Boston (the author), 1848. Abrasive anti-slavery tract.

52. Sumner, Charles. Report on the war with Mexico. Old South Leaflet, no. 32, Boston, 1904. Although he was one of the leading abolitionists, Sumner did not seem to be as greatly wrought up over the war as some of his colleagues and wrote very little about it—in opposition, of course.

53. Thomas, Thomas Ebenezer. Covenant breaking, and its consequences; or the present posture of our national affairs, in connection with the Mexican War . . . two discourses preached at Hamilton, Ohio. . . . Rossville, Ohio (Christy), 1847. Same abolitionist arguments: war was caused by a greedy slave power and the Texas boundary was the Nueces. See also No. 39.

54. Tuttle, I. F. "Our late conquest," New Englander, VI (1848), 524–34.

55. Wetmore, Prosper Montgomery. Observations on the origin and conduct of the war with Mexico. New York, 1847.

ALABAMA IN THE WAR

56. Cook, Z. S. "Mexican War reminiscences," Ala. Hist. Qrtly., XX (1957), 435–60.

ANNEXATION QUESTION;
SEE ALSO TEXAS BACKGROUND

57. Almonte, Juan Nepomuceno. Correspondencia entre los señores J. N. Almonte, Arrangoiz, consul de N. Orleans, a los sres. Pedro Fernandez del Castillo y Joaquin Velazquez de Leon, sobre Texas y los E.E.U.U., 1841–1843. Mexico (Vargas Rea), 1949.

58. Bucholaer, H. Texas question. New York (Baillie), 1844. Political cartoons.

59. Cuevas, Luis Gonzaga. Que las cámaras de los Estados Unidos del norte por un decreto . . . han resuelto incorporar el territorio de Tejas. Mexico, 1845.

60. [————]. Reflexiones sobre la memoria del ministerio de relaciones, en la parte relativa a Tejas. . . . Mexico, 1845. Texan independence is *de facto* and Mexico must decide between recognition stipulating Texas remain independent or annexation by the U.S.

61. Federación y Tejas. By the editors of Voz del Pueblo. Mexico, 1845. Discusses request of Luis G. Cuevas, minister of foreign relations, for authority to hear Texas's proposition and to enter into a treaty with Texas.

62. Fulmore, Zachary Taylor. "The annexation of Texas and the Mexican War," SWHQ, V (1901), 28–48.

63. Hall, Charles W. "The admission of Texas and the Mexican War," National Mag., XII (1900), 72–76.

64. La cámara de representantes a la nación. . . . Mexico (Lara), 1845. A twelve-page untitled pamphlet denouncing the U.S. annexation of Texas and urging Mexicans to prepare to arm themselves.

65. Luelmo, Julio. Los anti-esclavistas norte-americanos: la cuestión de Texas y la guerra con Mexico. Mexico (Sec. de Educ. Pública), 1947.

66. Romero, Matías. Estudios sobre la anexión de Mexico a los Estados Unidos. . . . Mexico (Imp. del Gobierno), 1890. A Mexican study of the movement in the United States to annex all of Mexico. Romero was Mexican minister to the United States at the outbreak of the Civil War and was exiled by Maximilian.

67. Smith, Justin Harvey. The annexation of Texas. New York (Barnes and Noble), 1911, reprinted 1941.

68. Stenberg, Richard R. "President Polk and the annexation of Texas," Southwestern Soc. Sci. Qrtly., XIV (1934), 332–56. Presi-

dent-elect Polk worked to get the joint resolution of annexation passed by Congress. Stenberg found fraud and intrigue in it.
SEE ALSO NOS. 36, 37, 46, 47.

ARKANSAS IN THE WAR

69. Brown, Walter Lee. "The Mexican War experiences of Albert Pike and the 'Mounted Devils' of Arkansas," Ark. Hist. Qrtly., XII (1953), 301–15.
70. Buhoup, Jonathan W. Narrative of the central division, or army of Chihuahua. . . . Pittsburgh (Morse), 1847. Buhoup served with a regiment of Arkansas volunteers under Albert Pike.

ARMY AND CAMP LIFE

71. Bailey, Thomas. "Diary of the Mexican War," Ind. Mag. Hist., XIV (1918), 134–47. Bailey was a musician in the Fifth Indiana Regiment.
72. Ballentine, George. Autobiography of an English soldier in the U.S. Army. New York (Stringer and Townsend), 1853. Later published as *The Mexican War* . . . ; see No. 447. Ballentine served with Scott's army. The book, which was apparently written from memory, contains observations that seem accurate, although the author did not have the revulsion for camp life and military discipline that most soldiers expressed.
73. Chamberlain, Samuel Emery. My confession: the recollections of a rogue. New York (Harper), 1956. This dramatic first-hand account and its color sketches did not come to light until 1955 when, amid some controversy regarding its authenticity, it was abridged in *Life* magazine. There remains little doubt today of its validity. It is especially valuable for soldier and camp life.
74. Chapman, William. "Letters from the seat of war—Mexico," Green Bay Hist. Bltn., IV (1928), 1–24. See No. 82.
75. Collins, Francis. Journal of Francis Collins, an artillery officer in the Mexican War. Ed. by Maria Clinton Collins. Cincinnati (Abingdon), 1915.
76. Cooke, Philip St. George. Scenes and adventures in the army; or, romance of military life. Philadelphia (Lindsey and Blakiston), 1857. Reissued 1859.

77. DeVoto, Bernard. "Anabasis in buckskin: an exploit of our war with Mexico," Harper's, CLXXX (1940), 400–410.

78. Donnavan, Corydon. Adventures in Mexico experienced during a captivity of seven months in the interior, having been captured at Camargo by Canales' band of guerrillos . . . and sold into slavery . . . final escape, and perilous journey to the United States; with a view of the present war. Cincinnati (Robinson & Jones), 1847; Boston (Holbrook), 1848. This was one of the most popular of the contemporary books. The author was a civilian who purported to have been captured, sold into slavery, and escaped to return to the United States. With the help of several artists he prepared a large "panorama" of various scenes in Mexico which he exhibited throughout the country. The book was sold in conjunction with the exhibition. It went through many editions, including a German translation printed in Pennsylvania in 1848.

79. Elderkin, James D. Biographical sketches and anecdotes of a soldier of three wars, as written by himself; the Florida, the Mexican War, and the Great Rebellion. Detroit, 1899.

80. Furber, George C. The twelve months volunteer; or journal of a private in the Tennessee regiment of cavalry in the campaign in Mexico, 1846–7. Cincinnati (James), 1848. Other editions 1850 and 1857. The author was a veteran of Scott's campaign. This is one of the best contemporary works. It emphasizes four topics: camp life, physical description of the country, manners and customs of Mexicans as Furber saw them, and military operations. To Furber, Mexico caused the war: "The conduct of Mexico now left no doubt but that she was determined upon war; and that war she soon commenced." Furber shows no animus for Mexicans, but compares the system of peonage unfavorably with slavery. See also No. 34. Furber also wrote fiction about the war under the title *Ike McCandliss and other stories.* . . . Cincinnati (James), 1852.

81. George, Isaac. Heroes and incidents of the Mexican War, containing Doniphan's expedition. . . . Written from dictation by J. D. Berry. Greensburg, Pa. (Review), 1903. About half of this book is anecdotal.

82. Hamilton, Charles S. "Letters written from the seat of war in Mexico, 1847," Metropolitan Mag., XXVII (1908), 313–21, 439–45. See No. 74.

83. ———. "Memoirs of the Mexican War," Wis. Mag. Hist., XIV (1930), 63–92.

84. Hartman, George W. A private's own journal. Greencastle, Pa. (Robinson), 1849.

85. Johnson, William S. "Private Johnson fights the Mexicans, 1847–1848," ed. by John Hammond Moore, S. Car. Hist. Mag., LXVII (1966), 203–28. Johnson's diary, with the South Carolina "Palmetto" Regiment, from Vera Cruz to Mexico City. Contains numerous references to sickness and disease suffered by troops in Mexico.

86. McWhiney, Grady, and Sue McWhiney (editors). To Mexico with Taylor and Scott, 1845–1847. Waltham, Mass. (Blaisdell), 1969. A collection of excerpts from contemporary sources.

87. Oswandel, J. Jacob. Notes of the Mexican War. . . . Philadelphia (the author), 1885. Smith and Judah (No. 94) suggest that Oswandel may have based his work on an unpublished diary kept by a fellow soldier named John Kreitzer. Oswandel enlisted in the 1st Regiment of Pennsylvania Volunteers attached to Scott's army. His reminiscences are not particularly valuable except for one rather striking observation: "After the close of the war we returned home with impaired health . . . ; shattered with a disease, contracted in a strange country and a hot climate, which, in a few years after the war had taken from their homes more than half of those who returned."

88. Payne, Darwin. "Camp life in the army of occupation: Corpus Christi, July 1845 to March 1846," SWHQ, LXXIII (1969), 326–42.

89. Perry, Oran. Indiana in the Mexican War. Indianapolis (Burford), 1908. Many quotations from Indiana newspapers and letters of soldiers. Excellent for army life.

90. Powell, Lawrence Clark. "Thomas C. Lancey, chronicler of '46," Pac. Hist. Rev., XVI (1947), 11–17.

91. Robinson, Fayette. An account of the organization of the army of the United States. Philadelphia (Butler), 1848.

92. Scribner, Benjamin F. Camp life of a volunteer: a campaign in Mexico; or a glimpse at life in camp. . . . Philadelphia (Grigg Elliot), 1847. Scribner was a private in the 2nd Regiment of Indiana volunteers, attached to Taylor's army, served through Buena Vista, and then was discharged.

93. Sedgwick, John. Correspondence of J. Sedgwick. 2 vols. New York (Battel), 1903. Sedgwick was a young lieutenant with Taylor, then with Scott, participating in every major battle of the war. The first volume consists of Mexican War letters to his family —among the best contemporary letters available.

94. Smith, George Winston, and Charles Judah. Chronicles of the gringos: the U.S. Army in the Mexican War, 1846–1848. Albuquerque (U. N. Mex.), 1968. This is a rather unusual and delightful book, hooking together in a loosely chronological fashion excerpts from first-hand accounts of participants in the war. Its use is made awkward because of the placement of the notes at the end of the book, which makes it difficult to identify excerpts quoted.

95. Tennery, Thomas D. The Mexican War diary of Thomas D. Tennery. Norman (OU), 1970.

96. Turnley, Parmenas Taylor. Reminiscences. . . from diaries. . . . Chicago (Donahue and Henneberry), 1892. Contains a section on his service in the Mexican War.

97. Vandiver, Frank E. "The Mexican War experiences of Josiah Gorgas," Jour. S. Hist., XIII (1947), 373–94.

98. Viall, Nelson. "Recollections of the Mexican War," R.I. Hist. Soc. Coll., XXX (1937), 65–82, 102–16.

99. Viola, Herman J. "Zachary Taylor and the Indiana volunteers," SWHQ, LXXII (1969), 335–46.

100. Welter, Everhard. Forty-two years of eventful life of two wars. Washington, 1888.

101. Wynkoop, J. M. (editor). Anecdotes and incidents. . . . Pittsburgh, 1848.

ARMY OF OCCUPATION IN TEXAS

102. Allen, Lewis Leonidas. Pencillings of scenes upon the Rio Grande. New York, 1848. A 48-page pamphlet written by a chaplain with Taylor and originally published in the St. Louis American. Contains several graphic and perhaps too imaginative anecdotes and has a glowing account of the heroism of the Great Western.

103. Crimmins, Martin L. "First stages of the Mexican War; initial operations of the army in 1846," Army Ord., XV (1935), 222–25.

104. Duncan, Louis C. "A medical history of General Zachary Taylor's army of occupation in Texas and Mexico, 1845–1847," Mil. Surg., XLVIII (1921), 76–104.

105. [Hill, Daniel Harvey]. "The army in Texas," Sou. Qrtly. Rev., IX (1846), 434–57. Severe castigation of supply system at the beginning of the war; hardship on Taylor's forces of lack of sup-

plies. Marcy is blamed. In a footnote the author casually dismisses Texas's claim to the Rio Grande as entirely unjust.

106. Nichols, Edward Jay. Zach Taylor's little army. New York (Doubleday), 1963. Appears well researched but lacks documentation; a readable narrative.

107. Scott, Florence Johnson. Old Rough and Ready on the Rio Grande. San Antonio (Naylor), 1935.

108. Thorpe, Thomas Bangs. Our army on the Rio Grande. . . . Philadelphia (Carey and Hart), 1846. An account of the army through the occupation of Matamoros; the author seems to have been an observer.

109. Whiting, Daniel Powers. Army portfolio. New York (Endicott), 1847. Five large colored lithos; one of the encampment at Corpus Christi, four of Monterrey, Mexico. Whiting was a captain in the 7th Infantry.

SEE ALSO NO. 88.

ATTITUDE OR BEHAVIOR OF AMERICAN TROOPS

110. Bloom, John Porter. "New Mexico viewed by Americans, 1846–1849," N. Mex. Hist. Rev., XXXIV (1959), 165–98.

111. Heyer, C. H. "A Mexican War letter," Mag. of Hist., XVI (1913), 238–41.

112. Lemoine, Villacuña Ernesto. Crónica de la ocupacion de Mexico por el ejercito de los Estados Unidos. Mexico, 1950.

113. McCall, George Archibald. Letters from the frontiers. . . . Philadelphia (Lippincott), 1868. Contains a section on Mexican War experiences.

114. McKeown, James Edward. "Social problems among the Anglos during their occupation of New Mexico, 1846–1847," Historia, XXX (1953), 91–109.

115. McSherry, Richard. El purchero; or a mixed dish from Mexico embracing General Scott's campaign, with sketches of military life, in field and camp, of the character of the country. . . . Philadelphia (Lippincott), 1850. A series of letters to David Holmes Conrad written while the author served as a surgeon with the Marine Corps. Excellent descriptions of McSherry's observations and experiences. Exhibits a friendly view of the Mexican people but a critical view of the structure of their society. Has less than one could hope for about camp diseases and mili-

tary medicine, but is nevertheless one of the best of the physi-
cians' reminiscences.

116. [Robertson, John Blount]. Reminiscences of a campaign in Mexico by a member of the "Bloody First," . . . Nashville (York),
1849. Dedicated to the privates of the First Regiment of Tennessee Volunteers, these reminiscences were first published in installments in the Nashville *Union*. Later they were gathered
into book form with a brief history of Mexico and discussion of
the origin of the war prefixed. The primary cause of the war
was Mexican hostility over the annexation of Texas. The regiment fought with Taylor to Buena Vista, then with Scott to
Mexico City. Friendly attitude toward Mexican people is evidenced.

117. Spell, Lota M. "The Anglo-Saxon press in Mexico," AHR,
XXXVIII (1932), 20–31.

118. Wallace, Edward S. "Deserters in the Mexican War," HAHR, XV
(1935), 374–83. Story of two companies that deserted and enlisted in the Mexican army, were captured and punished.

119. Wallace, Isabel. Life and letters of General W. H. L. Wallace
(1821–1862). Chicago (Donnelly), 1909. Includes some letters
during his service as a lieutenant in the Mexican War.

SEE ALSO NOS. 48, 80, 94.

ATTITUDE OF AMERICANS AT HOME

120. Brent, Robert Arthur. "Mississippi and the Mexican War," Jour.
of Miss. Hist., XXXI (1969), 202–14.

121. ———. "Reaction in the United States to Nicholas Trist's mission
to Mexico, 1847–1848," Rev. Hist. Am., XXXV (1953), 105–18.

122. Ellsworth, Clayton Sumner. "The American churches and the
Mexican War," AHR, XLV (1940), 301–26. Discuss the
churches' problem of reconciling nineteenth-century patriotism
with pacifism and pacifism with anti-Catholicism.

123. Fakes, Turner J. "Memphis and the Mexican War," W. Tenn.
Hist. Soc. Papers, II (1948), 119–44.

124. Gilley, Billy H. "Tennessee opinion of the Mexican War as reflected in the state press," E. Tenn. Hist. Soc. Pbl. XXVI (1954),
17–26.

125. Goldin, Gurston. "Business sentiment and the Mexican War with
particular emphasis on the New York business man," New York

Hist., XXXIII (1952), 54–70. A good understanding of mercantile interests, but a gross misunderstanding of the background for war.

126. Hinckley, Ted C. "American anti-Catholicism during the Mexican War," Pac. Hist. Rev., XXXI (1962), 121–38. Demonstrates that anti-Catholic attitudes were surprisingly negligible during the war. See also Nos. 122, 333, 335, 337.

127. Minnigerode, Meade. The fabulous forties, 1840–1850. New York (Putnam), 1924. Almost nothing on the Mexican War, but an interesting social and cultural account without documentation, but with many identified quotations. The observation that the Mexican War did not seem to concern the bulk of the population is borne out by this quasi-history.

128. Pugh, N. M. "Contemporary comments on Texas, 1844–1847," SWHQ, LXII (1959), 367–70.

129. Royce, Josiah. California, from the conquest in 1846 to the second vigilance committee in San Francisco: a study in American character. Boston (Houghton Mifflin), 1886.

130. Streeter, Floyd Benjamin. Political parties in Michigan, 1837–1860. Lansing (Mich. Hist. Comm.), 1918. Contains political controversy over the Mexican War.

ATTITUDE OR BEHAVIOR
OF MEXICAN TROOPS OR CIVILIANS

131. Allen, G. N. Mexican treacheries and cruelties. Incidents and sufferings in the Mexican War; with accounts of hardships endured; treacheries of the Mexicans; battles fought, and success of American arms; . . . by a volunteer returned from the war. Boston, 1848. Insignificant except as an example of jingoistic journalism.

132. Brack, Gene M. "Mexican opinion, American racism, and the war of 1846," Western Hist. Qrtly., I (1970), 161–74. A study of Mexican public opinion on the eve of the war, citing numerous examples of anti-American feeling in Mexican newspapers and journals and demands for war following the annexation of Texas.

133. Carpenter, William W. Travels and adventures in Mexico. New York (Harper), 1851. Carpenter was in Taylor's army, was captured after the battle at Monterrey, later escaped and wandered

about Mexico until finally making his way to the coast and an American naval vessel.

134. Carrion, Jorge. "Efectos psicologicos de la guerra de 47 en el hombre de Mexico," Cuadernos Americanos, VII (1948), 116–32. An interesting excursion into libido and sex and the traumatic effects on the average Mexican of his encounter with the world of the gringos. The Mexican is characterized (p. 124) as juvenile, individualistic, mystic, and in love with death; the American as strong, socially realistic, basically collectivist, pragmatic, and in love with life.

135. Encarnacion prisoners: comprising an account of the march of the Kentucky cavalry from Louisville to the Rio Grande, together with an authentic history of the captivity of the American prisoners, including incidents and sketches of men and things on the route. By a prisoner. Louisville (Prentice and Weissinger), 1848. Several units of this cavalry regiment were captured at a hacienda named Encarnacion about fifty miles south of Saltillo. The unknown author, not surprisingly, had no warm feeling for Mexico.

136. Hale, Charles A. "The war with the United States and the crisis in Mexican thought," Americas, XIV (1957), 153–73. The loss of the war caused a reassessment of the Mexican political situation. Liberals demanded unification and renewed efforts at reform; conservatives more strongly than ever favored monarchy or some form of absolutism. This article is an excellent and provocative analysis.

137. Mason, R. H. Pictures of life in Mexico. 2 vols. London (Smith, Elder), 1852. Visited Mexico shortly after the end of the war in 1848 and 1849. One chapter discusses Mexican views of Americans. The average Mexican had "the most horrible ideas" of American "cruelty and rapacity" before the coming of U.S. troops. But afterward, "by slow degrees," many developed "a great respect for the people of the United States." On the causes of the war, Mexico brought it on herself by "haughty and sneering refusals" to negotiate the issues, and "rushed into hostilities with their usual precipitancy, confident of easy victory on account of their multitude: though the number of their armies is always much exaggerated."

138. Ramirez, José Fernando. México durante su guerra con los Estados Unidos. Ed. by Genario Garcia. Mexico (Bouret), 1905. Vol. 3 in Garcia's *Documentos Inéditos* . . . (q.v.). A translation by Elliot B. Scherr, edited by Walter V. Scholes, appeared as *Mex-*

ico during the war with the United States. Columbia, Missouri (UM), 1950. This item is a collection of Ramirez's letters and other papers. Ramirez, in addition to serving in high public office, was a prolific and scholarly historian. He found the procrastination, vacillation, and vanity of the Mexican officials to be the principal cause of war and the defeat to be merited, from which he hoped the Mexican nation could learn an important lesson.

SEE ALSO NOS. 78, 112.

BAJA CALIFORNIA

139. Chamberlain, Eugene Keith. "Nicholas Trist and Baja California," Pac. Hist. Rev., XXXII (1963), 49–63.
140. Gerhard, Peter. "Baja California in the Mexican War, 1846–1848," Pac. Hist. Rev., XIV (1945), 418–24.
141. Meadows, Don. The American occupation of La Paz (Lower California, 1847–49). Los Angeles (Dawson), 1955.

BATTLES, CAMPAIGNS, AND MILITARY OPERATIONS; SEE ALSO NAVAL OPERATIONS

142. Alcaraz, Ramon, and others. Apuntes para la historia de la guerra entre México y los Estados Unidos. Mexico (Payno), 1848. Reprinted Mexico, 1952. A contemporary translation was made by Albert C. Ramsey: *The other side; or, notes for the history of the war between Mexico and the United States.* New York (Wiley), 1850. This work was a joint effort by Alcaraz and a dozen other Mexican participants in the war who met in Queretero in 1847 to record their accounts of the war. Bancroft says ". . . The candor and fairness they evince is in the highest degree praiseworthy." The work accuses U.S. of shameless territorial aggression in Texas, but little mention is made of California and none of slavery as causes. Tends to exonerate Mexico of culpability, yet calls the Paredes revolution shameful. Excellent accounts of the military actions but disappointingly little on internal Mexican politics. Numerous maps and plans of battle.
143. Alcorta, Lino J. Reglamente del estado mayor del ejército que

debe operar sobre Tejas. Mexico (Lara), 1844. An eleven-page pamphlet describing the organization of the Mexican army at that time.

144. Aldrich, M. Almy. History of the United States Marine Corps. Boston (Shepard), 1875.

145. Anderson, Robert. An artillery officer in the Mexican War, 1846-7. New York (Putnam), 1911. A collection of letters of Robert Anderson, a captain with Scott's army.

146. Armstrong, Andrew. "The Brazito battlefield," N. Mex. Hist. Rev., XXXV (1960), 63-74.

147. Babcock, James Fairchild. Fate of Fred D. Mills. New Haven, 1848. Mills was the first American killed in the attack on the gate of San Antonio Abad on the outskirts of Mexico City.

148. Backus, Electus. "A brief sketch of the battle of Monterrey," Historical Magazine (Morrisana, N.Y.), X (1866), 207-13; 255-57.

149. Barbour, Philip Norbourne. Journals of the late brevet Major Philip Norbourne Barbour . . . written during the war with Mexico. Ed. by Rhoda van Bibber Tanner Doubleday. New York (Putnam), 1936. A handsome book, but without notations. Covers the period March 28 to September 20, 1846, when Barbour was with Taylor. He was killed at Monterrey, Mexico.

150. Battles of Mexico; containing an authentic account of all the battles fought in the republic from the commencement of the war until the capture of the city of Mexico; with a list of the killed and wounded. New York (Martin and Ely), 1847. Justin Smith attributes the work to E. Hutchinson who copyrighted it.

151. Baylies, Francis. "The march of the United States troops, under the command of General John E. Wool, from San Antonio, Texas, to Saltillo, Mexico, in the year 1846," Stryker's American Register, IV (1850), 297-312.

152. ————. A narrative of Major-General Wool's campaign in Mexico, in the years 1846, 1847, and 1848. Albany (Little), 1851.

153. Belote, Theodore T. "Military medals of the war with Mexico and the Civil War," D.A.R. Mag., LVI (1922), 275-85.

154. Bishop, W. W. Journal of the 12 months' campaign of Gen. Shields's brigade in Mexico, 1846-47. St. Louis, 1847.

155. Brackett, Albert Gallatin. General Lane's brigade in central Mexico. New York (Derby), 1854.

156. Bradley, Glenn Danford. Winning the Southwest: a story of conquest. Chicago (McClurg), 1912. Popularized biographical sketches of Carson, Stockton, Kearny, Fremont, and others.

157. Buchanan, A. Russell. "George Washington Trahern: Texan cow-

boy soldier from Mier to Buena Vista," SWHQ, LVIII (1954), 60–90.

158. Buley, R. C. "Indiana in the Mexican War," Ind. Mag. Hist., XV (1919), 260–92, 293–326; XVI (1920), 46–68. Last installment covers Buena Vista controversy.

159. Burgess, Harry. "The influence of bridges on campaigns," Mil. Engineer, XIX (1927), 146–48, 228–34. Has a section on campaigns in Mexico.

160. Carreño, Alberto María. Jefes del ejército Mexico en 1847. Mexico, 1914.

161. Castañeda, Carlos E. "Relations of General Scott with Santa Anna," HAHR, XXIX (1949), 455–73.

162. Castillo Nájera, Francisco. Invasión norte-americana, efectivos y estado de los ejércitos beligerentes, consideraciones sobre la compaña. Mexico, 1947. Reprinted in Memorias y Revista de la Academia Nacional de Ciencias, LVI (1948), 265–331. A somewhat jingoistic apologia of Mexican military prowess during the war.

163. Churubusco en la acción militar del 20 de agosto de 1847. Mexico (Museo Historico de Churubusco), 1947.

164. Coy, Owen C. The Battle of San Pasqual. Sacramento (Cal. Hist. Survey Comm.), 1921. A small pamphlet with special reference to the location of the battleground.

165. Davis, George T. M. Autobiography of the late Col. Geo. T. M. Davis, captain and aid[e]-de-camp, Scott's army of invasion (Mexico), from posthumous papers. New York (Jenkins and McGowan), 1891.

166. Dowling, R. L. "Infantry weapons of the Mexican War," Antiques, XXXVIII (1940), 228–29.

167. Downey, Fairfax Davis. "The flying batteries," Army, VII (1957), no. 4, 66–72; no. 6, 60–64. On the use of artillery in the war.

168. Duncan, James. "Letter of James Duncan: the battle of Monterey," Collect., XV (1902), 45–46.

169. Dunovant, R. G. M. The battles in the valley of Mexico. Edgefield, S. C., 1895. Another item from the Justin Smith bibliography which has not been located.

170. Dupuy, Trevor N. Military heritage of America. New York (McGraw-Hill), 1956. A chapter on the war with Mexico.

171. Eglin, H. W. T. "General Scott's landing at Vera Cruz, March 9, 1847," Coast Artillery Jour., LXVIII (1928), 244–47.

172. Fallo definitivo del supremo tribunal de la guerra, al examinar la conducta militar del Exmo. Sr. General D. Mariano Arista. . . .

Mexico (Torres), 1850. Investigation of Arista for his loss of Palo Alto and Resaca de la Palma. See also Nos. 398, 626.

173. Fisher, George J. B. "Buena Vista—a western Thermopylae," Coast Artillery Journ., LXXII (1930), 141–50.

174. French, Samuel Gibbs. Two wars: an autobiography. . . . Nashville (Confederate Veteran), 1901. Considerable reminiscent material on the Mexican War.

175. Frias, Heriberto. Episodios militares mexicanos: prinicpales campañas, journados, batallos, combates y actos heroicos que ilustran la historia del ejército nacional desde la independencia hasta el triunfo definitivo de la república. 2 vols. Mexico (Bouret), 1901.

176. Gibson, Thomas W. Letter descriptive of the Battle of Buena Vista. . . . Lawrenceburgh, Indiana (Hall), 1847. Twelve-page pamphlet.

177. [Giddings, Luther]. Sketces of the campaign in northern Mexico . . . by an officer of the First Ohio Volunteers. New York (Putnam), 1853.

178. Greer, James K. Colonel Jack Hays, Texas frontier leader and California builder. New York (Dutton), 1952. Hays commanded the Texas Ranger regiment which fought first with Taylor, then with Scott. Ten chapters deal with these experiences.

179. Hardie, Francis Hunter. "The Mexican War," Jour. Mil. Serv. Inst. of the U.S., XV (1894), 1203–11.

180. Hart, Burdett. The Mexican War. New Haven (Peck & Stafford), 1847.

181. Henry, William Seaton. Campaign sketches of the war with Mexico. New York (Harper), 1847. A diary of Taylor's operations. Henry was brevetted major at Monterey.

182. Herrick, W. B. "Surgery at Buena Vista," Ill. & Ind. Med. & Surg. Jour., II (1846).

183. Hitchcock, Ethan Allen. Fifty years in camp and field: diary of Major General Ethan Allen Hitchcock, U.S.A. Ed. by W. A. Croffut. New York (Putnam), 1909.

184. Hunter, John Marvin. "General John E. Wool in Texas (1846)," Frontier Times, XXX (1953), 301–7.

185. Ibarra, Domingo. Churubusco, 20 de agosto de 1847. Grato recuerdo a los valientes mexicanos que defendieron el territorio nacional. Mexico (Correo), 1889.

186. ———. Un recuerdo en memoria de los mexicanos que murieron en la guerra contra los norte americanos en los años de 1836 á

1848. Mexico (Velasco), 1888. Ibarra was a military historian; another work covers Mexican military history from 1838 to 1860 but excludes the Mexican War.

187. Jacobs, James R. "Our first expeditionary force across the sea," Inf. Jour., XXXIII (1928), 20–24. Scott's expedition.

188. Jamieson, Milton. Journal and notes of a campaign in Mexico. Cincinnati (Franklin), 1849.

189. Kearny, Thomas. General Philip Kearny, battle soldier of five wars. . . . New York (Putnam), 1937. Kearny, a true military adventurer, served as Scott's personal bodyguard. He lost an arm leading a charge at Churubusco. Scott called him "the bravest man I ever knew." See No. 490.

190. Kendall, George Wilkins. The war between the United States and Mexico illustrated, embracing pictorial drawings of all the principal conflicts, by Carl Nebel, . . . with a description of each battle by Geo. Wilkins Kendall. New York (Appleton), 1851. This beautiful work was printed in Paris, royal folio size. The twelve lithographs (also done in Paris) are hand colored, with some variation in coloring from one copy to another. Kendall, editor of the New Orleans *Picayune,* was present at most of the engagements and wrote detailed accounts for his paper, thus becoming the world's first modern war correspondent. His accounts of the battles in this book remain among the best written. Each account ends with a paragraph about the accompanying litho.

191. Lander, Alexander. A trip to the wars. Monmouth, Ill. (Atlas), 1847.

192. Lane, Walter Paye. Adventures and recollections of General Walter P. Lane. Marshall, Texas (News Messenger), 1928.

193. Lane, William Bartlett. "Our cavalry in Mexico," United Serv. Mag., XIV (1895), 301–13.

194. Lavender, David Sievert. Climax at Buena Vista: the American campaigns in northeastern Mexico, 1846–1847. Philadelphia (Lippincott), 1966. Lightly documented and somewhat superficial. Three chapters on background of the war.

195. Lewis, Lloyd. Captain Sam Grant. Boston (Little, Brown), 1950.

196. Lippard, George. Legends of Mexico; or, the battles of Old Rough and Ready. . . . Philadelphia (Peterson), 1847.

197. Loperna, Ignacio. Observaciones sobre el contrato de armamento que con el supremo gobierno de la República célebre D. Ignacio Loperena en representacion de la casa inglesa de los Sres.

Walter, Longan y compañia, en 8 de junio de 1847. Mexico (Torres), 1850.

198. López Uraga, José. Sumaria mandada formar a pedimento del Sr. Coronel del 4° regimiento de infantería. Mexico (Navarro), 1846. A 34-page defense of the actions of Mexican officers at Palo Alto and Resaca de la Palma.

199. Maguire, T. Miller. "The United States versus Mexico," Royal Unit. Serv. Inst. Jour., LVIII (1914), 605–10, 764–70. An Englishman's arraignment of U.S. policy and conduct of the war. Second installment treats Taylor's campaign. Quotes extensively, and naïvely, from Grant's *Personal Memoirs* (No. 357).

200. Manigault, Arthur Middleton. "A letter from Vera Cruz in 1847," SWHQ, XVIII (1914), 215–18. Manigault was a first lieutenant in the Palmetto regiment.

201. Mansfield, Edward Deering. The Mexican War: a history of its origin, and a detailed account of the victories which terminated in the surrender of the capital; with the official despatches of the generals. Cincinnati (Derby, Bradley), 1848. To Mansfield the basic cause of the war was the annexation of Texas. "The diplomatic correspondence of our government shows, that it apprehended war—that it knew well the sole cause by which war would come and that in the minds of the President and his cabinet, the annexation of Texas, and its disputed boundaries, was the sole foundation for any rupture with Mexico." On the actual campaigns, this is a surprisingly good work for a contemporary account, apparently written before the Treaty of Guadelupe Hidalgo.

202. Maury, Dabney H. Recollections of a Virginian in the Mexican, Indian, and Civil wars. New York (Scribner's), 1894. Young Lieutenant Maury, fresh from West Point, participated in the seige and capture of Vera Cruz and was brevetted for bravery at Cerro Gordo.

203. McClintock, William A. "Journal of a trip through Texas and northern Mexico in 1846–1847," SWHQ, XXXIV (1930), 20–37, 141–58.

204. McMillen, Fred E. "San Juan de Ulua under the American flag," U.S. Naval Inst. Proc., LXII (1936), 1155–66. Capture of the fortress in Vera Cruz harbor in 1847 and 1914.

205. Meade, George Gordon. The life and letters of George Gordon Meade, Major General, United States Army. New York (Scribner's), 1913. Operations under both Taylor and Scott.

206. [Mejía, Francisco]. Sumaria mandada formar a pedimento . . . en los puntos del Palo Alto y Resaca de Guerrero. Mexico (Navarro), 1846. One of several "explanations" of the defeats, a 40-page pamphlet.

207. The Mexican War and its heroes: being a complete history of the Mexican War, embracing all the operations under Generals Taylor and Scott, with a biography of the officers. Also an account of the conquest of California and New Mexico. . . . Philadelphia (Lippincott, Grambo), 1850.

208. Military Historical Society of Massachusetts. Civil and Mexican wars, 1861. Boston (the Society), 1913. Buena Vista, by W. B. Franklin, 543–47; Contreras and Churubusco, by G. H. Gordon, 559–98; Molino del Rey and Chapultepec, by G. H. Gordon, 598–639.

209. Moore, H. Judge. Scott's campaign in Mexico: from the rendezvous on the island of Lobos to the taking of the city, including an account of the siege of Puebla. . . . Charleston (Nixon), 1849. Moore was a member of South Carolina's Palmetto regiment.

210. Neff, Jacob K. Thrilling incidents of the wars of the United States . . . by the author of "The Army and Navy of the United States." Philadelphia (Carey and Hart), 1848. Later editions 1857, 1860. About 60 pages deal with battles of the Mexican War. Authorship has been attributed by some to John Frost.

211. Official list of officers who marched with the army under the command of Major General Winfield Scott, from Puebla upon the city of Mexico, the seventh, eighth, ninth, and tenth of August, one thousand and eight hundred and forty-seven, and who were engaged in the battles of Mexico. Mexico (American Star Print), 1848.

212. Paredes y Arrillaga, Mariano. [Manifiesto]. Mexico, 1846. A 3-page untitled item dated April 4, 1846, outlining the organization of the military establishment.

213. ———. Reglamento para el corso de particulares contra los enimigos de la nacion. Mexico (Aguila), 1846. A 20-page pamphlet giving information on military arrangements at the beginning of the war. A 23-page pamphlet is reported in the Beineke collection at Yale under the title: *Reglamento para el corso de particulares en la presente guerra,* Mexico (Aguila), 1846.

214. ———. Reglamento sobre la organizacion del cuerpo de artilleria. Mexico (Aguila), 1846.

215. Peterson, Charles Jacobs. The military heroes of the war with

Mexico with a narrative of the war. Philadelphia (Leary), 1848. This handsomely illustrated book was very popular and went through many editions. The author's viewpoint is decidedly racist; the narrative of the campaigns is undocumented and somewhat imaginative; and the biographical section is little better. The Huntington Library copy of the first edition is interleaved with a collection of Mexican War manuscripts, for the most part autographed letters from prominent officers, including about a score of Winfield Scott letters and a number relating to the Scott-Worth controversy.

216. Peterson, Clarence Stewart. Known military dead during the Mexican War, 1846–1848. Baltimore, 1957.

217. Piatt, Donn. General George H. Thomas: a critical biography . . . with concluding chapters by Henry V. Boynton. Cincinnati (Clarke), 1893. Little space in the book is devoted to the Mexican War, which the author believes was the result of aggressive slaveocracy. Johnson was a lieutenant in Taylor's campaign, but after the battle of Buena Vista, served the remainder of the war at Brazos Santiago.

218. Ponce de Leon, Antonio. "Parte oficial de la acción de armas de Temascalitos," N. Mex. Hist. Rev., III (1928), 381–89. Official Mexican report of the battle of Brazito in 1846, translated by F. M. Gallaher.

219. ¡Pro-patria! Cronica de la heroica defensa, sitio, y capitulacion gloriosa de Vera Cruz, el año terrible 1847. . . . Vera Cruz, 1912.

220. Rangel, Joaquin. Tercera brigada de infanteria del ejército Mexicano. Mexico, 1847.

221. Relacion, de los sucesos acaecidos en la ciudad de Puebla, del 14 al 27 de mayo de 1847. Mexico (El Tiempo), 1901.

222. Roberts, Thomas D. "Resaca de la Palma, a traditional episode in the history of the Second Cavalry," Am. Mil. Hist. Found. Jour., I (1937), 101–7.

223. Roberts, William Barton. "Colonel William Barton Roberts in the Mexico City campaign—1847," ed. by Bert Anson, West Pa. Hist. Mag., XXXIX (1958), 243–63.

224. Robinson, Fayette. Mexico and her military chieftans. . . . Philadelphia (Butler), 1847.

225. Robinson, Mary Nauman. "In command at Vera Cruz, 1847–1848," Lancaster Co. Hist. Soc. Pap., XVIII (1914), 157–60. Compiled from letters of Col. George Nauman. See also No. 654.

226. Robinson, William M., Jr. "The engineer soldiers in the Mexican War," Mil. Engineer, XXIV (1932), 1–8.

227. Ruhlen, George. "Brazito; the only battle in the Southwest between American and foreign troops," Password, XI (1957), 4–13.

228. Sánchez Lamego, Miguel A. El colegio militar y la defensa de Chapultepec en septiembre de 1847. Mexico, 1947.

229. Santa Anna, Antonio López de. Apelación al buen criterio de los nacionales y estrangeros. Informe que el Escm. Sr. General de Division . . . dio por acuerdo de la seccion del gran jurado sobre las acusaciones presentadas por . . . Ramon Gamboa. . . . Mexico (Cumplido), 1849. Santa Anna's explanation and defense of his conduct of the war in answer to charges made against him by Ramon Gamboa (see No. 693). The first 71 pages, written by Santa Anna in Kingston, Jamaica, contain his own account. The remainder of the 184-page book consists of documents related to the affair, some of which are unobtainable in printed form elsewhere.

230. Schulz, Enrique E. "Batalla de Padierna, Agosto 16 de 1847," Boletin de Ingenieros, IV (1913), 217–42. Known in American annals as the Battle of Contreras. This is one of the very few items missed by Justin Smith.

231. Scott, Winfield. Memoirs of Lieutenant General Scott. . . . New York (Sheldon), 1864.

232. Semmes, Raphael. The campaign of General Scott in the valley of Mexico. Cincinnati (Moore & Anderson), 1852.

233. ———. Service afloat and ashore in the Mexican War. Cincinnati (Moore), 1851.

234. Shields, Elise Trigg. "The storming of Chapultepec," Confed. Vet., XXVI (1918), 399–401.

235. Smith, Gustavus Woodson. Company "A," Corps of Engineers, U.S.A., 1846–1848, in the Mexican War. Willets Point, N.Y. (Battalion), 1896.

236. Smith, Justin Harvey. "Official military reports," AHR, XXI (1915), 96–98. A brief essay on the trustworthiness of military reports for historical purposes.

237. ———. "Our preparations for the war of 1846–1848," Mil. Hist. and Econ., II (1917), 27–42.

238. [Smith, Robert Hall]. A series of intercepted letters, captured by the American guard at Tacubaya, August 22, 1847. Mexico (American Star Print), October 1847. Extremely rare; earliest known issue of the press of the American Army of Occupation. Also New Orleans, 1847, and Columbus, 1847. The letters, dated

in August 1847 and written by high-placed Mexicans, furnish evidence that Scott could have entered Mexico City after the battle of Churubusco on August 20 virtually unopposed. The letters also demonstrate the ample supply of arms and ammunition possessed by the Mexican army and its confidence in victory before the battle.

239. [Southern Quarterly Review]. "[Battles of the Mexican War]," S. Qrtly. Rev., XXI (1852), 121–53; 373–426; XXII (1852), 285–96; XXIII (1853), 1–52; XXIV (1853), 93–123. A series of articles on the battles of the Mexican War, each titled separately and signed "H."

240. Steele, Matthew Forney. American campaigns. Washington (Adams), 1909. Includes lectures at Fort Leavenworth on Taylor's and Scott's campaigns.

241. Stevens, Hazard. The life of Isaac Ingalls Stevens. 2 vols. Boston (Houghton Mifflin), 1900. Covers Stevens's Mexican War service as an engineer attached to Scott's staff.

242. Stevens, Isaac Ingalls. Campaigns of the Rio Grande and of Mexico, with notices of the recent work of Major Ripley. New York (Appleton), 1851. A critique of Ripley (1849) and a defense of Taylor and Scott as competent generals whose judgment was the largest element in American military success in Mexico.

243. [Stiff, Edward]. A new history of Texas . . . and a history of the Mexican War. . . . Cincinnati (Conclin), 1847. The history of the Mexican War is a brief appendage of about 20 unnumbered pages tracing Taylor's campaign through the capture of Monterey.

244. Thomlinson, M. H. "The dragoons and El Paso, 1848," N. Mex. Hist. Rev., XXXIII (1948), 217–24.

245. Thorpe, Thomas Bangs. Our army at Monterrey. . . . Philadelphia (Carey and Hart), 1847. A contemporary history, fairly well done.

246. Todd, Charles Burr. The battles of San Pasqual. . . . Pomona (Progress), 1925. A guide to the battlefield.

247. Torrea, Juan Manuel. "Un héro máximo de la intervención americana; Xicoténcatl," Soc. Mex. de Geog. y Estadistica, XXXIX (1929), 1–6, 63–79. Defense of Chapultepec.

248. United States Infantry School. Battle of Monterrey. Camp Benning (the school), 1921.

249. Vermilya, Lucius H. The battles of Mexico. Prattsville, N.Y. (Hackstaff), 1849. Cover title: The battles of Mexico from the beginning to the end of the war [!], with a sketch of Cali-

fornia. Vermilya was a commissary sergeant with the New York volunteers attached to Scott's forces.

250. Woodward, Arthur. Lances at San Pascual. San Francisco (Cal. Hist. Soc.), 1948. A fine in-depth study of the battle. Woodward is well-known in both historical and archeological circles as, among other things, a pioneer historical archeologist.

251. Wynne, James. Memoir of Major Samuel Ringgold. . . . Baltimore (Murphy), 1847. A 16-page eulogy containing little information.

SEE ALSO NOS. 31, 32, 35, 75, 91, 92, 93, 105, 106, 108, 133.

BEAR FLAG REVOLT; SEE ALSO CALIFORNIA; FREMONT

252. California Historical Society. "The Bear Flag movement," Cal. Hist. Soc. Qrtly., I (1922), 72–95, 178–91.

253. Hickman, C. J. "Fremont and the Bear Flag," Overland, LXVIII (1916), 448–51.

254. Hussey, John Adam. "Bear Flag revolt," Am. Heritage, I (1950), 24–27.

255. ———. "Commander John B. Montgomery and the Bear Flag revolt," U.S. Naval Inst. Proc., LXV (1939), 937–80.

256. Martin, A. H. "The Bear Flag revolution," Americana, VII (1912), 867–71.

257. Thompson, Robert A. Conquest of California. Capture of Sonoma by Bear flag men June 14, 1846. . . . Santa Rosa (Sonoma Democrat), 1896.

BEAUREGARD, P. G. T.

258. Basso, Hamilton. Beauregard, the great creole. New York (Scribner's), 1933. Contains an inconsequential chapter on Beauregard as a lieutenant with Scott.

259. Beauregard, Pierre Gustave Toutant. With Beauregard in Mexico; the Mexican War reminiscences of P. G. T. Beauregard. Ed. by T. Harry Williams. Baton Rouge (LSU), 1956. Edited from the original journal in the Missouri Historical Society. Written by Beauregard after the war, it was based on diaries now in the Library of Congress which he kept during the war.

260. Williams, T. Harry. P. G. T. Beauregard: Napoleon in gray. Baton Rouge (LSU), 1954. Contains an excellent chapter on Beauregard with Scott.

BIBLIOGRAPHY

261. Bolton, Herbert Eugene. Guide to materials for the history of the United States in the principal archives of Mexico. Washington (Carnegie), 1913.
262. Brown, Robert Benaway. "Doniphan's expedition: a problem for bibliographers," Hist. and Phil. Soc. Ohio Bltn., IX (1951), 50–55. Concerned with various editions of John T. Hughes's work.
263. Haferkorn, Henry Ernest. The war with Mexico. Washington Barracks, D.C., 1914. Reprinted New York (Argonaut), 1965. A bibliography of the causes, conduct, and political aspects of the war.
264. [Harper, Lathrop C.]. Catalogue 12: Books, pamphlets, broadsides printed in Mexico, 1813–1850. New York, [1964]. This catalogue of this fine book dealer is one of the best bibliographic aids to Mexican imprints of the times.
265. Lawson, William Thornton. Essay on literature of the Mexican War. New York (Columbia College), 1882. A 21-page pamphlet written as a senior essay at Columbia. Interesting appraisals of a half-dozen works then standard.
266. Smith, Justin Harvey. "Sources for a history of the Mexican War, 1846–1848," Mil. Hist. and Econ., I (1916), 18–32.
267. Trask, David F., Michael C. Meyer, and Roger R. Trask (comps. and editors). A bibliography of United States-Latin American relations since 1810: a selected list of eleven thousand published references. Lincoln (Neb. U.), 1968. An excellent and useful work.
268. Yale University Library. "The Mexican War, 1846–1848: a collection of contemporary materials presented to the Yale University Library by Frederick W. Beinecke," compiled by Jerry Patterson, Yale Univ. Lib. Gaz., XXXIV (1960), 94–123. A badly misinformed survey of important materials.
269. Zorilla, Luis G. Historia de las relaciones entre Mexico y los Estados Unidos de America, 1800–1858. 2 vols. Mexico (Editorial Porrua), 1965. The best Mexican work on the subject of U.S.-

Mexican diplomacy and among the best in both languages. Appears to be objective and straightforward without the whining jingoism of so many Mexican works. For scope and depth of research it compares with Nos. 24, 27, 407, 413, 421. For utilization of Mexican materials it is unequalled. Zorilla also presents an extensive and useful bibliography.

BENTON, T. H.

270. Benton, Thomas Hart. Thirty years' view; or a history of the working of the American government for thirty years, from 1820 to 1850. 2 vols. New York (Appleton), 1854–56. Material directly relating to the Mexican War is in vol. 2, pp. 639–736.
271. Chambers, William N. Old bullion Benton: senator from the new West. Boston (Little, Brown), 1956.
272. Roosevelt, Theodore. Thomas Hart Benton. New York (Houghton, Mifflin), 1914.

BOUNDARY SURVEY

273. Bartlett, John Russell. Personal narrative of exploations and incidents in Texas, New Mexico, California, Sonora, and Chihuahua, connected with the United States and Mexican boundary commission, during the years 1850, '51, '52, and '53. New York (Appleton), 1854. A recent reprint with an introduction by Professor Odie B. Faulk was issued by the Rio Grande Press. This work is basic to the history of the boundary survey and is included here as something of a classic. No other works on this subject, except Faulk's *Too Far North . . . Too Far South,* which has an extensive bibliography, are included here.
274. Faulk, Odie B. Too far north . . . too far south. Los Angeles (Westernlore), 1968. The only definitive study of the boundary dispute following the Treaty of Guadalupe Hidalgo.

BRACKENRIDGE, H. M.

275. Brackenridge, Henry Marie. Mexican letters written during the progress of the late war between the United States and Mexico. Washington (Waters), 1850.

276. Cleven, N. Andrew N. "Henry Marie Brackenridge, diplomat," Penn. Hist., V (1938), 213–22.

BRAZITO, BATTLE OF

SEE NOS. 146, 218, 227.

BUCHANAN, JAMES

277. Bemis, Samuel Flagg (editor). The American secretaries of state and their diplomacy. Vol. V. New York (Knopf), 1928. This volume covers the Mexican War period; the section on Buchanan was written by St. George Leakin Sioussat.
278. Buchanan, James. Works. . . . Ed. by John Bassett Moore. 12 vols. New York (Antiquarian), 1960. Vol. 6 contains speeches, state papers, and letters relating to the Mexican War.
279. Curtis, George Ticknor. Life of James Buchanan. 2 vols. New York (Harper), 1883. Not as useful for Mexican War as No. 277.

BUENA VISTA, BATTLE OF

280. Benham, Henry Washington. Recollections of Mexico and the Battle of Buena Vista. . . . Boston, 1871.
281. Carleton, James Henry. The Battle of Buena Vista, with operations of the "Army of Occupation" for one month. New York (Harper), 1848. A minute and detailed description, probably the best, of the battle. Carleton was an intelligent observer, commanded a company of dragoons at the encounter, and collected other eye-witness accounts. An appendix contains extracts from a number of letters and reports, both Mexican and American, together with tables of wounded, etc. Carleton remained in the army and later had a distinguished career in the West.
282. Wellman, James Ripley (editor). Decisive battles of America. New York (Harpers), 1909. Includes "The rupture with Mexico, 1843–1846," by George P. Garrison; "The Battle of Buena Vista, 1847," by John Bonner; and "Scott's conquest of Mexico, 1847," by John Bonner.
SEE ALSO NOS. 158, 173, 176, 182, 194.

BUTLER, ANTHONY

283. Mayo, Bernard. "Apostle of Manifest Destiny (Anthony Butler)," Amer. Merc., XVIII (1929), 420–26.
284. Stenberg, Richard R. "Jackson, Anthony Butler and Texas," Southwestern Soc. Sci. Qrtly., XIII (1932), 264–86. Jackson is the imperialist villain in this piece.

CALIFORNIA

285. Barker, Eugene Campbell. "California as the cause of the Mexican War," Texas Review (now Southwest Rev.), II (1917), 213–21.
286. Bigelow, John. Memoir of the life and public services of John C. Fremont. New York (Derby), 1856.
287. Bigler, Henry William. Chronicle of the West; the conquest of California, discovery of gold, and Mormon settlement, as reflected in Henry Bigler's diaries. By Erwin G. Gudde. Berkeley (UC), 1962. Strong on the Mormon battalion.
288. Bruce, H. Addington. The romance of American expansion. New York (Moffat, Yard), 1909. Includes conquest of California.
289. Bryant, Edwin. What I saw in California. New York, 1848. Reprinted Palo Alto (Osborne), 1967.
290. California Historical Society. "Documentary," Cal. Hist. Soc. Qrtly., II (1924), 350–62; III (1924), 84–88, 178–90, 270–89. Documents relating to the conquest of California.
291. ———. "The Fremont episode," Cal. Hist. Soc. Qrtly., IV (1925), 81–87, 374–91; V (1926), 184–95, 296–310; VI (1927), 77–90, 181–91, 265–80, 364–74; VII (1928), 79–85. Letters and documents relating to Fremont in 1846.
292. Colton, Walter. Three years in California. New York (Barnes), 1850. The author was made military alcalde of Monterey by Stockton and records observations of California life, 1846–49.
293. Cooke, Philip St. George. The conquest of New Mexico and California: an historical and personal narrative. New York (Putnam), 1878. Reprinted Oakland (Biobooks), 1942.
294. Cutts, James Madison. Conquest of California and New Mexico. Philadelphia (Carey and Hart), 1847. Reprinted Albuquerque (Horn & Wallace), 1965.

295. Ellison, William Henry. "San Juan to Cahuenga: the experiences of Fremont's battalion," Pac. Hist. Rev., XXVII (1958), 245–61.

296. Escobar, Augustín. "The Gabilan Peak campaign of 1846," ed. by Richard H. Dillon, Hist. Soc. S. Cal. Qrtly., XXXV (1953), 11–18. Reminiscences written in 1877 concerning Fremont's activities near Monterey, Cal.

297. Fremont, John Charles. Geographical memoir upon upper California. . . . Washington (Wendell & Van Benthuysen), 1848. An 1849 edition (Philadelphia, McCarty) contains extensive material on Oregon.

298. Giffen, Guy A. California expedition; Stevenson's regiment of First New York Volunteers. Oakland (Biobooks), 1951. Story of the landing of troops at Monterey.

299. Graebner, Norman A. Empire on the Pacific: a study in American continental expansion. New York (Ronald), 1955. Graebner's dissertation at Chicago (1949) was on the background and formation of the Treaty of Guadalupe Hidalgo. He appears to have become convinced that the heterogeneity of the United States could be anthropomorphized into a unified personality during the 1840's, bent upon territorial rapine. Although this study is thoroughly researched and well documented, primarily from political materials, the choice of words and selection of details provide a bias. For example, American settlers migrating under Mexico's open immigration policies of 1824 and 1825 are described as "infiltering" (implying of course some kind of conspiratorial purpose), and Graebner studiously ignores Mexico's generous land policy which was basic to the movement. The book is curiously assembled from articles published by Graebner in 1951, 1952, and 1953, many paragraphs being used verbatim or nearly so, although not in the same juxtaposition as in the articles. The articles received much praise, as did the book, and apparently none of the reviewers detected the patchwork literary approach which was ambiguously glossed over in the preface.

300. Griffin, John S. A doctor comes to California: the diary of John S. Griffin, assistant surgeon with Kearny's dragoons, 1846–47. San Francisco (Cal. Hist. Soc.), 1943.

301. Guinn, J. M. (editor). "Commodore Stockton's report," S. Cal. Hist. Soc. Pbl., X (1916), 116–23.

302. Hawgood, John A. (editor). First and last consul: Thomas Oliver Larkin and the Americanization of California; a selection of letters. San Marino (Hunt. Lib.), 1962.

303. Hittell, John Shertzer. A history of the city of San Francisco and incidentally of the state of California. San Francisco (Bancroft), 1878. Contains opinions on the conquest of California.

304. Hussey, John Adam. "The New Mexico-California caravan of 1847–1848," N. Mex. Hist. Rev., XVIII (1943), 1–16.

305. Jones, William Carey. "The first phase of the conquest of California," Cal. Hist. Soc. Papers, I (1887), 61–94.

306. Kearny, Thomas. "The Mexican War and the conquest of California: Stockton or Kearny conqueror and first governor?" Cal. Hist. Qrtly., VIII (1929), 251–61.

307. Kelsey, Rayner W. The United States consulate in California. Berkeley (UC), 1910. Has been superseded by later work on Larkin (see next entry).

308. [Larkin, Thomas Oliver]. The Larkin papers: personal, business, and official correspondence of Thomas Oliver Larkin, merchant and U.S. Consul in California. Ed. by George Peter Hammond. 10 vols. Berkeley (UC), 1951–64. Vols. 4 and 5 are pertinent to the Mexican War.

309. Marti, Werner H. Messenger of destiny: the California adventures, 1846–1847, of Archibald H. Gillespie, U.S. Marine Corps. San Francisco (Howell), 1960. Written as a Ph.D. thesis at UCLA, the book deals with Gillespie's role as a secret agent of Polk.

310. McClellan, Edwin North. "The conquest of California," Marine Corps Gaz., VIII (1922), 177–211.

311. McWhorter, George Cumming. Incident in the war of the United States with Mexico, illustrating the services of William Maxwell Wood, surgeon, U.S. Navy, in effecting the acquisition of California. New York (Sherwood), 1872.

312. Meyers, William H. Naval sketches of the war in California, reproducing 28 drawings made in 1846–47. . . . Text by Dudley W. Knox; introduction by Franklin D. Roosevelt. New York (Random House), 1939. One thousand copies San Francisco (Grabhorn), 1939. Roosevelt acquired the original sketchbook for his private collection of naval drawings. The late president incidentally took the position here that fear of European intervention in both Texas and California, and, therefore, implementation of the Monroe Doctrine led to the U.S. position in 1846. "The war between the United States and Mexico came in an era when it was the fashion for strong European powers to build up empires by hoisting their flags over weakly held territories in all quarters of the globe. Only a generation previously the Monroe

Doctrine had been set forth with a view to preventing such encroachments within the Western Hemisphere. Yet rumor, suspicion and fear continued to play upon the American imagination while covetous statesmen in Europe did not cease to scheme for the control of more lands on the continents across the Atlantic."

313. Neeser, Robert Wilden. "The navy's part in the acquisition of California, 1846–1848," U.S. Naval Inst. Proc., XXXIV (1908), 267–76. Expresses the fairly common view of that time that California would have been seized by Great Britain or some other power if the United States had not taken it, because the Mexican government there was a farce.

314. ———. Statistical and chronological history of the United States Navy. New York (Macmillan), 1909.

315. Palomares, José Francisco. Memoirs of José Francisco Palomares. Trans. by Thomas W. Temple. Los Angeles (Dawson), 1955. Actions against Americans in California.

316. Parker, Robert J. "Secret affairs of the Mexican war: Larkin's California mission," Hist. Soc. of S. Cal. Qrtly., XX (1938), 22–24.

317. Porter, Valentine Mott. "General Stephen W. Kearny and the conquest of California, 1846–7," Ann. Pblc. Hist. Soc. of S. Cal., VIII (1911), 95–127.

318. Revere, Joseph Warren. A tour of duty in California. . . . New York (Francis), 1849. Reprinted Oakland (Biobooks), 1947. Revere was one of Stockton's lieutenants on naval duty in California.

319. Richman, Irving Berdine. California under Spain and Mexico, 1535–1847. Boston (Houghton Mifflin), 1911. Presumably based on original sources in Spanish and Mexican archives.

320. Sherman, Edwin A. The life of the late Rear Admiral John Drake Sloat of the United States Navy who took possession of California and raised the American flag at Monterrey. . . . Oakland (Carruth and Carruth), 1902.

321. Smith, Justin Harvey. "Polk and California," Mass. Hist. Soc. Proc., XXX (1917), 83–91. Presents evidence to refute the contention that Polk brought on the war in order to gain California.

322. Stenberg, Richard R. "Polk and Fremont, 1845–1846," Pac. Hist. Rev., VII (1938), 211–27. Polk and Fremont were "secret confederates in a filibustering interprise" against Mexico.

323. ———. "President Polk and California: additional documents," Pac. Hist. Rev., X (1941), 217–20.

324. Stockton, Robert F. "Report of Commodore Stockton of his opera-

tion on the coast of the Pacific," S. Cal. Hist. Soc. Pblc., XV (1932), 292–302. Taken from 30 Cong., 2 sess., H. Ex. Doc. 1, 1848.

325. Tays, George. "Fremont had no secret instructions," Pac. Hist. Rev., IX (1940), 157–71.

326. Underhill, Reuben Lukens. From cowhides to golden fleece: a narrative of California, 1832–1858. Palo Alto (Stanford), 1939. Based on correspondence then unpublished.

327. Wise, Henry Augustus. Los gringos; or an inside view of Mexico and California. . . . New York (Baker and Scribner), 1849. Wise, a naval officer, later wrote frequently under the pen name, Harry Gringo. This book is his reminiscences of two and a half years at sea, most of it on the Pacific coast during the Mexican War.

328. Zobell, Albert L., Jr. "The Mormon battalion in California, 1847," Improvement Era, LIV (1951), 242–49.

SEE ALSO NOS. 129, 252, 254, 255, 256, 257.

CARSON, KIT

329. Kearny, Thomas. "Kearny and 'Kit' Carson as interpreted by Stanley Vestal," N. Mex. Hist. Rev., V (1930), 1–16. Demolishes Vestal's interpretation of the animosity between Kearny and Carson.

330. Vestal, Stanley [pseud.]. Kit Carson, the happy warrior of the old West. Boston (Houghton Mifflin), 1928.

CASS, LEWIS

331. McLaughlin, Andrew Cunningham. Lewis Cass. Boston (Houghton Mifflin), 1919. Peripheral material.

CATHOLICISM AND ANTI-CATHOLICISM, INCLUDING CHURCH-STATE CONFLICT IN MEXICO

332. Abbot, Gorham Dummer. Mexico and the United States: their mutual relations and common interests. New York (Putnam),

1869. Has a definite anti-Catholic bias; written to support the Juarez rebellion; contains a few small chapters on the Paredes government of 1846.

333. Blied, Benjamin Joseph. "Catholic aspects of the Mexican War," Social Justice Rev., XL (1948), 367–71.

334. Bustamente, Carlos María de. Compaña sin gloria y guerra como la de los cacomixtles. . . . Mexico (Cumplido), 1847. Vituperative denunciation of the Mexican government's policies toward the Church during the war.

335. Cloud, William F. Church and State; or Mexican politics from Cortez to Díaz. Under X-rays. Kansas City (Peck and Clark), 1896. Anti-Catholic bias. Divided into two parts; second part treats Texas and the Mexican War. Lays entire blame for the war on Mexican belligerency.

336. Downey, Fairfax Davis. "Tragic story of the San Patricio battalion," Am. Heritage, VI (1955), 20–23.

337. McEniry, Sister Blanche Marie. American Catholics in the war with Mexico. Washington (Cath. Univ. of Am.), 1937. Primarily interesting for its objective analysis of the attitude toward Catholics in the army. Has a chapter on the San Patricio deserters.

338. Meehan, Thomas F. "Archbishop Hughes and Mexico," U.S. Cath. Hist. Rec., XIX (1929), 33–40. A note on Polk's suggestion that Hughes go to Mexico early in 1846 to attempt to disabuse the Mexican clergy of any idea that the U.S. had designs on Church property there.

339. ———. "Catholics in the war with Mexico," U.S. Cath. Hist. Rec., XII (1918), 39–65. Deals primarily with the San Patricio deserters and only incidentally with Catholic soldiers and chaplains in the war.

340. [Rosa, Luis de la]. Los reveses que ha sufrido el ejército en la lucha que la lealtad y el patriotismo sostienen. . . . Mexico, 1847. A 16-page explanation of why the government wanted the clergy to surrender some of its vast properties for war use.

341. Sweeny, William M. "The Irish soldier in the war with Mexico," Am. Irish Hist. Soc. Jour., XXVI (1927), 255–59.

342. "Was Bishop Hughes offered a peace mission to Mexico by President James K. Polk?" Am. Cath. Hist. Rec., XXII (1911), 202–5.

SEE ALSO NOS. 122, 126.

CAUSES AND ORIGINS OF THE WAR

343. Berry, Philip. A review of the Mexican War on Christian principles; and an essay on the means of preventing war. Columbia, S.C. (Johnston), 1849. Reprinted from the *Southern Presbyterian Review*. A surprising treatise denying the justice of the war on moralistic principles without reference to slavery or expansionism. Supports annexation of Texas; defends Texas's claim to Rio Grande on the south; says the western boundary could have been negotiated. States the U.S. had an obligation to defend the Rio Grande, but should have acted defensively and should not have declared war or crossed the river. ". . . When the enemy retired beyond the Rio Grande . . . after the battles of Palo Alto and Resaca de la Palma, the war might have been desisted from with greater honour to the United States. . . . It is hardly credible that Mexico would have attempted another invasion . . ."

344. Bosch Garcia, Carlos. "Antecedents historicos del principio de no intervención en torno a la guerra de 1847," Ciencias Politicos y Sociales, VIII (1962), 15–25.

345. ———. "Dos diplomaticos y una problema," Historia Mexicana, II (1952), 46–55.

346. ———. Historia de los relaciones entre Mexico y los Estados Unidos, 1819–1848. Mexico (Escuela Nacional), 1961.

347. Breve reseña historica de los principales acontecimientos ocurridos con motivo de la rebelión de la colonia de Tejas y guerra con los Estados Unidos de Norte America. Mexico (Editorial Orientaciones), 1941. Originally published in 1848.

348. Brooke, G. M., Jr. "The vest pocket war of Commodore Jones," Pac. Hist. Rev., XXXI (1962), 217–33.

349. Buenos Mexicanos, Los. O se hace la guerra de Tejas, o se pierde la nación. Mexico (Lara), 1845. A 7-page pamphlet vehemently crying for war with the United States because of the annexation of Texas.

350. Capen, Nahum. The republic of the United States of America: its duties to itself, and its responsible relations to other countries. Embracing also a review of the late war between the U.S. and Mexico. New York (Appleton), 1848. Definitely a polemic justification of the war, yet a carefully constructed one. Quotes numerous original documents and has an extensive appendix of original material. The view is that Mexico was wholly responsible for the war.

351. Causes and justice of the Mexican War containing ninety-five instances of wanton murder . . . by the Mexican authorities upon the persons and property of American citizens. Concord, N.H. (Patriot), [1846]. Signed "Mount Washington." Lists and describes 95 of the claims against Mexico filed with the secretary of state. Interesting as an example of contemporary New Englad literature violently antiabolitionist and prowar. Cites the claims as the cause of the war. "[The reader] will find that there has been much more to condemn in the forbearance of our government under these numerous and long continued injuries, insults and outrages, than in the course which it is now pursuing for redress."

352. Chase, Lucien B. History of the Polk administration. New York (Putnam), 1850. Eight of the twelve chapters deal with the Mexican War, and quite naturally support Polk's actions and decisions. The third chapter contains a most comprehensive discussion of the so-called Nueces-Rio Grande boundary controversy. The Texas issue is considered the principal background for war, and the attack upon Taylor as the principal cause. Only a brief mention is made of the claims and none of California as causes. The book is unusually well documented for a mid-nineteenth-century work, although the footnotes are a little difficult to trace. An extensive appendix contains the text of Scott's accusations of W. L. Marcy and Marcy's letter in defense. Chase was a Democrat and member of the House of Representatives during the war.

353. Dictamen de las comisiones unidas de relaciones y de guerra. Mexico, 1846. An 8-page report of the committee to draft the declaration of war for the Congreso Nacional. Recites the grievances of Mexico against the United States.

354. Esquenazi-Mayo, Roberto. "Historiografía de la guerra entre Mexico y los EE. UU., Duquesne Hispanic Rev., II (1962), 34–77. Not so much historiography as a review of the causes of the war, focusing on Polk and the American government.

355. Fuentes Díaz, Vincente. La intervención norteamericana en Mexico, 1847. Mexico (Nuevo Mundo), 1947.

356. Gallatin, Albert. Peace with Mexico. New York (Bartlett & Welford), 1847. The annexation of Texas was tantamount to a declaration of war on Mexico and the occupation of the left bank of the Rio Grande was unprovoked aggression. Peace with Mexico should be sought on the basis of the Nueces as the Texas boundary and the settlement of the claims by Mexico. No other indemnity or territory should be required.

357. Grant, Ulysses Simpson. Personal memoirs. 2 vols. New York (Webster), 1885–86. Other editions 1895,1909, 1917, and 1952 (ed. by E. B. Long). Grant referred to the Mexican War as the most disgraceful one the country had ever fought.

358. Hart, Albert Bushnell. The foundations of American foreign policy. New York (Macmillan), 1901. This venerable American historian was too poorly informed on the subject to risk such conclusions as the Mexican War was waged to extend slavery and Polk enunciated that a major goal of his administration would be the acquisition of California.

359. Howe, Robert H. How we robbed Mexico in 1848. [New York (Latin American News Assoc.), 1916.]

360. Hunt, Samuel Furman. "The Mexican War: causes and results," in Orations and historical addresses, Cincinnati (Clark), 1909, 161–79.

361. La verdad desnuda sobre la guerra de Tejas, ó sea contestación al folleto titulado: la guerra de Tejas sin mascára. Mexico (Papel Mexicano), 1845. A 45-page answer to La Guerra to Tejas Sin Máscara (No. 559) signed "Los Defensores de la integridad del territorio mexicano." It is worth noting that in this as well as in other contemporary Mexican publications not one word is said of any boundary conflict. All of Texas—to the Sabine— belonged to Mexico.

362. Ladd, Horatio Oliver. History of the war with Mexico. New York (Dodd, Mead), 1883. Three chapters on background generally editorializing on U.S. culpability and the expansion of slavery. "The potent cause and ruling motive of the war with Mexico was the purpose to extend human slavery into free territory." Undocumented and superficial treatment of the war itself.

363. Largent, Robert J. "Legal and constitutional aspects of President Polk's Mexican policy," Marshall Rev., I (1937), 3–12. Very critical of Polk's assumption that the territory between the Nueces and the Rio Grande belonged to the United States, but concludes that he "clearly and undeniably acted within his constitutional prerogatives."

364. Mayer, Brantz. History of the war between Mexico and the United States, with a preliminary view of its origin. New York (Putnam), 1848. This work, divided into Book First and Book Second (all published), deals with the origin of the war. "The very threshold of this history is embarrassed by the party controversies [in Mexico] to which I have alluded. The origin of the war was attributed by the president [Polk] and his adherents to

the wrong doings of Mexico. . . . That grievances existed in the conduct of Mexico against us during a long series of years cannot be denied; but it is equally true, that, between governments well administered and entirely reasonable on both sides, none of these provocations justified war." War with the United States over Texas was at the heart of Paredes coup and it was Paredes who commenced hostilities. To Mayer, the so-called Nueces boundary dispute was not involved; the issue was all of Texas. Mayer also seems to have understood the complexities of the Centralist-Federalist dichotomy in Mexico as well as the central fact that the revolution in Texas from 1835 to 1836 was a reaction against the Centralist abrogation of the Constitution of 1824. Mayer served as secretary of the legation in Mexico from 1841 to 1842. Three additional chapters of Book Third exist in manuscript form, a typed copy of which was made by Henry Wagner in 1914 from the original then owned by W. H. Lowdermilk.

365. ———. Mexico as it was and as it is. 3rd edition, rev. Philadelphia (Zieber), 1847. The first edition was New York (Winchester), 1844, but the third contains an additional hundred or so pages related to events immediately preceding the outbreak of hostilities. Mayer presents translations of a number of Paredes's proclamations as well as the text of Polk's message to Congress in December 1846, of which he states he reserves the privilege to examine later.

366. ———. Mexico, Aztec, Spanish, and republican. 2 vols in 1. Hartford (Drake), 1851. Book III of this work is primarily about the Mexican War. Mayer reiterates, perhaps a little more strongly, that Paredes's belligerent posture really brought on the war, although it was the annexation of Texas that underlay it. "The true origin of the Mexican War was not this march of Taylor and his troops from the Nueces to the Rio Grande . . . hostilities were the natural result after the exciting annoyances upon the part of the Mexican government which followed the union of Texas . . . the Mexicans themselves taking the initiative."

367. McDonald, Archie D. (editor). The Mexican War: crisis for American democracy. Lexington, Mass. (Heath), 1969. A slim volume of readings in the Problems in American Civilization series.

368. Merk, Frederick. The Monroe Doctrine and American expansionism, 1843–1849. New York (Knopf), 1966. Views the Mexican War in the framework of an expanded Monroe Doctrine. Has an excellent chapter on the so-called Nueces boundary contro-

versy. This work is especially important because it points up American fear of foreign intervention on the continent, especially British, and shows that the Manifest Destiny and expansionism of the forties was in part, and for many people, not that at all, but instead a defensive gesture to prevent European expansion.

369. "The Mexican War—its origin and conduct," U.S. Mag. and Dem. Rev., XX (April 1847), 291–99. Mexico's violation of the claims arbitration and her belligerent and hostile attitude was the cause of the war. The annexation of Texas could not justly be considered a cause of the war since Texas was independent and Mexico, at least tacitly, recognized this.

370. Owen, Charles Hunter. The justice of the Mexican War: a review of the causes and results of the war, with a view to distinguishing evidence from opinion and inference. New York (Putnam), 1908. Owen was an attorney who aimed "to vindicate the justice of the war" and "to acquit the United States . . . of the most serious, if not the only, charge ever laid against her honor . . ." by approaching the subject as a lawyer would brief a case. "I confess myself," he said, "to be in love with my conclusions." His conclusions, however, are difficult to ascertain, except for his criticism of Brady (No. 499) and other historians for espousing the theses of conspiracy of the slaveocracy and/or conspiracy of Polk and expansionists.

371. Paredes y Arrillaga, Mariano. Ultimas comunicaciones entre el gobierno mexicano y el envado estraordinario y ministro plenipotenciario de los Estados Unidos, sobre la cuestión de Tejas. . . . Mexico (Cumplido), 1846. Inflammatory public dismissal of Slidell with accusations against the United States. This 22-page pamphlet also contains copies of correspondence between Slidell and Castillo y Lanzas, the foreign minister.

372. ———. Manifiesto. . . . Mexico (Aguila), 1846. A 19-page pamphlet dated July 26, 1846, condemning the United States for attacking Mexico without warning or provocation and blaming the trouble on the United States cabinet.

373. Paz, Eduardo. La invación norte-americana en 1846. Mexico (Paz), 1889.

374. Peña y Peña, Manuel de la. Comunicacion circular . . . 1845 . . . para dirigirla a los gobiernos y asembleas departamentales, sobre la cuestion de paz or guerra. . . . Queretaro (Lara), 1848. This circular was written, and presumably printed, in December 1845 and was sent to the various state governments ostensibly asking

for advice on the question of negotiating with Slidell. Peña y Peña, then foreign minister for the Herrera government, was actually fighting a last ditch stand for support for the government which was accused by the radical Paredes of offering to alienate the Mexican claim to Texas. Peña y Peña recognizes in this pamphlet that refusal to see Slidell will bring on war, and his question is: peace or war? Mexico is justified, he says, in going to war to defend her honor, but the cost will be high and Texas is not worth it. "War with the United States in order to dislodge the occupation of Texas is an abyss without bottom which will devour an indefinite series of generations and treasure which the imagination is unable to calculate and in the end will submerge the republic with all its hopes for the future." It was obviously reprinted in 1848 to display the author's patriotism and foresight. A 2-page introduction is affixed to the 1848 reprint. Reprinted in Peña y Reyes (1930) [see No. 647], pp. 3–25, as Circular del ministro de relaciones esteriores. . . .

375. Porter, Charles T. Review of the Mexican War. . . . Auburn, N.Y. (Alden & Parsons), 1849. The cause of the war was not slavery or slavery expansion or even the annexation of Texas which was defensible, but territorial greed of the people of the United States who must take all the blame for the war. "It was sustained alike by the north and the south. The spirit which impelled it was confined to no section of the country. The north rivalled the south in greediness after the possessions of another, and in causeless vindictiveness toward a weak and distracted nation." The influence of the war was to introduce crime and vice into American society, to awaken a spirit of conquest, and to lower the standard of public morality. Taylor's move from the Nueces to the Rio Grande was an act of war.

376. Price, Glenn W. Origins of the war with Mexico: the Polk-Stockton intrigue. Austin (UT), 1967. Although two recent and excellent studies (Nos. 368, 669) discharge Polk of responsibility in preannexation schemes in Texas, Price finds just the opposite about the "unscrupulous" president. Stockton, Price characterizes as "narrow, chauvinistic." Both men are called aggressive expansionists and this term must appear at least a hundred times in the book; it is the key to the bias which is supported not so much by facts as by scores of value-laden words interpreting the facts. The kernel of Price's "conspiracy" is a report in 1859 by the embittered and egotistical Anson Jones—one long known to historians of Texas and the southwest. Likewise, most of the

documents used to "prove" the existence of conspiracy have long been in print. In fact, Price adds little, if anything, to the charges leveled by Stenberg (Nos. 381, 382) and fails to cite Stenberg's publication of the Stockton-Bancroft letters. By selection, omission, and adjectival fulmination, Price finds the pair of villains guilty as charged.

377. Reid, Whitlow. The Monroe Doctrine, the Polk doctrine, and the doctrine of anarchism. New York (De Vinne), 1903.·

378. Rippy, James Fred. The United States and Mexico. Rev. ed. New York (Crofts), 1931. First chapter is a well-thought-out discussion of the causes of the war. Texans were entirely innocent of conspiracy or ulterior motives of any kind, having migrated for cheap land. Annexation brought on Mexican attack on Taylor. War would probably have been averted if it had not been for this attack, for Polk would not have resorted to war to collect the claims. "Once entered upon, the war necessarily became one of conquest . . . [the] claims could be adjusted only by the acquisition of territory for . . . Mexico was bankrupt . . . and had nothing else with which to meet these obligations."

379. Ruiz, Ramón Eduardo (editor). The Mexican War—was it Manifest Destiny? New York (Holt, Rinehart and Winston), 1963. In American Problem series. Readings on the question of the cause of the war. Ruiz's introduction is judicious and scholarly. His selections, however, tend to lead the student to view the United States as the aggressor.

380. Scott, L. M. "Oregon, Texas and California, 1846," Ore. Hist. Qrtly., XXXVI (1935), 154–62.

381. Stenberg, Richard R. "The failure of Polk's Mexican War intrigue of 1845," Pac. Hist. Rev., IV (1935), 39–68. This and the following article (see also Nos. 68, 284, 322, 323, 747) came out of Stenberg's doctoral dissertation, American Imperialism in the Southwest, 1800–1837 (University of Texas, 1932). This is the so-called Polk-Stockton conspiracy which rests on an incidental account in Anson Jones's memoirs and a letter by Charles Elliot. These sources have long been known, and reliable historians have always dismissed them as unimportant. Stenberg's effort to find villany precedes Price's (No. 376) by nearly forty years.

382. ———. "Intrigue for annexation," Southwest Rev., XXV (1939), 58–69. Letters from Stockton to Secretary of the Navy Bancroft while Stockton was stationed on the Texas coast in 1845. Price cites these letters when trying to weave his own web of conspiracy but fails to credit Stenberg with collecting and publishing them.

383. Varios Mexicanos. Consideraciones sobre la situación política y social de la República mexicana, en el año 1847. . . . Mexico
(Valdes y Redondas), 1848. May have been written by Mariano
Otero. Describes Mexico at the depths of the war and attempts
to explain American successes. Mexico as a whole seemed to sit
as a disinterested spectator instead of taking part in the struggle.
Social affliction had left the country hopelessly divided, and in
Mexico "that which is called national spirit does not nor has
been able to exist, for there is no nation."

384. Ware, Moses W. "A hidden cause of the Mexican war," Hist.
Teach. Mag., V (1914), 74–77. The extensive indebtedness of the
Republic of Texas to citizens of the United States, both north
and south, was a potent force in bringing on the war.

385. ———. "Land speculation and the Mexican war," Hist. Outlook,
XIX (1928), 317–23.

SEE ALSO NOS. 5, 18, 22, 24, 27, 32, 41, 49, 50, 53, 55, 63, 137, 138, 199,
201, 282.

CHAPULTEPEC, BATTLE OF

SEE NOS. 228, 234, 247.

CHURUBUSCO, BATTLE OF

SEE NOS. 163, 185.

CLAIMS QUESTION

386. Alamán, Lucas. Liquidacion general de la deuda exterior de la
República Mexicana. Mexico (Cumplido), 1845.

387. Bolles, Albert Sidney. Financial history of the United States,
1789–1860. New York (Appleton), 1894. Deals briefly with the
claims question. A better treatment is in No. 391.

388. Conquest of Mexico! An appeal to the citizens of the United
States on the justice and expediency of the conquest of Mexico.
. . . Boston (Jordan & Wiley), 1846. Defends the revolution of
Texas against Mexico, its annexation to the U.S., the Rio
Grande boundary, and finds the principal cause for the war in

the claims question. Concludes with a forthright statement of what later was called Manifest Destiny: "The conquest and right government of Mexico would be sanctioned by high considerations of *philanthropy*, as well as patriotism. Who can question whether the extension of our political institutions, our freedom of religion, our educational plans, and our industrial enterprise over that country, would be a blessing to its depressed people?"

389. Coxe, Richard Smith. Review of the relations between the United States and Mexico, and of the claims of citizens of the United States against Mexico. Washington (Ritchie & Heiss), 1845. Another printing New York (Wilson), 1846. Originally issued in installments in 1844 and 1845 in various newspapers. Finds the cause of the Texas Revolution to be the abrogation of the Mexican Constitution of 1824 and of the Mexican War to be the claims issue together with Mexico's belligerent posturing.

390. Dewey, Davis Rich. Financial history of the United States. New York (Longman's, Green), 1903.

391. Kohl, Clayton Charles. Claims as a cause of the Mexican War. New York (NYU), 1914. A thorough and complete discussion of the claims issue in which Kohl clearly demonstrates the recalcitrance of Mexican diplomats, the exasperation of the Americans, and the fact that, in mid-nineteenth-century thinking, the claims and the Mexican failure to negotiate were adequate cause for war. His brief conclusion, however, contradicts his work indirectly by stating that the claims were not a significant cause.

392. Murphy, Tomás. Memoria sobre la deuda esterior de a república Mexicana desde su creacion hasta fines de 1847. Paris (Blondeau), 1848.

393. Sumpter, Arthur. The lives of General Zachary Taylor and General Winfield Scott. . . . New York (Phelps), 1848. With an outline history of Mexico and a brief history of the Mexican War. The claims, and Mexican hostility over them, caused the war.

394. Thompson, Waddy. Recollections of Mexico. New York (Wiley and Putnam), 1846. Valuable to the Mexican War as background and for a chapter on the difficulty of negotiations over the claims.

SEE ALSO NOS. 17, 351.

CLAY, CASSIUS

395. Clay, Cassius Marcellus. The life of Cassius Marcellus Clay. Cincinnati (Brennan), 1886.

CONNER, DAVID

396. Conner, Philip Syng Physick. The castle of San Juan Ulloa. Philadelphia, 1897. Reprinted from United Service [Mag.], February 1897. Commodore Conner's son defends his father's insistence upon a combined land and sea operation against Ulloa and Vera Cruz.

397. ————. The Home squadron under Commodore Conner in the war with Mexico. . . . Philadelphia, 1896. Written from his father's papers; includes in appendix William G. Temple, "Memoir of the landing of the United States troops at Vera Cruz in 1847."

COOKE, PHILIP ST. GEORGE

398. Ampudia, Pedro de. El ciudadano general Pedro de Ampudia ante el tribunal respetable de la opinion pública, por los primeros sucesos ocurridos en la guerra á que nos provaca, decreta y sosiene el gobierno de los Estados-Unidos de America. San Luis Potosi (Gobierno en palacio, á cargo de Ventura Carrillo), 1846. Pamphlet explaining loss of battles of Palo Alto and Resaca de la Palma.

399. Bieber, Ralph (editor). The southwest historical series. . . . 12 vols. Glendale (Clark), 1931–45. The following volumes have material related to the war. (Vol. 1) Webb, James Josiah. Adventures in the Santa Fe trade, 1844–1847. (Vol. 3) Gibson, George Rutledge. Journal of a soldier under Kearny and Doniphan, 1846–1847. (Vol. 4) Marching with the Army of the West, 1846–1848. Contents: Abraham Robinson Johnston, Journal of 1846; Marcellus Ball Edwards, Journal of 1846–1847; Philip Gooch Ferguson, Diaries, 1847–1848; Muster roll of Co. D, First Regiment of Missouri Mounted Volunteers, June 1846. (Vol. 5) Exploring southwestern trails. Contains Philip St. George Cooke, Journal of the march of the Mormon battalion.

400. Cooke, Philip St. George. Report of Lieut. Col. P. St. George
Cooke of his march from Santa Fe, New Mexico, to San Diego,
Upper California. In Notes of a military reconnaissance. . . .
U.S. 30th Cong., 1st sess., H. Ex. Doc. 41. An edited version of
this report on the march of the Mormon battalion appears
under the same title, ed. by Hamilton Garder, in Utah Hist.
Qrtly., XXII (1954), 15–40.
SEE ALSO NOS. 76, 293.

CONTRERAS, BATTLE OF

SEE NO. 230.

DIPLOMATIC RELATIONS

401. Bailey, Thomas A. A diplomatic history of the American people.
7th ed. New York (Appleton-Century-Crofts), 1964. Leans
slightly toward Polk as provacateur and California as the basic
cause of the war.
402. Barker, Eugene Campbell. Mexico and Texas, 1821–1835. Dallas
(Turner), 1928. Of Barker's many works, this and No. 285 have
the most relevancy to the Mexican War. Barker has some sharp
and sarcastic comments about apologists for the United States
and detractors of Polk's actions, but withal he seemed to believe
in the inevitability of American westward expansion.
403. Bemis, Samuel Flagg. A diplomatic history of the United States:
an historical interpretation. New York (Harcourt, Brace), 1943.
Fifth edition. New York (Holt, Rinehart), 1965.
404. ———. The Latin American policy of the United States. New
York (Harcourt, Brace), 1943. Presents a strong defense of Polk's
actions.
405. Bosch Garcia, Carlos. Material para la historia diplomática de
Mexico. Mexico (Escuela Nacional), 1957. Official Mexican documents and some Spanish translations of U.S. documents. Basis
of No. 346.
406. Bourne, Edward Gaylord. "The United States and Mexico,
1847–1848," AHR, V (1900), 491–502.
407. Callahan, James Morton. American foreign policy in Mexican re-

lations. New York (Macmillan), 1932. Excellent factual reporting on the basis of documents in the state department.

408. Carreño, Alberto María. La diplomacia extraordinaria entre Mexico y Estados Unidos, 1789–1947. 3 vols. Mexico (Editorial Jus),
1951.

409. ———. Mexico y los Estados Unidos de America. Mexico (Victoria), 1922.

410. Duflot de Mofras, Eugene. Expéditions des Espagnols et des
Américains au Mexique en 1829 et en 1847. Paris (Panckouke),
1862. A 39-page pamphlet defending the Maximilian regime.

411. Hicks, Robert S. "Diplomatic relations with Mexico during the
administration of James K. Polk," S. Cal. Hist. Soc. Pblc., XII
(1922), 5–17.

412. Koebel, W. H. "The United States and Mexico in the forties,"
New World, III (1920), 231–35. An extensive review of Smith's
War with Mexico (No. 27).

413. Manning, William R. Diplomatic correspondence of the United
States: inter-American affairs, 1831–1860. Mexico. Vols. 8 and 9.
Washington (Carnegie endowment), 1932–39.

414. ———. Early diplomatic relations between the United States and
Mexico. Baltimore (Johns Hopkins), 1916. By all odds one of
the few thoroughly researched works on U.S.-Mexican relations.
Ends, however, in 1829 and is pertinent to the Mexican War
only for background.

415. Mares, José Fuentes. Poinsett: historia de una gran intriga. Mexico (Editorial Jus), 1951. A slanted view of early diplomatic intercourse in Mexico.

416. Memoria de la primera secretaría de estado y del despacho de relaciones interiores y exteriores . . . ; memoria de ministerio de
relaciones exteriores; memoria de la secretaria de relaciones ex-
teriorers; etc. Mexico, 1822——. An elusive series of annual reports of the Mexican foreign office under various names. Justin
Smith cites a Colección de memorias which he said contained
the published reports of the departments of Relaciones Exteriores (y Interiores), Guerra y Marina, Hacienda, Justicia, etc., in
9 vols. 1822–46.

417. Nichols, RoyFranklin. The stakes of power, 1845–1877. New
York (Hill and Wang), 1961.

418. "A proposed league of nations in 1845," N.Y. Hist. Soc. Bltn., III
(1919), 8–11. A petition calling for a world court, circulated in
1845, possibly for the purpose of preventing the crisis in Mexico or with England over Oregon.

419. Reeves, Jesse S. American diplomacy under Tyler and Polk. Baltimore (Johns Hopkins), 1907. The Mexican War was not a result of the annexation of Texas; it was waged for the purpose of conquest because of Polk's designs on California. Virtually no consideration is given the claims or slavery as causes.

420. Rippy, James Fred. "Britain's role in the early relations of the United States and Mexico," HAHR, VII (1927), 2–24.

421. Rives, George Lockhart. "Mexican diplomacy on the eve of the war with the United States," AHR, XVIII (1913), 275–94. An excellent study, based largely on manuscripts in Mexico, of the efforts of Mexican diplomats to enlist European aid in the cause against Texas and the United States.

422. Sears, Louis Martin. John Slidell, 1793?–1871. Durham (Duke), 1925.

423. ———. "Slidell and Buchanan," AHR, XXVII (1922), 709–30.

424. ———. "Slidell's mission to Mexico," So. Atlan. Qrtly., XII (1913), 12–26.

425. Smith, Ralph A. "Contrabando en la guerra con Estados Unidos," Historia Mexicana, II (1962), 361–81. An excellent study of a little known but important aspect of U.S.-Mexican relations during this period.

426. Thompson, Henry Tazewell. Waddy Thompson, Jr. . . . Columbia, S.C., 1929. A 35-page pamphlet; a major biography of Thompson is needed.

427. Van Alstyne, Richard W. The rising American empire. Oxford (Blackwell), 1960.

428. Velasco Gil, Carlos Mario. Nuestro buenos vecinos. Mexico (Ediciones Paralelo), 1957. A Mexican view of U.S.-Mexican relations.

429. Williams, Mary Wilhelmine. "Secessionist diplomacy of Yucatan," HAHR, IX (1929), 132–43.

SEE ALSO NOS. 15, 24, 269, 274, 275, 276, 277, 278, 283, 332, 345, 346, 348, 358, 371, 374, 378, 394.

DONIPHAN'S EXPEDITION

430. Allen, D. C. "Builders of the great American west; remarkable experiences of Alexander Doniphan," Jour. Am. Hist., IV (1910), 511–24.

431. Conquest of Santa Fe and subjugation of New Mexico . . . by a

captain of volunteers. Philadelphia (Packer), 1847. Includes a brief history of Doniphan's Chihuahua campaign.

432. Edwards, Frank S. A campaign in New Mexico with Colonel Doniphan. Philadelphia (Carey & Hart), 1847.

433. Gist, William H. H. "Letters of William H. H. Gist, a volunteer from Weston, Missouri, in the war with Mexico," ed. by Vivian K. McLarty, Mo. Hist. Rev., XLVIII (1954), 237–48.

434. Hughes, John Taylor. Doniphan's expedition. Cincinnati (James), 1848. Many editions. See No. 262 for bibliographic discussion. One of the best editions was edited by William Elsey Connelley, as *Doniphan's Expedition and the Conquest of California*, Topeka, 1907, which contains also the diary of John T. Hughes.

435. Kearful, Jerome. "Doniphan's artillery," Field Artillery Jour., XL (1950), 70–71.

436. Magoffin, Susan Shelby. Down the Santa Fe trail and into Mexico; the diary of Susan Shelby Magoffin, 1846–1847. Ed. by Stella M. Drumm. New Haven (Yale), 1926. This is one of the most delightful of all Southwestern reminiscences—a sensitive young bride's observations of New Mexico and Chihuahua at the time of the American occupation.

437. Porter, Valentine Mott. A history of Battery "A" of St. Louis: with an account of the early artillery companies from which it is descended. St. Louis (Missouri Hist. Soc. Collections), 1905. This battery was with Doniphan in New Mexico and Chihuahua.

438. Powell, E. Alexander. The road to glory. New York (Scribner's), 1915. Section on Doniphan's expedition.

439. Puckett, Fidelia Miller. "Ramón Ortiz (1813–1896): priest and patriot," ed. by Angelico Chavez, N. Mex. Hist. Rev., XXV (1950), 265–95. Particular reference to the conduct of Ortiz, who was a priest at El Paso and Juarez, during Doniphan's expedition.

440. Richardson, William H. Journal of William H. Richardson, a private soldier in Col. Doniphan's command. Baltimore (Robinson), 1847. Second and third editions in 1847 and 1848 and reprinted, with an introduction by William B. McGroarty, in Mo. Hist. Rev., XXII (1928), 193–236, 331–60, 511–42. Referred to by Doniphan himself as one of the best accounts of the expedition.

441. Robinson, Jacob S. A journal of the Santa Fe expedition under Colonel Doniphan. Portsmouth, N.H. (Journal), 1848. Reprinted several times, including Tarrytown, N.Y., 1927, and Princeton, 1932.

442. Smith, Heman C. "The hero of Sacremento, Alexander W. Doniphan," Jour. Hist., IV (1911), 338–56.

443. Smith, Ralph A. "The 'King of New Mexico' and the Doniphan expedition," N. Mex. Hist. Rev., XXXVIII (1963), 29–55.

444. Wislizenus, Adolphus. Memoir of a tour to north Mexico. Washington (Tippin and Streeper), 1848. Also published as S.M. Doc., 30 Cong., 1 sess. His tour with Doniphan.

SEE ALSO NOS. 81, 262, 399.

DUPONT, SAMUEL F.

445. DuPont, Samuel Francis. Official dispatches and letters of Rear Admiral DuPont. Wilmington (Ferris), 1883.

446. The war with Mexico: the cruise of the U.S. ship Cyane during the years 1845–8. Naval Inst. Proc., VIII (1882), 419–37. Taken from the papers of the ship's captain, Rear Admiral S. F. DuPont.

ENGLISH ACCOUNTS

447. Ballentine, George. The Mexican War, by an English soldier. New York (Townsend), 1860.

448 Ruxton, George Frederick Augustus. Adventures in Mexico from Vera Cruz to Chihuahua in the days of the Mexican War. Ed. by Horace Kephart. New York (Outing), 1915. Taken from the ever-popular Adventures in Mexico and the Rocky Mountains. . . . First published London (Murray), 1847.

449. Smith, Justin Harvey. "Great Britain and our war of 1846–1848." Mass. Hist. Soc. Proc., XLVII (1914), 451–62.

450. Whitworth, Robert. "From the Mississippi to the Pacific: an Englishman in the Mormon battalion," ed. by David B. Gracy, II, and Helen J. H. Rugeley. Ariz. and the West, VII (1965), 127–60.

451. Wiltse, Ernest A. "The British vice consul in California and the events of 1846," Cal. Hist. Soc. Qrtly., X (1931), 99–128. James Alexander Forbes, the vice consul, may have intended to request his government's intervention in California.

SEE ALSO NOS. 72, 137, 199, 420.

FARRAGUT, D. G.

452. Farragut, Loyall. The life of David G. Farragut. New York (Appleton), 1879. Farragut succeeded Conner at Vera Cruz and received the surrender of the city. See No. 397 for a slightly different account.
453. Mahan, Alfred Thayer. Admiral Farragut. New York (Appleton), 1892. An excellent biography but of little Mexican War interest since Farragut's role was insignificant.

FLORIDA IN THE WAR

454. Davis, T. Frederick. "Florida's part in the war with Mexico," Fla. Hist. Qrtly., XX (1942), 235–59.
455. [Proctor, Alfred N.]. "A Massachusetts mechanic in Florida and Mexico—1847," ed. by Arthur W. Thompson, Fla. Hist. Soc. Qrtly., XXXIII (1954), 130–41.

FREMONT, JOHN C.

456. Dellenbaugh, Frederick Samuel. Fremont and '49. New York (Putnam), 1914.
457. Duncan, Charles T. "Fremont in California: hero or montebank?" Neb. Hist., XXIX (1948), 33–54. Contrasts treatments of Nevins and DeVoto.
458. Fremont, John Charles. Memoirs of my life. . . . Chicago (Belford, Clarke), 1887.
459. Goodwin, Cardinal. John Charles Fremont (1813–1890): an explanation of his career. Palo Alto (Stanford) and London (Oxford), 1930. Deprecates slightly the role played by Fremont in the Bear Flag affair and the conquest of California.
460. Nevins, Allan. Fremont, pathmaker of the West. New York (Longman's, Green), 1939.
461. ———. Fremont, the West's greatest adventurer. New York (Harper), 1928.
462. Preuss, Charles. Exploring with Fremont. Norman (OU), 1958.
463. Upham, Charles Wentworth. Life, explorations and public services of John C. Fremont. Boston (Tickner and Fields), 1856.

464. Wiltse, Ernest A. The truth about Fremont: an inquiry. San Francisco (Nash), 1936. A defense of Fremont's conduct and purpose.

SEE ALSO NOS. 253, 286, 291, 295, 296, 297, 322, 325.

GEORGIA IN THE WAR

465. Kurtz, Wilbur G., Jr. "The First Regiment of Georgia Volunteers in the Mexican War," Geo. Hist. Qrtly., XXVII (1943), 301–23.

GRANT, ULYSSES S.

466. Garland, Hamlin. "Grant in the Mexican War," McClure's Mag., VIII (1897), 366–80.

467. [McPherson, John D.]. The evolution of the myth, as exemplified by Gen. Grant's history of the plot of President Polk and Secretary Marcy to sacrifice two American armies in the Mexican War of 1846–1848. By Senex. Washington (Morrison), 1890. Objects to the statement in Grant's *Personal Memoirs* (No. 357) that Polk and his administration intrigued against both Scott and Taylor because the generals were Whigs. Attempts to prove that any supply problems the armies may have had were not the result of petty political jealousy.

SEE ALSO NOS. 195, 357.

GREENHOW, ROBERT

468. Barbee, David Rankin. "Robert Greenhow," Wm. and Mary Qrtly., 2nd ser., XIII (1933), 182–83. Brief biographical sketch with announcement that his diary during the secret mission of 1839 has been given to William and Mary.

HERRERA, J. J.

469. Cotner, Thomas Ewing. The military and political career of José Joaquín de Herrera, 1792–1854. Austin (UT), 1949. A fine study, and the only one, of this central figure.

ILLINOIS IN THE WAR

470. Canady, Dayton. "Voice of the volunteer, 1847," Ill. St. Hist. Soc. Jour. (1951), 199–209.
471. East, Ernest Edward. "Santa Anna's wooden leg," Ill. Lib., XXXVI (1954), 163–70. It was seized by Illinois troops at Cerro Gordo and ultimately came into the possession of the Illinois State Library.
472. Elliott, Isaac Hughes. Illinois soldiers in the Mexican War. Springfield, 1882.
473. Englemann, Adolph. "The Second Illinois in the Mexican War," Jour. Ill. St. Hist. Soc., XXVI (1933), 357–452. Letters of Adolph Englemann during Taylor's campaign, originally written in German, and translated and edited by Otto B. Englemann.
474. Henderson, Alfred J. "A Morgan County volunteer in the Mexican War," Jour. Ill. St. Hist. Soc., XLI (1948), 383–401.
475. Norton, Lewis Adelbert. Life and adventures. . . . Oakland (Pacific), 1887. Norton served in an Illinois infantry regiment.

INDIANA IN THE WAR

476. Lane, Henry Smith. The Mexican War journal of Henry S. Lane," Ind. Mag. of Hist., LIII (1957), 383–434.
477. New, Harry S. "The importance of a single vote," Ind. Mag. Hist., XXXVI (1935), 104–8. The vote of a DeKalb County farmhand decided the election of a state legislator, who in turn decided the election of Hannegan as U.S. senator from Indiana, who in turn cast the decisive vote in a Senate caucus on the declaration of war.
478. Smith, Isaac. Reminiscences of a campaign in Mexico: an account of the operations of the Indiana brigade. . . . Indianapolis (Chapmans and Spahn), 1848.
SEE ALSO Nos. 71, 89, 92, 99, 158.

IOWA IN THE WAR

479. Upham, Cyril B. The Mexican War. Iowa City (I. St. Hist. Soc.), 1918. Pamphlet No. 12 in the series Iowa and War. There was only one company of Iowa volunteers in the war.

IRISH IN THE WAR

SEE NO. 341.

JACKSON, T. J.

480. Arnold, Thomas Jackson. Early life and letters of T. J. Jackson. New York (Revell), 1910. There are perhaps a score of biographies of Thomas Jonathon Jackson, most of which were written shortly after the Civil War; this work seems to be the best on his Mexican War experiences.
481. Cooke, John Esten. The life of Stonewall Jackson. New York (Richardson), 1863.
482. Dabney, Robert Lewis. Life and campaigns of Lieutenant General Thomas J. Jackson. New York (Blilock), 1866.

JOHNSTON, JOSEPH E.

483. Johnson, Bradley Tyler. A memoir of the life and public service of Joseph E. Johnston. Baltimore (Woodwards), 1891.

KEARNY, STEPHEN W.

484. Clarke, D. L. Stephen Watts Kearny, soldier of the West. Norman (OU), 1961.
485. Kearny, Stephen Watts. "Kearny letters," [ed. by Lansing B. Bloom], N. Mex. Hist. Rev., V (1930), 17–37, 216–17.
486. Kelly, George H. "Coming of the Kearny expedition," Ariz. Hist. Rev., I (1928), 33–49.
487. Ruhlen, George. "Kearny's route from the Rio Grande to the Gila River," N. Mex. Hist. Rev., XXXII (1957), 213–30.
488. Taylor, Mendell Lee. "The Western services of Stephen Watts Kearny, 1815–1848," N. Mex. Hist. Rev., XXI (1946), 169–84.
489. Vestal, Stanley [pseud.]. "Expedition for conquest," N. Mex. Mag., XVI (1938), 18–19, 41–42.

SEE ALSO NOS. 300, 306, 317, 329, 330, 399.

KEARNY, PHILIP

490. De Peyster, John Watts. Personal and military history of Philip Kearny, Major General of United States volunteers. New York (Bliss), 1869. Philip Kearny, a nephew of Stephen W. Kearny, fought with Scott. The book has two chapters on the Mexican War.

SEE ALSO No. 189.

KENDALL, GEORGE W.

491. Copeland, Fayette. Kendall of the Picaijune. Norman (OU), 1943. An excellent biography of this most remarkable man who accompanied both Taylor and Scott as one of the nation's first war correspondents and who himself published a book on the war.
492. Teja Zabre, Alfonso. "Historia y periodismo, el primer corresponsal de guerra en México," Investigaciones Históricas, I (1939), 399–403. Account of Kendall as war correspondent.

SEE ALSO No. 190.

KENTUCKY IN THE WAR

493. Cox, Leander Martin. "Mexican War journal of Leander M. Cox." ed. by Charles F. Hinds, Ky. St. Hist. Soc. Register, LV (1957), 29–52.
494. Crockett, John M. "Letter of John M. Crockett, 1846," Ky. Hist. Soc. Reg., LII (1954), 305–9. Dated September 20, 1846, from Camp Irvine (near Port Lavaca), Texas, describing the march of the Kentucky regiment to Texas.

SEE ALSO Nos. 135, 395.

LARKIN, THOMAS OLIVER

SEE Nos. 302, 307, 308, 316.

LEE, ROBERT E.

495. Freeman, Douglas Southall. R. E. Lee, a biography. 4 vols. New York (Scribner), 1934, 1935. First volume has detailed account of Lee's activities as an engineer in the Mexican War.

MANIFEST DESTINY OR EXPANSIONISM

496. Binkley, William C. The expansionist movement in Texas, 1836–1850. Berkeley (UC), 1925.

497. Bonsal, Stephen. Edward Fitzgerald Beale, a pioneer in the path of empire, 1822–1903. New York (Putnam), 1912.

498. Bourne, Edward Gaylord. "The proposed absorption of Mexico in 1847–1848." in Annual Report of the Am. Hist. Assoc. for 1899. Washington (GPO), 1900. An important work on the movement to annex all of Mexico.

499. Brady, Cyrus Townsend. Conquest of the Southwest. . . . New York (Appleton), 1905. Brady was a prolific novelist and journalist who saw conspiracy in every aspect of the Mexican War.

500. Cowan, John E. (comp.). Condensed history of the Mexican War and its glorious results. "By Hon. William McKay." New York ?, 1902? A 41-page pamphlet which includes reminiscences by Col. Daniel E. Hungerford and Col. Charles J. Murphy.

501. DeVoto, Bernard. The year of decision, 1846. Boston (Little, Brown), 1943. This flippantly written, poorly organized book has received wide praise from literary critics and historians alike. It deals primarily with matters in the West, blames Polk for the war, and credits a desire for California as the true cause of the war, with no discussion whatever of other factors. Perhaps DeVoto was unaware of them.

502. Fuller, John Douglas Pitts. The movement for the acquisition of all Mexico, 1846–1848. Baltimore (Johns Hopkins), 1936. In this, his Ph.D. dissertation, and in Nos. 503 and 663, Fuller demonstrates that proslavery forces as a unit were generally opposed to the acquisition of territory from Mexico.

503. ———. "The slavery question and the movement to acquire Mexico, 1846–1848," MVHR, XXI (1934), 31–48.

504. Garrison, George P. Westward expansion, 1841–1850. New York (Harper), 1906. Volume 17 in the American Nation series. The Mexican War receives three superficial chapters. So eminent a

historian as Garrison should have done a little more research in materials readily available to him. On the causes, his generalization may be true, but it is unwarranted on the basis of his writings: "No theory of a conspiracy is needed to explain the Mexican War . . . it was essentially a popular movement, both in Mexico and in the United States."

505. Merk, Frederick. Manifest Destiny and mission in American history: a reinterpretation. New York (Knopf), 1963. The greater part of this book is concerned with the Mexican War and the movement to annex all of Mexico, both of which are pictured as Manifest Destiny. Merk's thesis is that except for 1846 (and 1899) Manifest Destiny could not be considered a true expression of the American mind or of public opinion.

506. Parish, John Carl. The emergence of the idea of Manifest Destiny. Los Angeles (UC), 1932.

507. Pratt, Julius W. "The origin of 'Manifest Destiny,'" AHR, XXXII (1927), 795–99.

508. Weinberg, Albert K. Manifest Destiny: a study in nationalist expansionism. Baltimore (Johns Hopkins), 1935.

SEE ALSO NOS. 22, 283, 288, 299, 388, 438.

MARINE CORPS

509. Collum, Richard Strader. History of the United States Marine Corps. New York (Hamersly), 1903.

510. Metcalf, Clyde H. History of the United States Marine Corps. New York (Putnam), 1939.

511. Reynolds, John George. A conclusive exculpation of the Marine Corps in Mexico. . . . New York (Stringer and Townsend), 1853. A refutation of charges together with a copy of the general court-martial of the officer who made them.

512. [United States Marine Corps. Court-martial]. The Marine Corps in Mexico: setting forth its conduct as established by testimony before a court martial, convened at Brooklyn, New York, September, 1852, for the trial of First Lieutenant John S. Devlin, of the U.S. Marine Corps. Washington (Towers), 1852. Devlin was charged with writing an article for the *Brooklyn Daily Eagle* derogatory of the Corps, but at the trial a New York attorney, John Lomas, testified that he wrote it.

SEE ALSO NO. 144.

MARYLAND IN THE WAR

513. Archer, James J. "A Marylander in the Mexican War: some letters of J. J. Archer," ed. by C. A. Porter Hopkins, Md. Hist. Mag., LIV (1959), 408–22.
514. Kenley, John Reese. Memoirs of a Maryland volunteer. War with Mexico, in the years 1846–7–8. Philadelphia (Lippincott), 1873. The author commanded a company in the Baltimore battalion and apparently kept a diary of his experiences. This book is an expansion of that diary, with notes and additional material added. Kenly's company accompanied Taylor through the Monterey campaign, then marched overland to the coast and were transported to Vera Cruz to join Scott. This is, therefore, a rather full account of the war from a junior officer's view.

MC CLELLAN, GEORGE B.

515. Hilland, G. S. Life and campaigns of George B. McClellan. Philadelphia (Lippincott), 1864.
516. McClellan, George Brinton. The Mexican War diary of George B. McClellan. Ed. by William Starr Myers. Princeton (Prin. Univ.), 1917.
517. Michie, Peter Smith. General McClellan. New York (Appleton), 1901.

MC CULLOCH, BEN

518. Gunn, Jack W. "Ben McCulloch: a big captain," SWHQ, LVIII (1954), 1–21.
519. Reid, Samuel Chester. The scouting expeditions of McCulloch's Texas Rangers; or the summer and fall campaigns of the army of the United States in the Mexican War, 1846; including skirmishes with the Mexicans and an accurate detail of the storming of Monterey; also the daring scouts at Buena Vista together with anecdotes, incidents, descriptions of the country, and sketches of the lives of the celebrated partisan chiefs, Hays, McCulloch, and Walker. Philadelphia (Zieber), 1847. Reprint Austin (Steck), 1935.

520. Rose, Victor M. The life and services of Gen. Ben McCulloch. Philadelphia (Press), 1888. Reprinted Austin (Steck), 1958.

MEADE, GEORGE G.

521. Bache, Richard Meade. Life of General G. G. Meade. Philadelphia (Coates), 1897. Contains one short chapter on Meade as a lieutenant in the Mexican War. For a more recent biography, see No. 522.
522. Cleaves, Freeman. Meade of Gettysburg. Norman (OU), 1959. Three short chapters on Lt. Meade with Taylor's army.
SEE ALSO NO. 205.

MEDICAL HISTORY

523. Ashburn, Percy Moreau. History of the medical department of the United States Army. Boston (Houghton Mifflin), 1929. Has a brief section on the Mexican War.
524. Boston medical and surgical journal. Carried a few accounts of diseases in the army during the war years.
525. Brown, Harvey E. The medical department of the United States Army from 1775 to 1873. Washington (Surgeon General), 1873. Has part of a chapter on the Mexican War. Emphasis is on the organization of the medical department and the supply problem rather than health.
526. Castillo, Francisco Fernandez del. "La anestesia su aplicación durante la guerra de 1847," Memorias de la Academia Nacional de Historía y Geografía, IV (1948), 27–39. Ether was first used for surgery in the Massachusetts General Hospital on October 16, 1846. According to this article, Mexican surgeons picked up its use from U.S. army doctors early in 1847.
527. Duncan, Louis C. "A volunteer regiment in 1846–1847," Mil. Surg., LXV (1929), 709–13. Experiences of a Dr. H. R. Robards.
528. Foltz, Jonathan Messersmith. Scorbutus on board U.S. Squadron. Philadelphia, 1848. Foltz was a navy doctor.
529. Garrison, Fielding H. "Notes on the history of military medicine," Mil. Surg., L (1922), 578–602, 690–718. Pages 701–2 deal with the Mexican War.

530. Jarvis, Nathan S. "An Army surgeon's notes of frontier service, 1833–1848," Jour. Mil. Serv. Inst., XL (1907), 269–77, 435–52; XLI (1907), 90–105. The last two installments relate to the Mexican War.

531. Levy, Moses Albert. "Moses Albert Levy: letters of a Texas patriot," ed. by Saul Viener, Am. Jew. Hist. Soc. Pbl., XLVI (1956), 101–13. Levy served as a surgeon for a Texas volunteer unit and was captured.

532. New Orleans medical and surgical journal. A sophisticated medical journal, for its time, which carried numerous reports during the war years of diseases suffered by the troops.

533. Porter, John. "Surgical notes of the Mexican War," Am. Jour. of Med. Sci., 1852.

534. Smith, S. Compton. Chile con carne; or the camp and field. New York (Miller & Curtis), 1857. Also Milwaukee (Ford & Fairbanks), 1857. Smith came to Texas and joined the 1st Regiment of Texas Volunteer Rifles, received an appointment as surgeon, and accompanied his unit through the Monterey campaign, being relieved from duty in July 1847. His account is filled with anecdotal material of dubious authenticity and has very little on medicine, surgery, or disease.

SEE ALSO NOS. 85, 87, 104, 115, 182, 300, 311.

MEXICAN ACCOUNT OF THE WAR

535. Apuntes históricos sobre los acontecimientos notables de la guerra entre México y los Estados Unidos del Norte. Mexico, 1945.

536. Balbontin, Manuel. La invasion americana, 1846 á 1848; apuntes del subteniente de artilleria. . . . Mexico (Esteva), 1883. One of the earliest serious histories of the war published in Mexico; well balanced and important for first-hand observations.

537. Bocanegra, Jose María de. Memorias para la historia de Mexico independiente, 1822–1846. Mexico (Gobierno Federal), 1892.

538. Bustamente, Carlos María de. El nuevo Bernal Díaz del Castillo; o sea, historia de la invasion de los anglo-americanos en Mexico. 2 vols. Mexico (Garcia Torres), 1847. Reprinted Mexico (Sec. de Educacion Publica), 1949. One of the most important contemporary works, emphasizing internal Mexican politics. The first volume deals entirely with the background for the war. Texts of several of Paredes's manifestos are given. Santa Anna is particu-

larly disparaged. There is little on military action and less on causes. The U.S. is charged with aggression for annexing Texas, but nothing is said about the Nueces River.

539. Campaña contra los Americanos del norte. . . . Escrito por un oficial de infanteria. Mexico (Cumplido), 1846. Another pamphlet, 27 pages, giving the Mexican side of the battles of Palo Alto and Resaca de la Palma.

540. Mestre Ghigliazza, Manuel. Invasion norte-americana en Tabasco (1846–1847); documentos. . . . Mexico (Univ.), 1948.

541. Santa Anna, Antonio López de. Detall de las operaciones ocurridas en la defensa de la capital de la república, atacada por el ejército de los Estados Unidos del norte. Mexico (Cumplido), [1847]. Reprinted Mexico, 1961, with an English translation by J. Hefter. Santa Anna's defense of his conduct of the war and his excuses for the loss of Mexico City. Dated December 2, 1847.

542. ———. Las guerras de México con Tejas y los Estados Unidos. Ed. by Genaro García. Mexico (Bouret), 1910. Vol. 29 in García, Documentos inéditos . . . (no. 761).

543. ———. "Letters of General Antonio López de Santa Anna relating to the war between the United States and Mexico, 1846–1848," ed. by Justin H. Smith, Am. Hist. Assoc. Rep. for 1917, 355–431.

544. ———. [Conduct of the war controversy. Four pamphlets.] G.A.y N. Rápida ojeada sobre la campaña que hizo el Sr. General Santa Anna en el estado de Coahuila el mes de Febrero proximo pasado. . . . Mexico (Torres), 1847. Ordoñez Juan. Refutación al cuaderno titulado "Rápida ojeada. . . . Mexico (Arevalo), 1847. G.A.y N. Segunda parte de la rápida ojeada . . . o sea contestación al Sr. Don Juan Ordoñez. . . . Mexico (Torres), 1847. Ordoñez, Juan. Segunda parte de la refutación. . . . Mexico (Ortega), 1847.

545. Valadés, José C. Breve historia de la guerra con los Estados Unidos. Mexico (Editorial Patria), 1947. A popularized Mexican version of the war.

546. Valle, Rafael Heliodoro (editor). Héroes de 1847: seleccion y notes. Mexico (Sec. de Educacion Publica), 1947.

SEE ALSO Nos. 6, 25, 29, 142, 160, 162, 172, 175, 185, 186, 198, 206, 219, 220, 229, 247, 334, 383.

MEXICAN BACKGROUND AND POLITICS

547. Alamán, Lucas. Historia de Méjico desde los primeros movimientos que prepararon su independencia en el año 1808 hasta la época presente. 5 vols. Mexico (Lara), 1849–52. Last chapter of Vol. 5 has brief material on the Mexican War. Mostly valuable for background contemporary with the war.

548. Arrangoiz y Bezábal, Francisco de Paula de. Mexico desde 1808 hasta 1867. . . . 4 vols. Madrid (Perez Dubrull), 1871–72.

549. Bancroft, Hubert Howe. History of Mexico, 1824–1861. Vol. V. San Francisco (History Co.), 1887. Bancroft's interpretation of the causes of the war is probably the most pro-Mexican and anti-American of all.

550. ———. History of the north Mexican states and Texas, 1801–1889. Vol. II. San Francisco (Bancroft), 1889.

551. Bustamente, Carlos María de. Apuntes para la historia del gobiernos del general D. Antonio López de Santa Anna desde principios de octubre de 1841 hasta 6 de diciembre de 1844. . . . Mexico (Lara), 1845.

552. Causa criminal instruída al exmo. sr. presidente consitutional, general de divisíon D. Antonio López de Santa Anna, acusado del delito de traición contra la forma de gobierno. . . . Mexico (Lara), 1846. Thick documentary (425 pages) relating to the career of Santa Anna and the overthrow of his government in December 1844.

553. Cuevas, Luis Gonzaga. Porvenir de México, o juicio crítico sobre su estado político en 1821 y 1851. 3 vols. Mexico (Cumplido), 1851–57. Intensive review of Mexican history, 1821–28, with a reflective conclusion on the postwar situation in 1851. Because of political divisiveness, Mexico was in danger of losing its nationality and independence.

554. Gaxiola, Francisco Javier. La invasion norte-americana en Sinaloa; revisita histórica del estado, de 1845 á 1849. 2nd ed. Mexico (Rosas), 1891. For first edition, see No. 6.

555. Gilliam, Albert M. Travels in Mexico during the years 1843 and 1844. Aberdeen (Clark), 1847.

556. Granja, Juan de la. . . . Epistolario; con un estudio biografico preliminar por Luis Castill Ledón y notas de Neréo Rodriguez Barragán. Mexico (Museo Nacional . . .), 1937. Granja was a Spaniard who became a Mexican citizen in 1842 and served as Mexican consul to the U.S. until 1846 when he returned to

Mexico. He was elected to represent Jalisco in the Congress of 1848. Thus, though his most important achievement was the introduction of the telegraph in Mexico in 1851, his views of the war and its background are important.

557. Gutierrez de Estrada, José María. Mexico en 1840 y en 1847. Mexico (Torres), 1848.

558. Hutchinson, C. Alan. "Valentín Gómez Farías and the movement for the return of General Santa Anna to Mexico in 1846," in Essays in American history (Hackett memorial volume), Austin (UT Inst. Latin American Stud.), 1958, 169–91.

559. La guerra de Tejas sin máscara. Mexico (Torres), 1845. This 20-page "unmasking" of the Texas war is a bitter attack on Santa Anna and other Centralists who favor a war over Texas and who oppose the prospective treaty with Texas. For an answer, see No. 361.

560. Nicolau d'Olwer, Luis. "Santa Anna y la invasion vistos por Bermudez de Castro," Historia Mexicana, IV (1954), 47–65. Bermudez de Castro was the Spanish minister to Mexico who arrived just before the fall of the Herrera government and in his dispatches to Madrid made cogent observations on the war and Santa Anna's role. In 1847 he wrote: "The invasion and the war were not in Mexico national questions because the spirit of patriotism did not exist." The average man did not comprehend the defense of a country that was only a name to him and the patriotic spirit of moderate leadership was confused by divisiveness and economic interests.

561. Otero, Mariano. Ensayo sobre el verdadero de la cuestión social y política que se agita en la República Mexicana. 2nd ed. Guadalajara (Ediciones I.T.G.), 1952. Survey of the turmoil of Mexican politics—often considered a classic treatise. Otero was a well-known and volatile liberal and reformer.

562. Paredes y Arrillaga, Mariano. Breve exposición que el general . . . hace a sus conciudadanos sobre los motivos que lo impulsaron a regresar a su patria. Mexico (Lara), 1847. Dated at end Tulancingo, 29 September 1847. Explains his role in various actions of the war.

563. Peña y Peña, Manuel de la. Colección de los documentos mas importantes relativos a la instalación y reconocimiento del gobierno provisional del escmo. Sr. Presidente de la Suprema Corte de Justicia. . . . Mexico (Cumplido), 1847. Peña y Peña, president of the Supreme Court, assumed the office of provisional president of the republic on September 26, 1847, after the fall of Mexico City. This 79-page work is dated November 20, 1847.

564. Rodríguez de San Miguel, Juan Nepomuceno. La república mexicana en 1846, ó sea directorio general de los supremos poderes, y de las principales autoridades. . . . Mexico (Lara), 1845 [!]. An almanac of the Mexican government for the year 1846, listing names of officials, etc. Texas is blithely listed as one of the departments of Mexico under the Bases Orgánicos and a descriptive note is added without any reference to the revolution or independence of Texas.

565. Skinner, H. B. Mexico in miniature. Boston (Hall), 1847.

566. Smith, Justin Harvey. "La República de Rio Grande," AHR, XXV (1920), 660–75.

567. Smith, Ralph A. "Indians in American-Mexican relations before the war of 1846," HAHR, XLIII (1963), 34–64. Neither this article nor No. 571 is directly related to the war, but the Indian menace indirectly affected the prewar scene along the Rio Grande.

568. Suarez y Navarro, Juan. Historia de Mexico y del Santa Anna. . . . Mexico (Cumplido), 1850. This is not really a Mexican War item since the text breaks off abruptly for the year 1834 but is given here because it is often listed in Mexican War bibliographies.

569. Tornel y Mendívil, Jose María. Breve reseña histórica . . . de la nacion mexicana, desde el año 1821 hasta nuestros dias. . . . Mexico (Cumplido), 1852. Narrative extends to the author's death in 1828.

570. ———. Tejas y los Estados Unidos de America, en sus relaciones con la República Mexicano. Mexico (Cumplido), 1837. Of little value to the Mexican War except as an expression of one type of Mexican attitude toward the United States: "The dominant thought of the United States of America has been for more than fifty years . . . the occupation of a large part of the territory once Spain's and today Mexico's."

571. Vigness, David M. "Indian raids on the lower Rio Grande, 1836–1837," SWHQ, LIX (1955), 14–23.

572. Wright, Marie Robinson. Mexico: a history of its progress and development in one hundred years. Philadelphia (Barrie), 1911.

SEE ALSO Nos. 60, 64, 143, 197, 334, 340, 349, 364, 365, 366, 386, 405, 409, 421, 469, 537, 538.

MEXICAN OPPOSITION TO THE WAR

573. Armond, L. de. "Justo Sierra O'Reilly and Yucatecan-United States relations, 1847–1848," HAHR, XXXI (1951), 420–36.
574. Gómez, Marte R. "Sobre Justo Sierra O'Reilly," Historia Mexicana, III (1954), 309–27.
575. La célebre misión del doctor Don Justo Sierra O'Reilly a los Estados de norteamérican 1847 y 1848. Ed. by C. R. Menendez. Merida, 1945.
576. Sierra O'Reilly, Justo. Diario de nuestro viaje a los Estados Unidos (la pretendida anexión de Yucatan prólogo y notas de Héctor Pérez Martínez. Mexico (Porrúa), 1938. O'Reilly was the agent from the government of Yucatán to the U.S. to ask aid, protection, and recognition.
See also Nos. 136, 429, 554, 559, 560, 566.

MEXICO CITY, BATTLE OF

577. Wallace, Edward S. "The United States Army in Mexico City," Mil. Affairs, XIII (1949), 158–66.
See also Nos. 147, 223, 238, 541.

MILITARY GOVERNMENT IN MEXICO, AMERICAN

578. Gabriel, Ralph H. "American experience with military government," AHR, XLIX (1944), 630–43. Discussion of Scott's General Order 20 as the genesis of American military government.
579. Smith, Harry A. "Four interventions in Mexico: a study in military government," Infantry Jour., XVIII (1920), 125–31, 372–80.
580. Smith, Justin Harvey. "American rule in Mexico," AHR, XXIII (1918), 287–302.
581. Twitchell, Ralph Emerson. The history of the military occupation of the territory of New Mexico from 1846 to 1851 by the government of the United States. Denver (Smith-Brooks), 1909.
582. ———. The story of the conquest of Santa Fe, New Mexico, and the building of old Fort Marcy, A.D. 1846. Santa Fe (N. Mex. Hist. Soc.), 1921.
See also Nos. 114, 577.

MISSISSIPPI IN THE WAR

SEE NO. 120.

MONROE DOCTRINE AS CAUSAL FACTOR

583. Cushing, Charles S. "The contention of the nations for the San Francisco bay region," Cal. Pioneers Soc. Qrtly., VIII (1931), 83–97. Deals briefly with the Bear Flag Revolt.
584. Leggett, Aaron. "An important letter: Aaron Leggett to William L. Marcy, October 16, 1845," Cal. Hist. Soc. Qrtly., XI (1932), 33–34. Deals with the possibility of intervention by Great Britain in California.

SEE ALSO NOS. 312, 313, 368, 377, 449, 451.

MONTERREY (MEXICO), BATTLE OF

585. Ampudia, Pedro de. Manifesto del general Ampudia a sus conciudadanos. Mexico (Cumplido), 1847. A 10-page explanation by Ampudia of his loss of Monterrey.
586. Wallace, Edward S. General William Jenkins Worth: Monterrey's forgotten hero. Dallas (SMU), 1953.

SEE ALSO NOS. 109, 148, 168, 245, 248.

MORMON BATTALION

587. Bliss, Robert S. "The journal of Robert S. Bliss, with the Mormon Battalion," Utah Hist. Qrtly, IV (1931), 67–96, 110–28.
588. Creer, Leland Hargrave. Utah and the nation. Seattle (UW), 1929. Includes a section dealing with the calling of the Morman Battalion.
589. Gardner, Hamilton. "The command and staff of the Mormon Battalion in the Mexican War," Utah Hist. Qrtly., XX (1952), 331–51.
590. Golder, Frank Alfred (editor). The march of the Mormon Battalion from Council Bluffs to California. New York (Century), 1928. Taken from the joural of Henry Standage.

591. Hess, John W. "John W. Hess, with the Mormon Battalion," Utah Hist. Qrtly., IV (1931), 47–55.

592. Houston, Flora Belle. "The Mormon Battalion," S. Cal. Hist. Soc. Pblc., XIV (1930), 339–54.

593. Perkins, J. R. Mormon Battalion for service against Mexico was recruited here. Council Bluffs (Council Bluffs Board of Education), 1934.

594. Roberts, Brigham Henry. The Mormon Battalion: its history and achievements. Salt Lake City (Deseret News), 1919.

595. Schroeder, Theodore. "A question of Mormon patriotism," Am. Hist. Mag., I (1906), 279–91. Relation of the government to the Mormon Battalion.

596. Tyler, Daniel. A concise history of the Mormon Battalion in the Mexican War, 1846–1847. Salt Lake City, 1881. Reprinted Chicago (Rio Grande), 1964. DeVoto (No. 501): ". . . demonstrably wrong in practically everything it says. . . ."

597. Wells, Junius F. "The Mormon Battalion," Utah Geneal. and Hist. Mag., XVIII (1927), 97–105, 145–50. Address delivered at the dedication of the Mormon Battalion Monument in Salt Lake City.

SEE ALSO Nos. 287, 328, 399, 400, 450.

NAVAL OPERATIONS

598. Bauer, Karl Jack. Surfboats and horse marines: U.S. naval operations in the Mexican War. Annapolis (U.S. Nav. Inst.), 1969.

599. Betts, John L. "The United States Navy in the Mexican War," HAHR, XXXVI (1956), 370–71.

600. Briggs, Herbert Whittaker. The doctrine of continuous voyage. Baltimore (Johns Hopkins), 1926. On the development of maritime law, but cites case applicable to blockade and contraband in Mexican War.

601. Craven, Tunis A. M. "Naval conquest in the Pacific: the journal . . . during a cruise . . . in the sloop of war Dale, 1846–1849," Cal. Hist. Soc. Qrtly., XX (1941), 193–234.

602. Downey, Joseph T. The cruise of the Portsmouth, 1845–1847: a sailor's view of the naval conquest of California. Ed. by Howard Lamar. New Haven (Yale), 1958.

603. Feipel, Louis N. "The United States Navy in Mexico, 1821–1914," U.S. N. Inst. Proc., XLI (1915), 33–52, 489–97, 889–903, 1159–72, 1527–34, 1993–2002.

604. Goodrich, Caspar. "'Alvarado Hunter,' a biographical sketch," U.S. Navy Inst. Proc., XLIX (1918), 495–514. Account of the capture of the town of Alvarado, March 31, 1847, by Lt. Charles G. Hunter, commander of the U.S.S. *Scourge,* and of his subsequent court-martial.

605. Parker, William Harwar. Recollections of a naval officer, 1841–1865. New York (Scribner's), 1883. Several chapters relate his experiences during the Mexican War in the Gulf squadron under Conner.

606. Soley, James Russell. Admiral Porter. New York (Appleton), 1903. Soley wrote several naval biographies and naval histories; he was a professor at the Naval Academy.

607. Steedman, Charles. Memoir and correspondence of Charles Steedman, Rear Admiral, United States Navy, 1811–1890. Ed. by Amos Lawrence Mason. Cambridge (Riverside), 1912. Has one chapter on Mexican War.

SEE ALSO NOS. 312, 313, 318, 320, 324, 327, 348, 396, 397, 445, 446, 452, 528.

NEW MEXICO IN THE WAR

608. Abert, James William. Western America in 1846–47. . . . Ed. by John Galvin. San Francisco (Howell), 1966. The diary of Abert's exploration of New Mexico for the Corps of Topographical Engineers, with illustrations in color from his sketch book. Expanded from the 1848 version in the Congressional serial set. A beautiful edition of slight value as a Mexican War item, but contains intelligent impressions of the aftermath of Kearny's occupation of New Mexico.

609. Atherton, Lewis E. "Disorganizing effects of the Mexican War on the Santa Fe trade," Kans. Hist. Qrtly., VI (1937), 115–23.

610. Bender, A. B. "Frontier defense in the territory of New Mexico, 1846–1853," N. Mex. Hist. Rev., IX (1934), 249–72.

611. ———. "Government explorations in the territory of New Mexico, 1846–1859," N. Mex. Hist. Rev., IX (1934), 1–32.

612. Davies, T. M., Jr. "Assessments during the Mexican War: an exercise in futility," N. Mex. Hist. Rev., XLI (1966), 197–216.

613. Emory, William H. Notes of a military reconnaissance from Fort Leavenworth in Missouri to San Diego in California. Washington (Wendell & Van Benthuysen), 1848. Also issued as Sen. Ex. Doc. 7, 30 Cong., 1 sess.

614. Keleher, William A. Turmoil in New Mexico, 1846–1848. Santa Fe (Rydal), 1952. Almost a southwestern classic by an Albuquerque attorney.

615. ———. "The year of decision," N. Mex. Hist. Rev., XXII (1947), 8–17. Occupation of New Mexico by Kearny and Doniphan.

616. Loyola, Sister Mary. "The American occupation of New Mexico, 1821–1852," N. Mex. Hist. Rev., XIV (1939), 34–75, 143–99, 230–86.

617. Oliva, Leo E. Soldiers on the Santa Fe trail. Norman (OU), 1967. Has a section on the effect of the Mexican War in the Southwest.

618. "Report of the citizens of New Mexico to the president of Mexico, September 26, 1846 . . . of Manuel Armijo to the minister of foreign relations . . . , September 8, 1846; letter from Stephen Watts Kearny to Armijo, August 1, 1846; and Armijo's reply, August 12, 1846," N. Mex. Hist. Rev., XXVI (1951), 68–82.

SEE ALSO Nos. 42, 110, 114, 293, 294, 304, 399, 431, 436, 443, 486, 489, 581, 582.

NEW YORK IN THE WAR

619. Clark, Francis D. The First Regiment of New York Volunteers, commanded by Col. Jonathan D. Stevenson, in the Mexican War. New York (Evans), 1882. Service in California.

620. Hollingsworth, John McHenry. The journal of John McHenry Hollingsworth of the First New York Volunteers (Stevenson's regiment), September 1846–August 1849. San Francisco (Cal. Hist. Soc.), 1923.

621. [Lomard, Albert]. The "High Private." New York, 1848. A popular contemporary work on New York volunteers in the war.

622. Murphy, Charles J. Reminiscences of the war of the rebellion, and of the Mexican War. New York (Ficker), 1882. Murphy was a member of New York's Seventh Regiment in the Mexican War, but this work, written to support his Civil War claim against the government, has very little Mexican War material in it. The title is misleading.

623. ———. Reminiscences of the Mexican and Civil wars. [San Francisco, 1906?]. Title also misleading. A 4-page letter relating Civil War experiences.

624. Sweeny, Thomas William. "Narrative of army service in the Mexi-

can War and on the plains, 1846–1853," ed. by William M. Sweeny, Mag. of Hist., XXIV (1917), 17–27. Sweeny was one of the most interesting men to serve in the Mexican War. He was born in Ireland, migrated to the U.S., served as a lieutenant in the First New York Volunteers, lost an arm at the Battle of Churubusco, remained in the army, and retired as a brigadier general despite being tried for treason for an attempt to lead Irish revolutionaries in an invasion of Canada. This narrative is a transcript of his journal, which, incidentally, is not found in the Sweeny Collection at the Huntington Library.

SEE ALSO NOS. 125, 249, 298.

NORTH CAROLINA IN THE WAR

625. Wallace, Lee A. "Raising a volunteer regiment for Mexico, 1846–1847," N. Car. Hist. Rev., XXXV (1958), 20–33.

OHIO IN THE WAR

SEE NOS. 75, 177.

JUSTO O'REILLY AND YUCATAN

SEE NOS. 429, 573, 574, 575, 576.

PALO ALTO AND RESACA DE LA PALMA, BATTLES OF

626. Barasorda, Panfilo. Pedimentos presentados a la exma. primera sala del supremo tribunal de la Guerra y Marina en la causa formada al E. Sr. gral. Mariano Arista. . . . Mexico (Lara), 1849. A 35-page pamphlet relating to the military trial of Arista for his alleged errors at Palo Alto and Resaca de la Palma. See also No. 398.

SEE ALSO NOS. 172, 198, 206, 222, 251, 539.

PAREDES Y ARRILLAGA, MARIANO

627. Garcia, Genaro (editor). El general Paredes y Arillaga, su gobierno en Jalisco, sus movimientos revolucionares, sus relaciones con el general Santa Anna . . . segun su propio archivo. Mexico (Bouret), 1910. Vol. 32 in Documentos ineditos . . . (No. 761). Letters, July 5, 1833, to November 12, 1844.
SEE ALSO NOS. 212, 213, 214, 371, 372, 562.

PEACE NEGOTIATIONS

628. Beach, Moses Yale. "A secret mission to Mexico," Scribner's Monthly, XVIII (May 1879), 136–40. The story of Beach's secret mission and of the intrigues of Jane McManus Storm Cazeneau.
629. Brent, Robert Arthur. "Nicholas P. Trist and the Treaty of Guadalupe Hidalgo, 1847–1848," SWHQ, LVII (1954), 454–74. For a reinterpretation of the Trist mission, see No. 643.
630. Breve impugnación á las observaciones acerca del parecer fiscal y acuerdo de la suprema corte. . . . Mexico (Lara), 1848. A 28-page pamphlet giving reasons for Mexican objections to the Treaty of Guadalupe Hidalgo. Reprinted in No. 647.
631. Conmy, Peter Thomas. A centennial evaluation of the Treaty of Guadalupe Hidalgo, 1848–1948. Mimeo. Oakland Public Library, 1948.
632. Contestaciones habidas entre el supremo gobierno mexicano, el general en gefe del ejercito american, y el comisionado de los Estados Unidos. Mexico (Torres), 1847. A 37-page pamphlet relating to the peace negotiations of 1847.
633. Curti, Merl E. "Pacifist propaganda and the treaty of Guadalupe Hidalgo," AHR, XXXIII (1928), 596–98. A brief argument that the United States and/or pacifists in the U.S. did not cause the insertion of the arbitration clause (XXI) in the Treaty of Guadalupe Hidalgo.
634. Dentzel, Carl Schaefer. "The Treaty of Guadalupe Hidalgo," Westerners Brand Book for 1948 (Los Angeles Westerners), 1949, 32–39.
636. Esposición dirigida al supremo gobierno por los comisionados que firmaron el tratado de paz con los Estados-Unidos. Queretaro (Lara), 1848. A defense of the Mexican peace commissioners' actions at the conferences with Trist. For Mexican objections to

the treaty, see No. 630. The commissioners' frank admission (pp. 15–16) that the territory between the Nueces and Rio Grande had been lost to Mexico for ten years is an interesting one. Reprinted in No. 647 as Exposición de motivas presentada . . . , pp. 139–168.

637. Esposición de una persona residente en al república Mexicana sobre la guerra que actualmente sostiene con los Estados Unidos del norte. Mexico (Rafael), 1847. An interesting 16-page pamphlet by an unidentified author, apparently a European who had lived in Mexico for many years. He deplores the anarchy that has existed in Mexico for so long and seems to blame the personal ambitions of Mexican leaders for making war instead of peace. He supports the peace negotiations of 1847.

638. Esposición o programa, de los diputados pertenecientes al partido puro ó progresista, sobre la presente guerra, con motivo de una proposición del Sr. Otero, é imputaciones de ciertos periodicos que se publican en la capital, bajo la influencia del conquistador, y que se dejan correr libremente por el actual gobierno de la Union. Queretero (Frias), 1847. A 23-page pamphlet objecting to the treaty and to the alienation of territory, especially the Rio Grande boundary. Discusses Nos. 644 and 637. Signed by Gomez Farías and others. Reprinted in No. 647, pp. 93–105.

639. Hammond, George Peter (editor). The Treaty of Guadalupe Hidalgo, February second, 1848. Berkeley (Friends of Bancroft Library), 1949. Contains remarks on the protocol of Queretero, the treaty itself, the border controversy, and the contest over San Diego.

640. Hill, Charles Edward. Leading American treaties. New York (Macmillan), 1922.

641. Ketchum, Jack. "The thankless task of Nicholas Trist," Am. Heritage, XXI, No. 5 (Aug. 1970), 13–15, 86–90. Popularized version following Sears's (No. 649) concept of the diplomat with ideals.

642. Klein, Julius. "The making of the Treaty of Guadalupe Hidalgo on February 2, 1848," Univ. of Cal. Chronicles, VII (1905), 247–318. Has been superseded by later work on the treaty.

643. Nortrup, Jack. "Nicholas Trist's mission to Mexico: a reinterpretation," SWHQ, LXXI (1968), 321–46. A sound revision, depicting Trist as a bungler and a dupe of more sophisticated Mexican diplomats rather than as a diplomat with ideals.

644. Otero, Mariano. Comunicacion que sober las negociaciones diplomaticos hablidas en la casa de Alfaro entre los plenipotenciarios de los Estados Unidos y Mexico. . . . Mexico (Torres),

1847. Reprinted in No. 647, pp. 65–68. Otero was one of the leaders of the opposition to the peace negotiations and the treaty. The house of Alfaro was the place in Queretero where the negotiators met.

645. ———. Esposición que hace el ciudadano Mariano Otero. . . . Toluca, 1847; reprinted Mexico (Vargas Rea), 1847.

646. Pacheco, José Ramón. Esposición . . . con motivo de la comunicación oficial que acerca de las conferencias tenidas en agosto y septiembre con el comisionado de los Estados Unidos. Querétaro (Perez), 1847. Opposes the peace negotiations.

647. Peña y Reyes, Antonio de la (editor). Algunos documentos sobre el tratado de Guadalupe y la situación de Mexico durante la invasión americana. Mexico (Sec. de Rel. Exteriores), 1930, Vol. 31 of Archivo Historico Diplomatico Mexicano. A collection of Mexican documents relating to the peace negotiations and the treaty as well as the controversy these aroused. The work is not well arranged; that is, there appears to be no particular order in the placement of the documents; identification is difficult because authorship and/or correct titles are not always given; and some contemporary pamphlets relating to the treaty are not reprinted. For these reasons important items are listed separately in the present bibliography.

648. Rejón, Manuel Crecencio. Observaciones . . . contra los tratados de paz . . . precidias de la parte histórica relativa a la cuestión orignaria. Queretaro (Lara), 1848. Rejón, foreign minister in 1846, had denounced the United States at that time and had demanded that the U.S. acknowledge its guilt as aggressor before beginning peace negotiations. In this 62-page pamphlet he continues to oppose the U.S. and severely criticizes the treaty. Reprinted in No. 647, pp. 300–347.

649. Sears, Louis Martin. "Nicholas P. Trist: a diplomat with ideals," MVHR, II (1924), 85–98. For an opposite view, see No. 643.

650. Tratado de paz, amistad, limites y arreglo definitivo entre la república Mexicana y los Estados-Unidos de America, firmado en Guadalupe Hidalgo. . . . Queretaro (Lara), 1848. This early Mexican printing (probably the first) is often bound with No. 636 under a cover title: Tratado de paz, amistad y limites . . . y esposición de los comisionados. . . .

651. Van Winkle, Henry Livingstone. "The Treaty of Guadalupe Hidalgo," S. Cal. Pioneers Qrtly., II (1925), 45–56.

652. Wickersham, Virginia Voorheis. "Disobedient diplomat," Pac. Spectator, II (1948), 458–66. Popularized account of Trist.

SEE ALSO Nos. 40, 66, 112, 121, 139, 162, 342, 356, 358, 383, 498, 502, 503, 544, 561, 563, 578, 579, 580.

PENNSYLVANIA IN THE WAR

653. Coulter, Richard. "The Westmoreland guards in the war with Mexico," West. Pa. Hist. Mag., XXIV (1941), 101–20.

654. Nauman, George. "A Lancastrian in the Mexican War," contr. by Mary Nauman Robinson, Lancaster Co. Hist. Soc. Papers, XII (1908), 109–29. Letters by Colonel Nauman, May 20, 1846, to September 22, 1847, who was with Taylor on the Rio Grande, then joined Scott's forces at Vera Cruz, and after the capture of Mexico City, was in command of the castle of San Juan de Ulloa. See also No. 225.

655. [Skelly, James]. "Diary of a Pennsylvania volunteer in the Mexican War," ed. by James K. Greer, West. Pa. Mag. Hist., XII (1929), 147–54. Skelly was a volunteer in the 2nd Pennsylvania Regiment attached to Scott's command.

656. Stearns, Morton E. "Pittsburgh in the Mexican War," West. Pa. Hist. Mag., VII (1924), 235–42.

SEE ALSO Nos. 84, 87, 223.

PIERCE, FRANKLIN

657. Bartlett, David Vandewater Golden. The life of General Franklin Pierce, the Democratic candidate for President of the United States. Auburn (Serky and Miller), 1852.

658. Nichols, Roy Franklin. Franklin Pierce: young hickory of the granite hills. Philadelphia (Penn. U), 1931. Revised ed., 1958. Three chapters on the Mexican War.

PIKE, ALBERT

SEE Nos. 69, 70.

POINSETT, JOEL

659. Parton, Dorothy M. The diplomatic career of Joel Roberts Poinsett. Washington (Cath. Univ. of Amer.), 1934.
SEE ALSO No. 415.

POLITICS, UNITED STATES

660. Bruce, Harold R. American parties and politics: history and role of political parties in the United States. New York (Holt), 1927. A little material on domestic politics and the war.
661. Cole, Arthur Charles. Whig party in the South. Washington (Am. Hist. Assoc.), 1913.
662. Dodd, William E. "The West and the war with Mexico," Jour. Ill. St. Hist. Soc., V (1912), 159–72. Also Ill. Hist. Soc. Trans. 1914, 15–23.
663. Fuller, John Douglas Pitts. "Slavery propaganda during the Mexican War," SWHQ, XXXVIII (1935), 235–45. Describes the efforts of northern expansionists to remove the slavery issue from current politics.
664. Gallatin, Albert. War expenses. New York (Bartlett & Welford), 1848.
665. Gunderson, Robert Gray. The log cabin campaign. Louisville (UK), 1957.
666. Howe, Daniel Wait. Political history of secession, to the beginning of the American Civil War. New York (Putnam), 1914. Slavery as a cause of the Mexican War.
667. Morrison, Chaplin W. Democratic politics and sectionalism: the Wilmot Proviso controversy. Chapel Hill (U of NC), 1967.
668. Nevins, Allan. Ordeal of the union. 2 vols. New York (Scribner's), 1947. Early chapters of the first volume contain an excellent discussion of the war's aftermath as it affected the U.S. political scene.
669. Sellers, Charles. James K. Polk. 2 vols. Princeton (Princeton U.), 1957–1966. The second volume, James K. Polk, Continentalist, has material on the election of 1844 and the war.
670. Silbey, Joel H. The shrine of party: congressional voting behavior, 1841–1852. Pittsburgh (U. of Pittsburgh), 1967.

671. Wiltse, Charles M. John C. Calhoun: sectionalist, 1840–1850. New York (Bobbs Merrill), 1951.

SEE ALSO NOS. 130, 270, 278, 331, 352, 380, 417, 477.

POLK, JAMES K.

672. Jenkins, John Stilwell. The life of James Knox Polk. Auburn (Alden), 1850.

673. McCormac, Eugene Irving. James K. Polk: a political biography. Berkeley (UC), 1922.

674. McCoy, Charles A. Polk and the presidency. Austin (UT), 1960.

675. Morrell, Martha McBride. Young Hickory, the life and times of President James K. Polk. New York (Dutton), 1949.

676. "Polk-Donelson letters: letters of James K. Polk and Andrew J. Donelson, 1843–1848," ed. by George L. Sioussat, Tenn. Hist. Mag., III (1917), 51–74.

677. "Polk-Johnson letters: letters of James K. Polk to Cave Johnson, 1833–1848," Tenn. Hist. Mag., I (1915), 209–56.

678. "Polk-Laughlin correspondence: letters from James K. Polk to Samuel H. Laughlin, 1835–1844," ed. by Joseph H. Parks, East Tenn. Hist. Soc. Pbl., XVIII (1946).

679. "Polk-Nicholson letters: letters from James K. Polk to Alfred O. P. Nicholson, 1835–1849," ed. by Joseph H. Parks, Tenn. Hist. Mag., VIII (1924), 67–80.

680. "Polk-Pillow correspondence: correspondence between James K. Polk and Gideon J. Pillow in 1844," AHR, XI (1906), 832–43.

681. Polk, James Knox. Correspondence. . . . Ed. by Herbert Weaver and Paul Bergeron. A multi-volume project now in progress.

682. ———. Diario del Presidente Polk, 1845–1849. 2 vols. Mexico (Antigua Libería Robredo), 1948.

683. ———. The diary of James K. Polk, during his presidency, 1845–1849. Ed. by Milo Milton Quaife. 4 vols. Chicago (McClurg), 1910.

684. ———. Polk: the diary of a president. Ed. by Allan Nevins. New York (Longmans, Green), 1929. Extracts, with annotations, from the Quaife edition.

SEE ALSO NOS. 68, 309, 321, 322, 323, 352, 363, 381, 382, 404, 411, 467, 499, 669.

PORTER, D. D.

SEE No. 606.

PUEBLA, BATTLE OF

SEE No. 221.

QUITMAN, ANTHONY

685. Claiborne, John F. H. Life and correspondence of Anthony Quitman. New York (Harper), 1860.

REJÓN, CRECENCIO

686. Echanove Trujillo, C. La vida pasional e inquieta de Don Crecencio Rejón. Mexico, 1941.
SEE ALSO No. 648.

SAN PASQUAL, BATTLE OF

SEE Nos. 164, 246, 250.

SAN PATRICIO BATTALION

687. Hopkins, G. T. "The San Patricio Battalion in the Mexican War," U.S. Cav. Assn. Jour., XXIV (1913), 279–84.
688. McCornack, Richard Blaine. "The San Patricio deserters in the Mexican War," Americas, VIII (1951), 131–42. Probably the best account of this unit which is so well known and about which so little is known.

689. Wallace, Edward S. "The Battalion of Saint Patrick in the Mexican War," Mil. Affairs, XIV (1950), 84–91.
SEE ALSO NOS. 118, 336, 337, 339.

SANTA ANNA

690. Callcott, Wilfred Hardy. Santa Anna: the story of an enigma who once was Mexico. Norman (OU), 1936.
691. Crane, R. C. "Santa Anna and the aftermath of San Jacinto," West Tex. Hist. Assoc. Yearbook, XI (1935), 56–61.
692. Crawford, Ann Fears (ed.). The eagle: the autobiography of Santa Anna. Austin (Pemberton), 1967. Apparently a translation of Santa Anna's memoirs from the original manuscript in the University of Texas library.
693. Gamboa, Ramón. Impugnación al informe del Señor Gen. Santa Anna. . . . Mexico, 1849. Included as part 3 of No. 542.
694. Hanighen, Frank C. Santa Anna, the Napoleon of the West. New York (Coward-McCann), 1934.
695. Jones, Oakah L. Santa Anna. New York (Twayne), 1968.
696. Muñoz, Rafael F. Antonio López de Santa Anna. Madrid (Espasa-Calpe), 1936; Mexico (Editorial Mexico nuevo), 1937.
697. Santa Anna, Antonio López de. Esposición del . . . a sus compatriots. . . . San Luis Potosí, August 16, 1846. A 4-page speech upon his return to Mexico to assume leadership in the war.
698. ———. Mi historia militar y politica, 1810–1874: memorias ineditos. Mexico (Bouret), 1905. Vol. 2 in Garcia, Documentos ineditos . . . (No. 761).
699. Villa-Amor, Manuel. Biografía del General Santa Anna y convenia secreto que celebró con el [cabinete] de los Estados Unidos. . . . Mexico (Uribe), 1847. Reprinted 1849. A second edition was issued in 1857: Biografía del general Santa Anna, aumentada con la segunda parte. Mexico (Torres), 1857. Denounces Santa Anna as an evil genius whose actions have brought so much trouble to Mexico.
SEE ALSO NOS. 161, 229, 471, 541, 542, 544, 551, 552, 558, 559, 560.

SCOTT, WINFIELD, BIOGRAPHY

700. Elliott, Charles Winslow. Winfield Scott, the soldier and the man. New York (Macmillan), 1937.

701. Mansfield, Edward Deering. The life of General Winfield Scott, embracing his campaign in Mexico. New York (Barnes), 1848. An expanded version under a slightly different title was issued by the same publisher in 1852 and a later one in 1860.

702. Smith, Arthur D. Howden. Old Fuss and Feathers; life and exploits of Lieutenant General Winfield Scott. New York (Greystone), 1937.

703. Wright, Marcus J. General Scott. . . . New York (Appleton), 1894.
SEE ALSO NOS. 23, 231, 393.

SCOTT'S CAMPAIGN; SEE ALSO–SPECIFIC BATTLES

SEE NOS. 145, 161, 165, 169, 171, 187, 188, 189, 202, 209, 211, 215, 232, 241, 242, 249, 282, 514.

SHIELDS, JAMES

704. Condun, William H. Life of Major General James Shields: hero of three wars and senator from three states. Chicago (Blakely), 1900. Four chapters on the Mexican War and one on Shields's experience in California immediately after the war.
SEE ALSO NO. 154.

SLAVERY AND ANTISLAVERY; SEE ALSO ABOLITION

705. Boucher, Chauncey S. "In re that aggressive slaveocracy," MVHR, VIII (1921), 13–79. Demonstrates the lack of Southern unity on such questions as the annexation of Texas and the Mexican War.

706. Holst, Hermann Edward von. The constitutional and political history of the United States. Trans. by Alfred Bishop Mason. 7 vols. Chicago (Callaghan), 1876–92. To this German scholar, slavery versus antislavery was the primary theme in American history; consequently, he finds that an aggressive slaveocracy brought on the Mexican War.

707. Knapp, Frank Averill, Jr. "John Quincy Adams, ¿defensor de

Mexico?" Hist. Mexicana, VII (1958), 116–23. Adams was popular in Mexico because of his opposition to the annexation of Texas and his posture that Mexico was its rightful owner.

708. Palfrey, John Gorham. Papers on the slave power. Boston (Merrill Cobb), 1846. This famous New England minister and one-time editor of the *North American Review* found slavery expansion at the root of the Texas issue.

SEE ALSO Nos. 65, 362, 502, 503, 663, 666, 667.

SLIDELL, JOHN

SEE Nos. 374, 422, 423, 424.

SLOAT, JOHN D.

SEE No. 320.

SMITH, E. KIRBY

709. Noll, Arthur Howard. General Kirby-Smith. Sewanee (Univ. Press), 1907. Noll also authored several books on Mexican history.

710. Smith, Ephriam Kirby. To Mexico with Scott: letters of Captain E. Kirby Smith to his wife. Prepared by Emma Jerome Blackwood. Cambridge (Harvard), 1917.

SOUTH CAROLINA IN THE WAR

SEE Nos. 85, 200, 209.

STEVENS, ISAAC I.

SEE Nos. 241, 242.

STOCKTON, R. F.

711. [Bayard, Samuel John]. A sketch of the life of Commodore Robert F. Stockton . . . with an appendix, comprising his correspondence with the Navy department respecting his conquest of California, and extracts from the defense of Col. J. C. Fremont. . . . New York (Darby & Jackson), 1856. Although the book is not footnoted, much of the material in it is from original sources.

712. Brown, Madeline F. "A New Jersey sailor who served his country well," Jour. Am. Hist., XXII (1928), 298–302. About Robert F. Stockton.

713. Marshall, Thomas Maitland. "Stockton's proclamation to the San Diego insurgents," SWHQ, XX (1916), 151–53.

SEE ALSO Nos. 301, 306, 318, 324, 376, 381, 382, 601.

TABASCO IN THE WAR

SEE No. 540.

TAMAULIPAS IN THE WAR

714. Prieto, Alejandro. Historia, geografía y estadística del estado de Tamaulipas. . . . Mexico (Escalerillas), 1873.

TAYLOR ALMANACS

715. The General Taylor almanac for . . . 1848. By Charles F. Egelmann. Philadelphia (Griffith & Simon), [1848?]. A number of such "almanacs" were issued, none of which is of any value.

716. General Taylor and his staff: comprising memoirs of Generals Taylor, Worth, Wool and Butler; Colonels May, Cross, Clay, Hardin, Yell, Hays, and other distinguished officers . . . compiled from public documents and private correspondence. Philadelphia (Grigg, Elliot), 1848. All were glorious heroes, so says

the unknown author, but his book is hardly worthy of them, heroes or not.

717. General Taylor and the Mexican War. . . . New York (Blanchard), 1847.

718. Gen. Taylor's Rough and Ready almanac, 1848. Philadelphia (Turner & Fisher), [1848?].

719. General Zachary Taylor's Old Rough and Ready almanac, 1848. Philadelphia (Grigg, Elliot), [1848?].

720. Osgood, True (editor). The Rough and Ready. Weekly newspaper, December 12, 1846, to March 13, 1847, published in Concord, N.H.

721. The Rough and Ready almanac for 1848, containing all the battles fought in Mexico by old Zach Taylor. . . . Lafayette, Ind. (Rosser), [1847].

722. Rough and Ready almanac for the year 1848. New York (Tribune), [1847?].

723. The Rough and Ready annual; or, military souvenir. . . . New York (Appleton), 1848.

724. The Rough and Ready almanac for 1847 containing a complete life of General Taylor and sketches of the Battles of Palo Alto, Resaca de la Palma, and Monterrey. Cincinnati (Davenport), 1847.

725. [Thorpe, Thomas Bangs]. Taylor anecdote book. By Tom Owens [pseud.]. New York (Appleton), 1848.

TAYLOR, ZACHARY, BIOGRAPHY

726. Dyer, Brainerd. Zachary Taylor. Baton Rouge (LSU), 1946.

727. Frost, John. Life of Major General Zachary Taylor, . . . New York (Appleton), 1847.

728. Fry, Joseph Reese, and R. T. Conrad. A life of Gen. Zachary Taylor. . . . Philadelphia (Grigg, Elliot), 1847. Consists almost totally of letters of Taylor to the Adjutant General during the northern Mexico campaign.

729. Hamilton, Holman. Zachary Taylor, soldier of the republic. Indianapolis (Bobbs-Merril), 1941. The best biographical work on Taylor.

730. Howard, Oliver Otis. General Taylor. New York (Appleton), 1892.

731. The life of General Taylor, the hero of Okee Chobee, Palo Alto, Resaca de la Palma, Monterrey, and Buena Vista. Philadelphia (Lindsay & Blakiston), 1847.

732. The life and public services of Major General Zachary Taylor. Philadelphia (Turner & Fisher), [1847].

733. McKinley, Silas Bent, and Silas Bent. Old Rough and Ready: the life and times of Zachary Taylor. New York (Vanguard), 1946.

734. Montgomery, Henry. Life of Major General Zachary Taylor. Auburn (Derby and Miller), 1848, and many other editions.

735. Powell, C. Frank. Life of Major General Zachary Taylor. . . . New York (Appleton), 1846.

736. Quisenberry, Anderson Chenault. General Zachary Taylor and the Mexican War. Frankfort (Ky. State Hist. Soc.), 1911.

37. Rayback, Joseph G. "Who wrote the Allison letters? A study in historical detection," MVHR, XXXVI (1949), 51–72. On the authorship of two letters to J. S. Allison from Zachary Taylor.

738. Taylor, Zachary. Letters of Zachary Taylor, from the battlefields of the Mexican War: reprinted from originals . . . in the collection of William K. Bixby. Ed. by William H. Samson. Rochester, N.Y. (Genessee), 1908. Most of the letters are addressed to Taylor's son-in-law, Dr. R. C. Wood. In the appendix is a lengthy letter to Buchanan on the matter of his mistreatment by the war department.

739. ———. Old Rough and Ready speaks his mind: Zachary Taylor on the conduct of the war, a letter to T. Butler, Matamoros, June 19, 1846. Hartford (Beineke), 1960.

740. ———. "Prime ALS of Zachary Taylor," Month at Goodspeeds, XXVII (1956), 83–87.

741. ———. "A series of Zachary Taylor letters," Autograph, I (1911), 21–22, 48–50, 71–74.

SEE ALSO NOS. 51, 107, 393.

TAYLOR'S CAMPAIGN; SEE ALSO SPECIFIC BATTLES

SEE NOS. 106, 108, 133, 149, 154, 157, 177, 180, 181, 196, 203, 217, 243, 245, 514.

TENNESSEE IN THE WAR

742. Campbell, William Bowen. "Mexican War letters of Col. William Bowen Campbell, of Tennessee, written to Governor David

Campbell, of Virginia, 1846–1847," ed. by St. George L. Siousatt, Tenn. Hist. Mag., I (1915), 129–67.

743. Rutland, Robert. "Captain William B. Walton, Mexican War volunteer," Tenn. Hist. Qrtly., XI (1952), 171–79. Walton served with the First Regiment of Tennessee Volunteers with Taylor and later with Scott.

SEE ALSO NOS. 80, 116, 123, 124.

TEXAS BACKGROUND; SEE ALSO ANNEXATION

744. Berlandier, Luis and Rafael Chovell. Diario de viage de la comisión de límites que puso el gobierno de la república, bajo la dirección del exmo. sr. general de división don Manuel de Mier y Teran. . . . Mexico (Navarro), 1850. Not directly Mexican War, but excellent view of Anglo settlement in Texas.

745. Garrison, George P. Texas: a contest in civilizations. New York (Houghton, Mifflin), 1903. This first serious attempt at a scholarly history of Texas treats American expansion as inevitable.

746. Peña y Reyes, Antonio de la (editor). Don Manuel Eduardo de Gorostiza y la cuestion de Texas. . . . Mexico (Sec. de Rel. Exteriores), 1924, Vol. 8 of Archivo Historico Diplomatico Mexicano.

747. Stenberg, Richard R. "The Texas schemes of Jackson and Houston, 1829–1836," Southwestern Soc. Sci. Qrtly., XV (1934), 229–50. Preposterous.

SEE ALSO NOS. 284, 347, 384, 385, 496, 570.

TEXAS TROOPS IN THE WAR

748. Barton, Henry W. "Five Texas frontier companies during the Mexican War," SWHQ, LXVI (1962), 17–30.

749. Clark, Amasa Gleason. Reminiscences of a centenarian. . . . Bandera, Texas, 1930.

750. Ford, John Salmon. Rip Ford's Texas. Ed. by Stephen B. Oates. Austin (UT), 1963. Memoirs of John S. Ford. Contains extensive recollections of Ford while he was adjutant of Hays's Texas Ranger regiment with Taylor.

751. Holland, James K. "Diary of a Texas volunteer in the Mexican War," SWHQ, XXX (1926), 1–33.

752. Rogers, William P. "The diary and letters of William P. Rogers, 1846–1862," ed. by Eleanor Damon Pace, SWHQ, XXXII (1929), 259–99.

753. Smith, S. Compton. "Some incidents of the war in Mexico," Frontier Times, XXXI (1954), 406–33. Extract from No. 534.

SEE ALSO NOS. 157, 178, 518, 520, 531, 534.

THOMAS, GEORGE H.

754. Coppee, Henry. General Thomas. New York (Appleton), 1893.

SEE ALSO NO. 217.

ULLOA, SAN JUAN DE

SEE NOS. 204, 396, 654.

VERA CRUZ, BATTLE OF

755. Bauer, Karl Jack. "The Vera Cruz expedition of 1847," Mil. Affairs, XX (1956), 162–69.

756. "Capture of Vera Cruz, the. By an eyewitness," The Knickerbocker, or New York Monthly Mag., XXX (July 1847), 1–8.

SEE ALSO NOS. 171, 200, 219, 225, 452.

VETERANS AND VETERANS' ORGANIZATIONS

757. Davies, Wallace Evan. "The Mexican War veterans as an organized group," MVHR, XXXV (1948), 221–38. Veterans of the war leaned more toward the politics of the Democratic party than toward the Whigs or Republicans.

758. Robarts, William Hugh. Mexican War veterans: a complete roster of the regular and volunteer troops in the war between the United States and Mexico, from 1846 to 1848. . . . Washington (Brentano's), 1887. Lists officers only.

SEE ALSO NOS. 153.

WILMOT PROVISO

SEE NOS. 40, 667.

WOOL'S CAMPAIGN

SEE NOS. 151, 152, 184.

MISCELLANEOUS WORKS NOT SUBJECT-RELATED

759. Cullum, George Washington. Biographical register of officers and graduates of West Point. New York (Houghton, Mifflin), 1868.

760. Davis, J. The Mexican War and its results. New Orleans, 1876. Listed in Justin Smith but not located in catalogs of Ayers (Newberry), Bancroft (California), Huntington, Library of Congress, New York Public, Texas U., or Yale Western Americana.

761. García, Genaro (editor). Documentos inéditos ó muy raros para la historia de Mexico. 36 vols. Mexico (Bouret), 1905–11. See individual authors or titles in this monumental series for works related to the Mexican War.

762. Glazier, Willard. Heroes of three wars; comprising biographical sketches. . . . Philadelphia (Hubbard), 1880.

763. Grone, Karl von. Briefe über Nord-America und Mexico, und der zwischen beiden geführten krieg. . . . Braunschweig (Westermann), 1850.

764. Mitchell, James Tyndale (collector). The unequalled collection of engraved portraits of officers in the army and navy. . . . Philadelphia (Henkels), 1906. A catalog compiled to offer the collection for sale. Includes many Mexican War portraits.

765. Phillips, Edward Hake. "The Texas norther," SWHQ, LIX (1955), 1–13. Several pages concern the Mexican War.

766. Tilden, Bryant Parrot. Notes on the upper Rio Grande. Philadelphia (Lindsey and Blakiston), 1847. Tilden explored the Rio Grande by steamer as far upstream as Laredo and by dugout as far as Presidio in October and November 1846 under the orders of General Patterson. This rare little book is accompanied by detailed charts of the course of the river.

MAIN ENTRY LIST
FOR BIBLIOGRAPHY

THE NUMERICAL REFERENCES are to bibliography numbers. Cross-references are supplied for pseudonyms or confusing main entries. Titles are listed for anonymous works or works without authors. Journals, diaries, etc., are listed under the name of the actual author rather than the editor.

La cámara de representantes
. . . : 64.
La célebre misión . . . : 575.
La guerra de Tejas . . . : 559.
La verdad desnuda sobre . . . :
361.
Ladd, Horatio Oliver: 362.
Lamar, Howard: 602.
Lander, Alexander: 191.
Lane, Henry Smith: 476.
Lane, Walter Paye: 192.
Lane, William Bartlett: 193.
Largent, Robert J.: 363.
Larkin, Thomas Oliver: 308.
Lavender, David Sievert: 194.
Lawson, William Thornton: 265.
Leggett, Aaron: 584.
Lemoine, Villacuña Ernesto: 112.
Levy, Moses Albert: 531.
Lewis, Lloyd: 195.
Lippard, George: 196.
Livermore, Abiel Abbot: 43, 44.
Lomard, Albert: 621.
Lomas, John: See 512.
Loperna, Ignacio: 197.
Lopez Uraga, Jose: 198.
Lowell, James Russell: 45.
Loyola, Sister Mary: 616.
Luelmo, Julio: 65.
Lundy, Benjamin: 46, 47.

McCall, George Archibald: 113.
McClellan, Edwin North: 310.
McClellan, George Brinton: 516.
McClintock, William A.: 203.
McCormac, Eugene Irving: 673.
McCornack, Richard Blaine: 688.
McCoy, Charles A.: 674.
McDonald,Archie D.: 367.
McElroy, Robert McNutt: 19, 20.
McEniry, Sister Blanche Marie:
337.

McKeown, James Edward: 114.
McKinley, Silas Bent, and Silas
Bent: 733.
McLarty, Vivian K.: 432.
McLaughlin, Andrew Cunning-
ham: 331.
McMillen, Fred E.: 204.
McPherson, John D.: 467.
McSherry, Richard: 115.
McWhiney, Grady, and Sue Mc-
Whiney: 86.
McWhorter, George Cumming:
311.
Magoffin, Susan Shelby: 436.
Maguire, T. Miller: 199.
Mahan, Alfred Thayer: 453.
Manigault, Arthur Middleton:
200.
Manning, William R.: 413, 414.
Mansfield, Edward Deering: 201,
701.
Mares, José Fuentes: 415.
Marshall, Thomas Maitland: 713.
Marti, Werner H.: 309.
Martin, A. H.: 256.
Mason, Alfred B.: 706.
Mason, Amos L.: 607.
Mason, R. H.: 137.
Maury, Dabney H.: 202.
Mayer, Brantz: 364, 365, 366.
Mayo, Bernard: 283.
Meade, George Gordon: 205.
Meadows, Don: 141.
Meehan, Thomas F.: 338, 339.
Mejía, Francisco: 206.
Memoria de la primera . . . : 416.
Menendez, C. R.: 575.
Merk, Frederick: 368, 505.
Mestre Ghigliazza, Manuel: 540.
Metcalf, Clyde H.: 510.
Mexico (corporate author): See
author or title.

INDEX